Victorian Britain
Part I

Professor Patrick N. Allitt

THE TEACHING COMPANY ®

PUBLISHED BY:

THE TEACHING COMPANY
4151 Lafayette Center Drive, Suite 100
Chantilly, Virginia 20151-1232
1-800-TEACH-12
Fax—703-378-3819
www.teach12.com

ISBN 1-56585-810-7

Patrick N. Allitt, Ph.D.

Professor of History, Emory University

Patrick Allitt is Professor of History at Emory University. He was born and raised in central England and attended schools near his home in Mickleover, Derbyshire. An undergraduate at Hertford College, Oxford, he graduated (1977) with honors in British and European History. After a year of travel, he studied for the history doctorate at the University of California, Berkeley. He was a postdoctoral fellow at Harvard in the mid 1980s and since 1988 has been on the faculty of Emory University in Atlanta, Georgia. Professor Allitt is the author of three books, including *Catholic Converts: British and American Intellectuals Turn to Rome* (1997). He also writes frequent articles and reviews. In 1999, he won Emory's Excellence in Teaching Award and, in 2000, was appointed to the N.E.H./Arthur Blank Professorship of Teaching in the Humanities. Professor Allitt keeps in touch with his homeland by spending about two months every year on a working holiday in Britain, teaching the history of Victorian England with Emory's summer school, which is held at University College, Oxford. His wife, Toni, is American, a Michigan native, and they have a daughter, Frances, born in 1988.

Table of Contents

Victorian Britain
Part I

Victorian Britain

Scope:

Victorian Britain was a paradoxical society and one of extreme contrasts. On the one hand, it witnessed an unprecedented outpouring of inventions, scientific advances, and humanitarian reforms, backed by an array of outstanding literary and political figures. On the other hand, it practiced a harsh form of laissez faire capitalism at home, which resulted in chronic poverty for most of the population, and harsh imperial policies abroad, which subordinated many of the peoples of Africa and Asia to British control. This course aims to explain how the Victorians lived with these contradictions and how Britain changed between the 1830s and 1900, perhaps more rapidly than any society in world history up to that time.

Queen Victoria reigned for 64 years, longer than any other British monarch, and she stamped her vivid personality on the whole era, but she no longer enjoyed the sort of power that had been wielded by her ancestors. Instead, Britain moved cautiously toward a democratic political system. The oligarchy of 1830, in which only a small minority of men, and no women, enjoyed the vote and the right to sit in Parliament, was modified by Parliamentary Reform Acts of 1832, 1867, and 1884 so that by century's end, most men at least were entitled to vote. Simultaneously, religious restrictions on political participation were lifted, enabling Methodists, Quakers, Catholics, and Jews, as well as members of diverse social classes, to take seats in Parliament. Despite these changes, however, the traditional land-based aristocracy retained immense political power and social influence; successful manufacturers often devoted their fortunes to buying their way into these ranks.

Rapid social change was facilitated by the Industrial Revolution, which had been gathering force in the decades before Victoria's accession. The harnessing first of water power, then steam power, to the manufacture of cotton textiles in factories initiated the revolution. Developments in coal mining, iron and steel making, ceramics, and transportation accelerated it. First canals, then railways, which began to crisscross the land in the 1830s, speeded up the pace of economic life and increased its scale. The railway builders, particularly the father-and-son team George and Robert Stephenson, along with Isambard Kingdom Brunel, featured largely in this transformation;

Brunel's visionary genius was further shown in his construction of the world's first oceangoing steamships.

Along with industrialization came urbanization. Such industrial cities as Manchester, Liverpool, and Sheffield grew so fast that infrastructure development could not keep pace. In consequence, tens of thousands of industrial workers and their families found themselves living in squalid, hastily built houses, severely overcrowded, and without access to safe drinking water supplies or proper sanitation. These factors, along with overwork, poor nutrition, a smoke-filled environment, and dangerous working conditions, contributed to regular epidemics and a low life expectancy for most working-class communities. Death at any age was common and child mortality high. Many occupations, moreover, had characteristic illnesses of their own, such as the lung diseases suffered by Britain's hundreds of thousands of coal miners. A few impoverished areas in every city, such as London's squalid "rookeries," became breeding grounds of violent crime. Middle- and upper-class people moved away from these dangerous areas whenever they could, furthering the class gulf between Britain's haves and have-nots.

Britain's technological superiority enabled its industries to dominate world markets for the first two-thirds of the 19th century, especially when the industrialists' growing political influence had established a free trade regime. British imperial development accelerated at the same time. British merchants forced opium, grown in India, onto a reluctant China in a series of "Opium Wars" that seem particularly disgraceful in retrospect. After the Indian Mutiny of 1857, the British government took over direct control of this most important colony from the Honorable East India Company, which had run it privately for the last century. In suppressing the mutiny, in which atrocities had been committed against some of their civilians, the British demonstrated a ruthless ferocity. In the same years, hardy explorers, such as Richard Burton and David Livingstone, were charting the still-unknown interior of Africa, soon to be followed by trade, missionaries, and the Union Jack. In the last years of the 19th century, Britain's European rivals joined her in an undignified "scramble for Africa" and its potential sources of wealth.

Historians often treat the Great Exhibition of 1851 as a symbol of mid-Victorian prosperity and self-confidence. The exhibition was held in the Crystal Palace, a prefabricated structure of iron and glass that was quickly erected in Hyde Park; the structure was elegant, sturdy, and light and delighted visitors from all over Britain and abroad. Built by Joseph Paxton, its ultra-modern style, echoed in the glass arches of Paddington and St. Pancras railway stations, stands in strong juxtaposition to the other great public building style of Victorian Britain, Gothic Revival. Gothic's champions included Charles Barry and Augustus Pugin, the architects of the new Houses of Parliament (which are now probably the most well-known buildings in Britain), and George Gilbert Scott. Britain's wealth created a growing market for innovative architects, just as the growing middle class created a market for paintings and literature. The Pre-Raphaelite movement in art and the dramatic, serialized literature of Charles Dickens, Anthony Trollope, and George Eliot remain as yardsticks of the Victorians' creativity and inventiveness.

The later portions of the course will show how Britain began to lose its supremacy. The death of Prince Albert, Queen Victoria's husband, in 1861, cast a shadow of grief over the monarch herself from which she never fully emerged. Meanwhile, Union victory in the American Civil War and the unification of Germany in 1870 gave notice that two great industrial rivals were about to challenge Britain's supremacy. Despite the advantages of her early lead, Britain was unable to keep pace with German and American industrial innovations and gradually retreated to a policy of trading in the protected area of its worldwide empire. This strategy, successful in the short term, enabled Britain to postpone the day of reckoning. Paradoxically, however, it turned the appearance of immense world-striding strength into a growing liability, which would ensure the rapid decline of British power in the 20th century. The inner vulnerability of the empire could have been glimpsed earlier, not only with the Indian Mutiny but also in the catastrophic Irish famine of 1846–1850 and recurrent friction with South Africa's Dutch-descended Boers between 1880 and 1898.

Despite ominous signs, however, Britain still seemed to be master of the world in the last decades of the 19th century, when it enjoyed the leadership of such brilliant prime ministers as Benjamin Disraeli (the man who adapted British Conservatism to a more democratic era) and the sternly moralistic Liberal William Gladstone. Queen Victoria celebrated her Diamond Jubilee (60 years on the throne) in 1897 with a triumphal parade, including soldiers from every corner of the empire. The mood of the time was captured by the poet Rudyard Kipling when he urged Britons (and Anglo-Saxon Americans) to "take up the white man's burden" and bring the blessings of their Christian civilization to what he thought of as the less fortunate races of the world.

The growing strength of trade unions, and political recognition that they would become a permanent part of society, led to the rise, as the century turned, of the Labour Party, which was destined within 20 years to become and to remain one of the nation's two major political forces. War against the Boers from 1898 suddenly showed that British redcoats, complacent after years of easy victory against primitive societies, were not assured of automatic victory when they faced well-armed, well-trained guerrillas defending their homelands. When Queen Victoria died in 1901, she left the nation in a world full of potential enemies, no longer so amenable to British direction as it had been in the years of her early reign. Twentieth-century Britain was indelibly marked by the Victorian legacy, for good and ill, and the course ends with a glimpse at some of these lasting effects.

Lecture One
The Victorian Paradox

Scope:

This lecture outlines the main themes of the course: Victorian Britain was a paradoxical society and one of extreme contrasts between wealth and poverty, morality and cynicism, creativity and constriction, imperial grandeur and domestic squalor, and collectivity and individualism. It was a society committed to the ideals of material and moral progress, industrial and commercial expansion, and worldwide free trade. However, its vulnerability to fluctuations of the business cycle and to foreign competition entailed hardships for its majority, the poor and working classes, and severely unequal distribution of its benefits. It is a society still close enough to us to evoke our admiration in many ways, but also close enough to provoke our censure in many others. It is difficult not to admire many of its most brilliant characters but equally difficult not to condemn the moral narrowness and hardheartedness they sometimes displayed.

Outline

I. Victorian Britain (1837–1901) was a paradoxical society and one of extreme contrasts.

   A. Very wealthy and very poor people lived side by side.

   B. The society was immensely creative but burdened with a stifling social-class system.

   C. Britain took pride in its worldwide empire but was unable to control its oldest and closest colony, Ireland.

   D. It believed in its racial, religious, and civilizational superiority but could be brutally destructive and cynical, even going to war in 1839 to force opium on the reluctant Chinese.

   E. Many of Britain's most brilliant intellectuals were Victorians, but they lived in an under-educated and still largely illiterate society.

II. The Victorians believed, perhaps more strongly than any other British generation, in progress, in making the world better from year to year, both materially and morally. In many ways, they succeeded.

A. They built up Britain's worldwide empire.

    1. They ruled India with a small army and a talented group of administrators, first through the East India Company, then, after 1857, directly.

    2. They turned Australia from a prison colony into a thriving colony of farmers and settlers.

    3. They provided a steady flow of settlers to Canada, New Zealand, and South Africa and invented creative ways for these colonies to be self-governing while still connected to Britain.

    4. They dominated strategically important places around the world, including Gibraltar, Suez, and Aden, which safeguarded their imperial routeways.

B. The Victorians made Britain the world's most powerful trading nation, building up the world's largest merchant navy and protecting it with the largest military navy.

C. Britain made immense strides in industrialization, immediately before and during Victoria's reign.

    1. It was the first industrial capitalist nation, beginning with the mass production of cotton textiles, later industrializing mining, metallurgy, and other manufactures.

    2. It was the first country in the world to build a railway network, which speeded up the pace of economic life and made it possible for ordinary citizens to travel long distances for the first time.

    3. It pioneered in banking, insurance, and free trade legislation.

D. Victorian Britain moved toward a democratic political system but did not suffer the revolutionary upheavals that afflicted most of continental Europe in the same era.

    1. A series of Reform Acts, in 1832, 1867, and 1884, extended the vote to growing numbers of men (though not to women) in a variety of class positions.

2. Victoria herself, and her husband, Prince Albert, restored the prestige of the monarchy, which had been damaged by her disreputable predecessors.

3. Victorian politicians—including Peel, Palmerston, Gladstone, and Disraeli—were brilliant speakers and rank among the outstanding figures in the whole of British political history.

III. Along with its achievements, however, Victorian Britain had shortcomings and unsolvable problems.

A. Many Britons were very poor, and, as growing numbers went to work in industry, they became vulnerable to periodic slumps, unemployment, and acute privation. Charity was insufficient to deal with the scale of British poverty. The alternative, the "workhouse," was bitterly hated and resented.

B. A sharply defined class system closed off avenues of opportunity to most talented members of the lower classes. Snobbery and class distinction were sources of friction and discontent.

1. Class antagonism fueled the growth of the trade union movement, which in, turn, gave birth to the Labour Party in the 1890s.

2. Members of the upper classes sought work in government, the army, the navy, and the church; "trade," the basis of Britain's power, was regarded as beneath their dignity.

C. British industrialists did not maintain their lead over their rivals, notably in America and Germany.

1. They failed to modernize equipment.

2. They trained their sons to be gentlemen rather than businessmen.

3. They relied on the colonies as a protected market that permitted them to remain inefficient.

D. While taking pride in its far-flung empire, Britain was unable to deal satisfactorily with its closest colony, Ireland. The result was that the "Irish Question" hamstrung the work of British politicians, especially in the later Victorian era.

1. Ireland was virtually an agricultural monoculture, the potato being its almost exclusive crop.
2. Reliance on one crop led to disaster, when the potato blight struck Ireland in 1846, causing nationwide famine.
3. Many Irish laborers fled to England and the United States.
4. Catholicism was also a stumbling block to Home Rule: Irish Protestants opposed Home Rule, fearing they would suffer under Catholic domination.
5. Legislation for Irish Home Rule passed through the House of Commons in 1893 but failed in the House of Lords.

IV. Many colorful, larger-than-life figures lived and worked in Victorian Britain, and their work has resonance down to the present. Several of them we'll feature in this course.

   A. Queen Victoria herself, a strong-willed, imperious figure, knew how to make the most of the monarch's remaining prerogatives.

   B. Florence Nightingale, an even more determined and skillful worker behind the scenes, transformed nursing and public health in British life.

   C. Isambard Kingdom Brunel, the genius-engineer, built Britain's most luxurious railway and the first steam-powered transatlantic ship.

   D. Charles Darwin, the biologist, produced the great work *On the Origin of Species*, which revolutionized human understanding of the natural world.

   E. Benjamin Disraeli was a Jewish outsider who became a Conservative Party prime minister, empowered the queen as empress of India, and learned to adapt conservatism to a mass electorate.

   F. John Henry Newman, the brilliant Anglican churchman, shocked the nation by becoming a Roman Catholic in 1845 and went on to scandalize many of his new co-religionists by his intellectually adventurous ideas.

   G. Charles Dickens, the novelist, serialized stories that enthralled readers in England, America, and later around the world and pointed out many of the worst injustices and follies of British life.

V. The Victorians' reputation declined sharply in the early 20th century but has subsequently revived, in part.

    A. Lytton Strachey's *Eminent Victorians* (1918) lampooned Victorian high-mindedness.

    B. Post-World War I modernists in art and architecture reacted against Victorian decorative complexity in favor of austere simplicity.

    C. Scattered champions of Victoriana, such as John Betjeman and L. S. Lowry, were the exception.

    D. British political changes after 1980 contributed to a recovery of the Victorians' better aspects.

VI. The course will follow a generally chronological pattern.

    A. We first glance back to earlier developments, particularly the Industrial Revolution.

    B. Lectures on such issues as the lives of women and servants, music, art, and architecture will be less rigorously chronological.

Essential Reading:

W. D. Rubinstein, *Britain's Century: A Political and Social History, 1815–1905.*

K. Theodore Hoppen, *The Mid-Victorian Generation: 1846–1886.*

Supplementary Reading:

Lytton Strachey, *Eminent Victorians.*

Llewelyn Woodward, *The Age of Reform, 1815–1870.*

Questions to Consider:

1. Does Victorian Britain continue to fascinate the world because of its achievements or because of its strange internal contradictions?

2. What were the characteristics of "Victorianism"?

Lecture One—Transcript
The Victorian Paradox

Victorian England was a paradoxical society and a society of extreme contrasts between wealth and poverty, morality and cynicism, creativity and constriction, imperial grandeur and domestic squalor, and between collectivity and individualism. It was a society that was committed to the ideals of material and moral progress, industrial and commercial expansion, and the achievement of worldwide free trade. It was a vulnerable society as well. It was vulnerable to economic fluctuations, to the harshness of the prevailing ideas about capitalism. Eventually, foreign competition intensified Britain's vulnerability.

As a result, the big majority of the British people, the working classes and the poor, lived lives of chronic anxiety. The benefits of British society were unequally distributed. That was true throughout the entire period. Victorian Britain is a society still close enough to evoke our admiration in many ways, but it is also still close enough to us to provoke our sensia in many other ways. It is difficult not to admire some of the great Victorian characters that we will be studying in this course. It is equally difficult not to condemn the moral narrowness and hard-heartedness that some of them displayed.

It was a perverse society in the sense that it didn't value, reward highly enough, its own most necessary qualities. The thing that made Britain great was its commercial achievements. Yet, commerce was never a particularly highly valued activity within the British nation. At a very fundamental level, it was a dysfunctional place.

Queen Victoria came to the throne of Britain in 1837 when she was just 18 years old. She reigned for 64 years and died in 1901, in her eighties. She reigned longer than any other British monarch in history. She governed over a society that was riddled by paradoxes. One strange thing was that the very rich and the very poor lived extremely close together. Even the biggest city, London, was quite small. The palaces of the wealthy in the west end of London were often just a few hundred yards from the rookeries of squalor and crime and poverty, where some of the most intense suffering took place. It was an immensely creative society, and yet it was one that was burdened with a stifling social class system, and all the way through the course we will see the way that class limitations created problems within British society.

It took great pride, and sometimes justified pride, in its worldwide empire. Yet, it was unable to control its oldest and closest colony, Ireland. The "Irish Question" dogs Victorian British history. The Victorians took very seriously the idea that they were racially superior to the other people of the world, religiously superior as Anglicans, and that their civilization itself was better than anybody else's. Sometimes, it was brutally destructive and cynical. Perhaps the most notorious episode is that of the Chinese Opium Wars of the late 1830s and early 1840s, where a British army forced the illegal drug, opium, into the Chinese market.

Many of Britain's most brilliant intellectuals lived during the Victorian period, including an incredible category of eminent writers. Yet, they lived in a society which was largely illiterate. A minority of the British people could write at the beginning of Queen Victoria's reign. What I want to do in this first lecture is preview some of the things that Britain did right, some of its great qualities, then look at some of the things that they did wrong, then give some introductory thoughts about how the course will proceed from this point.

First, it was a society which took seriously the idea of progress. Progress is an idea; it is not a fact. It is a way of interpreting some of the things that have happened to say, "Things are better now. They are better materially, and they are better morally." It is one of the governing ideas of the Victorians. They did build up a great worldwide empire with consequences lasting right up to the present. The jewel in the crown, the centerpiece of the British Empire, was India.

An extraordinary development was the Indian Empire, in which, by the early 19th century, about 25,000 or 30,000 Britons ruled over an Indian population of more than 100 million, a tiny British presence in a massive Indian population. In the early Victorian period, India was run, not by the British government but by a private company, the honorable East India Company. After 1857, after a series of events called the Indian Mutiny, which we will study, the government took over directly and ruled India from then on right through to Indian independence in the 1940s.

At the beginning of the Victorian period, Australia was a prison colony, a place to which convicts were sent. But the convict shipping system lapsed, and Australia itself then became a thriving colony of white settlers. Throughout the Victorian period, Britain was sending out settlers, quite a lot to the United States of America, but more to its colonies, Canada, Australia, New Zealand, and to South Africa. In each case, Britain invented ways for these colonies to become self-governing while still connected to Britain.

Britain dominated strategically important places around the world. The reason the British had gone to South Africa in the first place was because the Cape of Good Hope was a staging post between Britain and India. In the days before the building of the Suez Canal, that is how you got to India, and that is why the Cape Colony was there. With the building of the Suez Canal in 1869, the best way to get to India from Britain was through the Mediterranean Sea. Britain controlled Gibraltar, at the western entrance to the Mediterranean, and it controlled Suez, and Aden at the mouth of the Red Sea and so on. So, it dominated strategically important places around the world to keep open its sea lanes to India and other colonies.

In the Victorian period, Britain became decisively the world's predominant trading nation, the most powerful trading nation, building up not only the world's most powerful military navy, The Royal Navy, but also the most powerful merchant marine. There was an enormous cult in the 19th century of Britain's great naval heroes. The greatest was Lord Nelson who died at the climax of the Battle of Trafalgar in 1805, defeating the French and Spanish navies. All the way through, there were adventure stories for boys about great English sailors, some of it right into the level of great literature. The novels of Robert Louis Stevenson are one example or, a little bit later, the great works of Joseph Conrad, a Polish sailor who became a great English novelist.

Britain's greatness was based on its industrialization. It was immediately before Victoria came to the throne that Britain went through the world's first industrial revolution. The first commodity which it made in an industrial way was cotton textile, the cotton coming very largely, incidentally, from the American south. The production of cotton textiles began the industrial revolution, and later it diversified into iron, steel, coal mining, and many other manufactures. It was based on water power, the use of water power to drive wheels to power the factories, but then it very quickly switched over to steam power. It was the work of people like James Watt in developing effective steam engines that goes right to the maturing of the British industrial economy.

Britain was the first nation in the world to build a railway network. That had an enormous impact on everything else in society. It brought every town in Britain within an easy day's journey of every other place. It made it possible to speed up economic life, bringing goods quickly into the places where they were manufactured and shipping them out again when they were finished. It made it possible for the first time for ordinary citizens to travel great distances. Until then, Britain had been intensely autochthonous—nearly everybody stayed in exactly the place where they started out, lived and died in the same place. This remains true to some extent, although it begins to break down as the Victorian period goes on. If you read the novels of Thomas Hardy, you can often find that the farm laborers, the locals, meet together in the molt house—the pub—and they have always been there, and their fathers have been there, and their grandfathers. It is an intensely localized society. The railway begins to break down some of that localism and it makes possible the creation of nationwide marketing networks.

For the first time, it became possible to make a commodity in one place and sell it everywhere in Britain, which previously had been very difficult. It is no coincidence that when the railway system was finished it became possible to have professional sports teams, because they could visit each other's cities. The trade unions became nationwide. Political campaigns became nationwide. One after the next, the activities which had previously been very local could expand.

Britain pioneered not only in industrial manufacturing but in all the things that go with it, that is, in the development of modern banking techniques and modern insurance methods and in legislation for free trade. So long as Britain was a commercial leader, it was advantaged by having easy access to foreign markets and by importing goods cheaply.

Victorian Britain was not a democracy. It moved gradually toward a democratic political system during the 19th century. It was blessed because it didn't suffer the revolutionary upheavals that were common in many other parts of the world and Europe. The French Revolution had taken place in the 1780s and 1790s, and fear that Britain might have an event like the French Revolution had caused tremors of anxiety and continued to do so throughout the 19th century as France recurrently went into revolution in 1815, 1830, 1848, and 1870. On each of these occasions, there were people in Britain very anxious that the same thing was going to happen there. Political stability is a great blessing and one of the achievements of the United States and Britain. Sometimes in history, we have to be attentive to what didn't happen. What didn't happen in Victorian Britain was a political revolution. The institutions changed, adapted, and evolved, but were never overthrown in some violent upheaval.

The British political system went through a series of changes, first, in 1832, then again in 1867, then again in 1884. By acts of Parliament the rules governing who could participate in political life were changed. The electorate was expanded so that more members of the middle and lower classes were brought into the franchise. Gradually, by 1884, it had become possible for working-class people to vote and even to become potentially members of parliament. That is the foundation for the creation of the Labour Party.

At the beginning of the Victorian period, political participation was also very narrowly restricted to members of the Church of England, but that gradually began to expand. First, non-Anglican Protestants could participate, then Roman Catholics, then Jews, then Atheists. Bit by bit, the political system was opening up to a larger number of people. Queen Victoria herself and her husband Albert restored the prestige of the monarchy, which had been very badly damaged by Victoria's immediate predecessors. The three monarchs who preceded Victoria were in many respects a very disreputable group.

They were George III, who was king during the American Revolution and who suffered from long periods of madness, George IV, and William IV—rakes, reprobates, people who brought the idea of the monarchy into disfavor. Victoria was their absolute antithesis. She was a paragon of decency, uprightness, and moral backbone, especially when she was married to Prince Albert, who brought an enormous gravity with him when he came to Britain.

By the end of the Victorian period the place of the monarchy in Britain's constitutional monarchical system was secure. Back in the 1830s it seemed a little bit tentative. Victoria was lucky in that she had a whole succession of extremely brilliant prime ministers. When she became queen, Lord Melbourne took her in hand. She was then 18, and he was in his late 50s or early 60s. Melbourne taught her her constitutional duties and was glad to find her so receptive. Robert Peel was his successor, a brilliant politician. Lord Palmerston was the Prime Minister in the 1850s and 1860s, then in the later part of her reign, two giants in political history, William Gladstone and Benjamin Disraeli, some of the most brilliant politicians in the whole history of the nation.

Along with all these achievements which are unquestionable, Victorian Britain had its shortcomings. Let's have a preview of some of those. First, most British people were very poor, and, as great numbers of people went to work in industry instead of agriculture, they became more vulnerable. After all, if you live as a farmer, the fluctuations of the business cycle don't particularly matter. As long as you are growing food in your own little plot, there is always going to be something to eat. Once you are working in industry for wages, if the work stops, so do the wages. That means that suddenly you are in a completely vulnerable position.

There was no welfare state at all for most of the Victorian period with a result that business fluctuations led to lives of chronic anxiety and instability for the majority of working-class people and could lead to very acute privation. There was a lot of charity. The Victorian middle classes were philanthropic. Nevertheless, there wasn't sufficient charity to deal with the magnitude of poverty which periodically afflicted the nation. If you were destitute, you had to go to the workhouse. The workhouse is a widely hated place. Members of the working class bitterly hated, feared, and resented the workhouse. There were constantly stories that, for example, the people who died there were used as food among people who had to go there. People would do anything to try to prevent descent into the workhouse itself.

There was a very sharply defined class system, and it had the effect of closing off avenues of opportunity to the most talented members of the lower classes. Britain has always been an enormously snobbish society. Class distinctions are very sharp. They become sources of friction and discontent. It was very easy in Victorian Britain to tell someone's social class by their accent. They are regionally very specific and also class specific. George Bernard

Shaw's play *Pygmalion* jokes on this. Henry Higgins is such an expert that he can even tell which end of the street somebody comes from by exactly how they speak. Although that is a slight exaggeration, it is only very slight. Regional accents are various and can be narrowly identified. This is true just as much of me as of anybody else. When I am in Britain, people can tell from how I sound where I come from. They can even speculate very accurately on my social origins and so on.

Class antagonism fueled the growth of the British trade union movement. In America there is a big ideology of gaining wealth, of being born in a log cabin but becoming president, of going from rags to riches. This is enshrined in the books of Horatio Alger. There is not the same kind of tradition in Britain. The assumption in Britain was, certainly then, that you are born into a certain class and that you stay there, that your children stay there as well.

That meant that it was relatively easy under those circumstances for a vigorous trade union movement to develop. People were ready to believe "Here we are in this position. Let's get the most that we can for ourselves in this place, because we are not going to be able to move off into some completely different realm of life." The trade unions grew gradually more powerful in the mid and late 19th century and eventually created their own political party, The Labour Party, at the very end of the 19th century. That, in turn, was going to displace one of the two major parties in the British political system and dominate political life throughout the 20th century.

For members of the British upper classes, the aristocracy, there were certain things they would do and certain things they wouldn't do. They would work in government, become members of Parliament, a very honorable profession. They would become army officers. They would become navy officers. They would become clergymen in the Church of England. What they wouldn't do is they would not go into trade. They wouldn't go into trade or commerce or business because they regarded it as socially beneath them, as clearly a mark of downward mobility to have to go into trade.

This is what I meant at the beginning when I said that it was a paradoxical society. It didn't reward—it didn't value adequately—the activities upon which its greatness was based. Trade would remain something slightly despised, beneath their dignity. This meant that British industrialists although created a lead—they had done everything first—they didn't maintain their lead over their rivals. By the late Victorian period, two rivals particularly, the United States and Germany, were catching up and passing by Britain. British manufacturers failed to modernize their equipment. American manufacturers—even someone like Andrew Carnegie, who was a Scottish immigrant to American, was a fanatic for modernizing his iron and steel equipment constantly. When he came back to Britain periodically and looked at the way the English steel and iron manufacturers were still using outmoded technology, he was astonished by their reluctance to continue to change.

British entrepreneurs who made a great fortune, rather than passing the business on to their sons and creating a father and son dynasty, would send their sons to the English private schools, the early private schools, from whence they would go into Oxford and Cambridge. There, they learned to get out of trade rather than stay in it. They wanted the status that came from buying a landed estate and living a life of leisure. Again, there tend not to be durable dynasties of British manufacturers in the way that there were in America and Germany. Eventually, British business relied on having a protected area, the British Empire, within which it could continue to conduct its inefficient business.

So, a glance at the map in 1900 will give you the impression that the British Empire bestrode the world and was magnificently powerful. That was true in a way, but in another way it had become a sign of weakness. It was a protected area within which British businesses could operate without having to face up to the harsh realities of German and American competition.

As I mentioned at the beginning, Britain was never able to deal adequately with the problem of Ireland. Ireland hamstrung the Victorian politicians, and it was a problem they were never able to solve. In the 1840s, 1846–1848, there was a terrible famine in Ireland. Ireland was agriculturally a monoculture. Potatoes were the dominant food of almost the whole population. A potato blight deprived the Irish population of almost any food at all. Perhaps as many as half a million people starved to death. A million people emigrated to England and to the United States. Even now, a century and a half later, the population of Ireland has not regained the level of the early 1840s when it was about eight million.

One of the other great problems in Ireland was that its majority population was Roman Catholic, whereas the majority population in England was Anglican. So, in addition to a national rivalry, there was a religious antagonism which intensified the conflict. In the 1880s, as we will see, there was a struggle for home rule. Ireland wanted to become self-governing within the British Empire, but a majority of British politicians fiercely opposed it. In 1886, William Gladstone, the Prime Minster, became converted to the idea of home rule and tried to pass legislation through Parliament to achieve it.

Legislation for Irish home rule passed through the House of Commons in 1893 but failed in the House of Lords. Why? Because the Conservative Party of Britain, which was a clear majority in the House of Lords, the second body of the legislature, was opposed to the idea of Irish home rule. They took the point of view of the protestant minority in Ireland. There are six counties in the northeast of Ireland, the Ulster counties, where the Protestants are a majority, and they were eager to prevent Irish home rule because then, they said, "We are going to be swallowed up in a Catholic majority." That is a problem which continued to fester throughout the Victorian period and finally was only resolved by a bitter revolutionary war between 1916 and 1922.

Many colorful and larger-than-life characters lived in Victorian Britain, and we are going to be looking at many of them in the course of this series. Their work has a resonance right down to the present, and we'll just glance at a few of them straightaway. First, Queen Victoria herself was a wonderful person, absolutely brimming with contradictions and paradoxes. She hated the idea of votes for women— she thought the English feminist movement was pernicious—yet she herself was a strong-willed, imperious, and very purposeful lady who knew exactly how to make the most of the monarchy's remaining prerogatives. Another strong and capable woman from the same period is Florence Nightingale, an upper-class woman who went off to the Crimean War in the 1850s and transformed the British medical system for the better by introducing elementary principles of cleanliness and sanitation and good diet and helped far more soldiers survive than had been doing so until then. It was she who made nursing a respectable profession for middle- and upper-class women where previously it had a very low social status.

We will be looking a little bit at the work of Isambard Kingdom Brunel, a man with a magnificent name. He was the man who engineered one of Britain's best railways and then built the first series of transatlantic oceangoing steamships, which marked an enormous jump in the safety and reliability of Atlantic crossings. We are going to look at Charles Darwin. It was Darwin who, in 1859, published a book called *On the Origin of Species by Natural Selection*. It had a revolutionary effect of understandings of the natural world. What is a species? Where does it come from? It was important not only for biology but also for religion because it contradicted the *Genesis* story of the creation which until then most people had assumed to be an actual description of what had happened, that God had made all the species distinctly. Darwin presented a picture where that was not to be true. In fact, species themselves have origins. The title itself embodies a contradiction.

We are going to be studying Benjamin Disraeli, who became the Conservative Prime Minister in the 1860s and 1870s. Nobody was less likely to be Prime Minister than he was, most of all because he came from a Jewish family in a society full of racial and religious prejudice. For a Jew, even a converted Jew who converted to Anglicanism, to become Prime Minister was an astonishing achievement. It was he who brilliantly adapted the conservative party to a much wider electorate and found ways to give it a continuing resonance into the 20th century.

We will take a look at John Henry Newman, one of the most brilliant Anglican churchmen of the early 19th century, who scandalized the entire nation in 1845 by doing one of the things that was then regarded as the most reckless act imaginable—he became a Roman Catholic. The whole civilized society went through tremors of horror at Newman's conversion. I'll explain why he did it, and he then went on to scandalize his new co-religionists, just as he had the old ones.

And we will be looking at the work of English writers, people like Charles Dickens. Dickens' novels were mainly serialized. They came out in episodes, and each episode would end with some cliff-hanging episode. People would be waiting for the next episode to come out. When the series had finished, sometimes a year and a half long, the book would be published in its entirety. He was not only a very good novelist, he was also a great social critic, and one of the ways that we get a sense of the nature of the debates is by his biting satires. He describes injustices in British life. From these people, and from many others like them, we can see the bright lights as well as the shadows that made Victorian Britain so distinctive.

The Victorians' reputation declined sharply in the early 20th century, but subsequently revived. It declined most sharply during the First World War, when the young generation which had to fight the war treated its elders, who had grown up in the Victorian period, as responsible for this terrible catastrophe. In 1918, Lytton Strachey published his book, *Eminent Victorians,* which lampooned Victorian high-mindedness. It took four famous Victorian people, General Gordon, Florence Nightingale, Cardinal Manning, and Thomas Arnold, people with immense reputations, and denigrated them. It is a masterpiece of belittling. It is a wonderful book, very entertaining, which I counsel you all to read if you haven't done so. After the first World War, the aesthetic style of modernism dominated: the art of Picasso, the international style of architecture. And over the very auspices of the elaborate decorativeness which had been so characteristic of the very arts and architecture of the Victorian period, simplicity was now the favored style instead of the lavish Victorian styles.

There were always scattered enthusiasts for Victoriana. One of them was the English poet, John Betjeman, and an otherwise eccentric and lovely artist called L.S. Lowry, who did lots of paintings of industrial cities, and the centerpiece of his paintings is Victorian churches covered in soot. Because Britain was a coal-based society, everything got covered in soot. Lowry loved black churches and painted them enthusiastically. Since the 1980s, the Victorians had enjoyed a recovery of reputation, partly because of Mrs. Thatcher, the great British Prime Minister of the 1980s. Summoned up in some of her actions and ideas are reminiscences of the Victorians. I don't want to compare the two people—they are very different—but they had something in common: They are very strong and capable women. It is true that Victoriana is popular once again. The art and the architecture of the Victorians is now valued and treasured in a way that it certainly wasn't throughout most of the earlier 20th century. Even some of the ideals of the Victorians have started to come back a little bit into popular circulation.

During this course, from here onwards, we are going to do two things: First, we will follow a chronological pattern starting in the

1830s and moving gradually forward to finish in 1901 at the time of Queen Victoria's death. We will have to look backwards a little first to understand the developments and changes in the economy to make sense of some of the political dynamics of her reign. Then, periodically, we will pause to look at things like the lives of servants, ideas about the relationships between men and women, and some of the music and the art which don't lend themselves quite so well to a chronological format. That is the way the course will go forward.

Lecture Two
Victoria's Early Reign—1837–1861

Scope:

Victoria came to the throne in 1837 at the age of eighteen. Her predecessors, George III, George IV, and William IV, had been unimpressive and had impaired the reputation of the monarchy. By her authority and example, she restored its reputation and dignity, embodying the era's mood of moral improvement. Along with her husband, Albert of Saxe-Coburg-Gotha, whom she married in 1840, Victoria made the most of what limited political power and influence the monarchy still retained, communicating regularly with her prime ministers. She bore nine children and enjoyed many of the material advantages of the industrial age. Her husband's death in 1861 was, to her, a shattering catastrophe.

Outline

I. Victoria became queen at the age of 18, succeeding her uncle, William IV.

    A. Born in 1819, Victoria did not seem likely, at first, to be heir to the throne. She was the daughter of George IV's younger brother, the Duke of Kent.

        1. Her father died when she was less than a year old.

        2. Her mother, a minor German princess, was left with only a tiny allowance.

        3. When William IV's legitimate children all died in infancy, the government realized that Victoria was the probable heir and gave her and her mother a much larger income.

        4. Victoria was fluent in German and French, written and spoken; understood Italian; was a regular diarist; and was familiar with many of England's stately and aristocratic houses.

        5. Most of her childhood was lonely. She was close to her governess, Louise Lehzen, but had no friends of her own age.

        6. She resented her mother's scheming with Sir John Conroy to make him regent in the event of her becoming queen when too young to rule.

B. Victoria was notified of her accession early in the morning of June 20, 1837, in her dressing gown, by the Archbishop of Canterbury and Lord Coyningham, the Lord Chancellor.

C. She relied on the advice of Whig Prime Minister Lord Melbourne in her first years as queen.

    1. He was a 58-year-old widower whose wife had been mentally unstable—she had been one of Lord Byron's lovers.

    2. Victoria regarded him as a father figure (she had never known her own father) and they got on extremely well. He trained her to run affairs, and they met or wrote letters to each other every day.

    3. Her superiority over her three predecessors, whom Sir Sidney Lee described as "an imbecile, a profligate, and a buffoon," soon made her popular among politicians and populace.

D. Victoria was upset when Melbourne resigned in 1839 and furious when Sir Robert Peel, the Tory leader, asked to change her Ladies of the Bedchamber, removing Whigs and adding Tories.

    1. Throughout her reign, Victoria resented prime ministers at first but later came to value them—by 1846 she was a great admirer of Peel.

    2. The exception was the great Liberal leader Gladstone, whom she always disliked.

E. Victoria found it difficult to accept that she was now only a constitutional monarch.

    1. In the late 1840s, she bitterly disliked Foreign Secretary Lord Palmerston because of his opposition to some European monarchs, her relatives.

    2. In 1850, she tried to demand that the Prime Minister, Lord John Russell, dismiss Palmerston or subordinate him to her will, but was unable to prevail.

F. She followed the progress of the Crimean War in 1854–1855 and created the Victoria Cross for gallantry, personally awarding it to common soldiers, as well as officers.

II. Victoria married Prince Albert of Saxe-Coburg-Gotha, her cousin, in 1840, but showed her determination to be monarch as well as housewife.

    A. Albert was earnest and well educated, at the University of Bonn.

    B. Victoria's uncle, King Leopold of the Belgians, had trained Albert for the role of Victoria's husband.

    C. Victoria disliked the idea of marrying Albert but thawed when he came to visit in 1839, because he was handsome, serious, and charming.

    D. British dislike of foreigners meant that he was given no official title until 1857 (when he was named Prince-Consort) and was not allowed to have German friends and advisers in his household.

        1. At first, Victoria froze Albert out of her political affairs altogether.

        2. Albert showed his abilities, however, by rationalizing the chaotic conduct of the royal household.

        3. When Victoria was about to give birth for the first time, Albert was admitted to the Privy Council and named regent in the event of her death.

    E. British politicians of both parties came to respect Albert, his hard work, active conscience, and high moral tone.

III. Victoria and Albert enjoyed many of the new amenities of industrial society.

    A. They bought and rebuilt two houses, Osborne House, on the Isle of Wight, and Balmoral, in the Scottish highlands, filling both with the most modern heating devices and using modern iron-frame technology.

        1. At Balmoral, Victoria sketched, painted, rode, and learned Scottish dances, while Albert tried to learn Gaelic and stalked deer.

        2. Victoria later published a book about Balmoral, *Leaves from a Journal of Our Life in the Highlands.*

    B. Victoria traveled by train in 1842 from London to Windsor—on Brunel's Great Western Railway.

        1. Later, she had a luxurious train built for her frequent travels to southern England and Scotland

2. Her royal yacht, *Victoria and Albert* (1842), used brand-new propeller technology instead of paddles.

C. Victoria accepted chloroform to help her in childbirth of Prince Leopold in 1853, the eighth of her nine children.

D. She suffered acute postpartum depression and often flew into rages against Albert, feeling penitent later.

E. She and Prince Albert opened the Great Exhibition, the first world's fair, in 1851.

IV. Prince Albert's death in 1861 sent Victoria into a profound depression and withdrawal from society.

A. She continued to have his shaving gear brought to their rooms every morning and his side of their work desk prepared each day.

B. She refused to attend public functions throughout the 1860s and made her prime minister, Lord Palmerston, fear that republicanism would gain ground.

C. She wore mourning for the rest of her life.

D. The Albert Hall, the Albert Memorial, and many other structures still visible today, were built and named in his memory in the 1860s and 1870s.

Essential Reading:

Christopher Hibbert, *Queen Victoria: A Personal History*.

Stanley Weintraub, *Albert, Uncrowned King*.

Supplementary Reading:

Lytton Strachey, *Queen Victoria*.

Juliet Gardiner, *Queen Victoria*.

Questions to Consider:

1. What qualities enabled Victoria to revive the popularity of the monarchy?

2. What were the benefits and drawbacks to Britain of maintaining a queen?

Lecture Two—Transcript
Victoria's Early Reign—1837–1861

Victoria came to the British throne in 1837 at the age of eighteen. Her predecessors, George III, George IV, and William IV had been unimpressive kings and they had impaired the reputation of the monarchy. By her authority and her example, Victoria restored its reputation and dignity and embodied, represented, the era's mood and moral improvement. Along with her husband, Prince Albert of Saxe-Coburg-Gotha, whom she married in 1840, Victoria made the most of what limited political power and influence the monarchy still retained within the British constitutional monarchy system. She communicated regularly throughout her entire reign with her Prime Ministers. She also bore nine children and enjoyed many of the advantages of the industrial society in which she was living.

Her marriage was in 1840, and she became very devoted to Prince Albert, so his death in 1861 was a shattering catastrophe. In this lecture we are going to follow Victoria from her birth up to that point. She was born in 1819 and at first didn't seem ever to be likely to become the monarch, the queen. The British system of succession is that if the king has a son, the son will always take the throne first. Only if there are no direct male heirs will the throne devolve onto a princess. That is what happened in this case. She finally succeeded her uncle William IV because none of his legitimate children survived to adulthood.

She herself was the daughter of the younger brother of King George IV, the Duke of Kent. Her grandfather was George III, and because he had gone mad for long periods, for the rest of her life she was terribly afraid that she also might suffer from madness, although only in events. She was extremely level-headed and sensible and down to earth. Her father, the Duke of Kent, died before she was one year old, so, in fact, she never knew him. Her mother, who was a minor German princess, (These were the days when Germany was divided up into dozens of little principalities.) was left with a tiny allowance that the rather grudging British government had given to her. Then, when William IV's children all died in infancy, it suddenly began to occur to the powers that she was likely to become the heir, and, as that probability increased, so did her mother's income and her mother's ability to give her a relatively first-class education. William IV, incidentally, had ten children who did survive, but they were all by one of his mistresses, so they were ineligible for succession to the throne.

Victoria's education was very strong in foreign languages. She was fluent in German and French, was good at Italian, and wrote a regular diary, so we know that from the age of 10 or 11 onwards, she was also a fluent prose stylist. One of her music teachers was Mendelssohn, one of the great composers of the day, and during her childhood she visited many of the great aristocratic houses of Britain, so she was already familiar with the kinds of circles in which she would move when she became the monarch. What she didn't have was childhood friends. Most of her childhood was very lonely. She was constantly in the society of adults but rarely with other children. Her closest friend was probably her governess, Louise Lehzen.

Louise Lehzen was herself a German woman, and the daughter of a Lutheran minister from Hanover, and her very strict standards had brought Victoria up to hold herself proudly and to think of herself as a queen. Later on in life, Victoria wrote a reminiscence of her own childhood. I'll read you a little passage from it. It is all in the third person. She often used the royal "we" but also refers to herself in the third person. "The princess (herself) had a great respect and even awe of her, beyond that the warmest affections. She would often amuse and play with the princess so as to gain her warmest affections. The princess was her only object and her only thought. She never, for the 13 years she was governess to princess Victoria, never once left her." It was also Lehzen who taught her not to gossip with the servants and to set a very high tone in her regal bearing.

While this is going on, particularly once it becomes clear that Victoria is probably going to succeed to the throne, her mother was scheming with one of her favorite courtiers, an Irishman called Sir John Conroy, to make him the regent. If she became queen while she was still not of age, a regency would follow, and the mother and Conroy were hoping to get it. She herself resented this scheming very bitterly. On the event, she was old enough to take on the responsibilities herself, with the result that the mother and Conroy were disappointed.

She was notified early in the morning of June 20, 1837 and was brought down in her dressing gown to meet the Archbishop of Canterbury and Lord Coyningham, the Lord Chancellor, who had come to notify her of what had happened, that she was now the queen. She wrote in her diary that night: "Since it has pleased providence to place me in this station, I shall do my utmost to fulfill my duty toward my country; I am very young and perhaps in many, though not all things, inexperienced, but I am sure that very few have more real good will and more real desire to do what is right than I have."

She was lucky in having the Prime Minister at that time, Lord Melbourne. He was a Prime Minister from the Whig Party, and he tutored her in her duties as queen. He was a widower, and he'd had a very stormy marriage. His wife was one of the English ladies who had run away with Lord Byron, the poet, and had a stormy affair with him and was thought to be mentally unstable, so he was thought to have an unhappy married life.

Victoria regarded him as a father figure, or perhaps even a grandfather figure, because she had never known her own father, but she got from Melbourne the kind of sympathetic attention, love, and help that she had not previously had from a male friend. He came there to run affairs, and on days when they were apart they wrote letters to each other every day. So, they were very close for the first four or five years of her reign. Melbourne used to tell her stories about her own wicked uncle, this shoddy cruster who'd been on the throne legally before her. He'd known Lord Nelson, and he had known Napoleon, for that matter. He'd lived right through the Napoleonic wars and so was able to pass on great stories to her of the defiance of the preceding generation.

He wasn't a very godly man, and when they would go to church together he would fall asleep and sometimes begin to snore. Although she had high standards, she thought, "Old Melbourne is terribly busy. We must be indulgent toward him." Here is a letter she wrote to her uncle Leopold, who was the king of Belgium and a man to whom she was very close:

> "Let me pause to tell you how fortunate I am to have at the head of the government a man like Lord Melbourne. I see him now every day, with the exception of Friday, and the more I see of him, the more I have confidence in him; he is not only a clever statesman and an honest man, but a good and kind-hearted man, whose aim is to do his duty for his country and not just for his party. He is of the greatest use to

me both politically and privately… It gives me the greatest pleasure to do my duty for my country and for my people, and no fatigue, however great, will be burdensome to me if it is for the welfare of the nation."

That is likely written after she had been queen for about a week.

Sir Sidney Lee, our commentator of the time, said her predecessors were an imbecile, a profligate, and a buffoon. With that low starting point, it was easy for her to restore the credibility of the monarchy, and she certainly did. As she went out in her carriage in the streets, people came out to cheer. She was pretty in those days and widely liked. However, in 1839, about two years after her accession, Lord Melbourne had to resign in a political crisis.

The leader of the Tory party, Robert Peel, was going to become the Prime Minister in Melbourne's place. One of the things Peel wanted to do was to replace the Ladies Of The Bedchamber, that is, the queen's household servants. He said when she became queen, Lord Nelson made a group of Whig ladies the Ladies Of The Bedchamber. "Now I want to put Tory ladies there. After all, one set of political sympathies has been well expressed. Now it is time for another set." The queen put her foot down and flatly refused. She liked her ladies, she liked the way things were already, and she absolutely refused to let this happen. This event in British history is remembered as the Bedchamber Crisis. It's not quite as interesting as it sounds.

Peel said, "If the queen won't accept these ladies, I refuse to take office," with the result that Melbourne came back and limped on as a kind of lame duck Prime Minister for a couple more years, and the changeover actually took place in 1841. The system of switching wasn't quite as smooth as it has subsequently become. This is a pattern that was set down and continued throughout her whole reign, almost whenever there was a change of government. She resented the newcomer at first, but it wasn't long before she came to like and admire him in turn and to grieve when he had to go. So, Peel, whom at first she didn't like at all, when he had to resign in 1846, she was devastated and said "I can't imagine how we are going to get on now that we haven't got Peel among us anymore." The only one whom she profoundly disliked was William Gladstone, the great Liberal leader, whom many people think of as one of Britain's greatest politicians ever.

She found it difficult to accept that she was now only a constitutional monarch; she didn't actually have political power. For example, in the late 1840s, the foreign secretary was Lord Palmerston, another of the great figures of mid 19th-century political history. She didn't like him particularly because his foreign policy toward Europe was sometimes antagonistic to states with which she had warm relations because her relatives were the monarchs there. She tried to persuade the Prime Minister John Russell to get rid of Palmerston altogether because she was unable to subordinate him to her will. Russell and Palmerston both knew that although the queen had influence, although her opinion ought to be solicited, it could no longer be the compelling factor in policy making.

When Britain went to war against Russia in the Crimea in 1854, she reviewed her troops, and she created a medal called the Victoria Cross which, from that time to the present, remained the very highest award for bravery that can be given to a British military person. She awarded it not only to officers who had won the medal but also to enlisted men, something which had never previously been done by a monarch. She wanted to get a little more directly involved in the lives of all the soldiers.

She married in 1840 one of her cousins, Prince Albert of Saxe-Coburg-Gotha, another of the little German principalities. In getting married and in the early years of the marriage, she was very keen to show him that, although he might be the *paterfamilias,* she was the queen. That was the thing which counted most. Albert himself was a very earnest young man, by all accounts rather humorless. He had been educated at the University of Bonn. He was an intelligent and very gifted person. This uncle whom I mentioned, the King of Belgium, King Leopold, had foreseen the possibility of a marriage between the two of them because they were exact contemporaries. Leopold had, in effect, trained Albert for the job of becoming Victoria's husband. It was a gamble because no one could ever be certain that the marriage was ever going to come off.

At first, Victoria didn't like the sound of it. She wasn't keen at all. When he came to Britain in 1839, she began to thaw because he was handsome and had excellent manners. He was serious and charming and many of the qualities she might have looked for in a husband "he seemed to embody," is what she wrote in her journal shortly after meeting him. One of the pleasures of studying diary entries and the like, and so many letters and so many memorandums, that we have tens of thousands of pages of her writing and, whatever the subject is, we can always find out what she thought. He was also very deep. Here is what she said:

> "Albert is really quite charming and so excessively handsome, such beautiful blue eyes, an exquisite nose, and such a pretty mouth with delicate mustachios and slight but very slight whiskers, a beautiful figure, broad in the shoulders and a slim waist. My heart is quite going. It is quite a pleasure to look at Albert when he gallops and waltzes. He does it so beautifully, holds himself so well with that beautiful figure… "

And so on. We can see that she is already getting enthusiastic. So, it wasn't long before she proposed to him. Normally, it would be the other way around, but she was the queen. She writes all about that as well. So, let's just go around and look at the diary.

> "I said to him…that it would make me too happy if he would consent to what I wished…we embraced each other over and over again, and he was so kind, so affectionate. To feel that I am loved by such an angel as Albert is too great a delight to describe. He is perfection; perfection in every way. In beauty, in everything…I thought it was the happiest moment of my life."

There we are. She is carried away but not to the extent that she is willing to surrender any of her prerogatives. Listen to a scene among them two or three days after the proposal. She is showing that she is in charge and he can have only a very subordinate role. "I signed some papers and warrants, etc,, and he was so kind as to dry them with blotting paper for me. We talked a good deal together and he clasped me so tenderly in his arms and kissed me again and again." That was his role, to hold, and blotting of papers.

In the early years of their marriage, which took place in 1840, at first he was clearly the subordinate figure. Here is a quotation from Lytton Strachey. He was the one who wrote *Eminent Victorians,* and then went on to do a biography of Victoria herself. It is a very entertaining book. Here is a little passage from it about him.

> "Albert, brought up in a regime of Spartan simplicity and early hours, found the great court functions intolerably wearisome and was invariably observed to be nodding off on the sofa at half past ten, while the queen's favorite form of enjoyment was to dance through the night, then, going out onto the portico of the palace, watch the sun rise on St. Paul's and the towers of Westminster."

The British people traditionally don't like foreigners. There is a long history of xenophobia in Britain, and the fact that Albert was German made him a subject of suspicion. The queen understood that and so did her ministers. It was necessary almost as a matter of policy not to give authority to this man who had just arrived from Germany. It wasn't until 1857 that he was given the title of Prince Consort, and just as the queen's choice of her bedchamber ladies had been restricted, so was his choice of companions. He wasn't allowed to bring with him from Germany members of his own household. Instead, British men were given him as servants and advisers, just as the queen had her people appointed.

At first he was rather awkward and rather frosty and difficult to get to know. Here is another little passage from Strachey.

> "Owing partly to a natural awkwardness, partly to a fear of undue familiarity, and partly to a desire to be absolutely correct, his manners were infused with an extraordinary stiffness and formality. Whenever he appeared in company, he seemed to be surrounded by a thick hedge of prickly etiquette."

The queen at first let him have no political authority at all. Gradually, his abilities began to show themselves and he started to be admitted into the interior circles of British political life. The first thing he did to get a good reputation was to restore the conduct of the royal household. The royal household was run in a chaotic way. Over the centuries, an accretion of special offices, duties, privileges, and rights had come in so that the palace was absolutely full of people, many of whom had very little jobs to do and for which they got very big salaries. For example, there were three different sets of servants, one to clear out the ashes from the grates, a second set to lay a new fire, and a third lot to actually light the fire. Not only was it cumbersome, it was very difficult to get the fire quickly changed when you needed it, that sort of thing.

Prince Albert took the whole thing in hand, rationalized the administration of the royal household from top to bottom, got rid of dozens of unnecessary servants and sinecure holders, with the result that the household was run better and at far less cost. You can imagine that the government is enthusiastic about anyone who can save it some money. It wasn't long before the ministers began to realize that Prince Albert was a real asset. "We can use him."

When she was starting to give birth for the first time, less than a year after their marriage, he was admitted to the Privy Council, the group of ministers immediately around the monarch, and was named regent in the event of her death. This is a time when death in childbirth was common. Women often died in their twenties and thirties giving birth. So, the possibility of a regency reemerged, and Albert was named. That is a measure of his admission into the favored circles.

Here is a letter that Albert wrote to his father in 1841, after a year and a half: "I study the politics of the day with great industry. I speak quite openly on all subjects. And I endeavor quietly to be as much use to Victoria in her position as I can be." Here is a letter from Victoria to her uncle Leopold. "Albert is indeed a great comfort to me. He takes the greatest possible interest in what goes on, feeling with me and for me, and yet abstaining to keep from biasing me either way. We talk much on every subject and his judgment is, as you say, good and calm." British politicians of both parties came to respect him for his hard work, active conscience and good judgment, and for his very high moral tone.

When we think about Victorian morality, we have an idea of an extraordinary stiffness, an intolerance. Certainly, some of that does come from Prince Albert. Finally, it was he who smoothed the transition from Lord Melbourne to Robert Peel as Prime Minister in 1841. Peel himself was grateful to Prince Albert and took him increasingly into his confidence.

Victoria and Albert, as the first family in the land, enjoyed many of the amenities of this new industrial society in which they were living. They bought and renovated two houses, Osborne House on the Isle of Wight and Balmoral Castle in the Scottish highlands, both of which you can now go to visit. They expensively rebuilt them, and they built them in archaic styles. Balmoral is Scottish Gothic. At a glance, they may look like ancient houses, but actually they are from the 1840s and 1850s. They took advantage of all the modern technologies, particularly iron-framed buildings. This is the century in which, for the first time, iron could be extensively used as a building frame instead of just masonry.

They spent a lot of time at Balmoral in Scotland, both loving it very much. It was there that Victoria sketched and painted, rode a lot with her servant John Brown, who was later to mean so much in her life, and learned Scottish dances. Prince Albert would go out stalking deer, and he tried to learn Gaelic, the Scottish language, although he didn't make very much progress. Later, after Albert's death, Queen Victoria wrote a little book called *Leaves from a Journal of Our Life in the Highlands.* It is really just a collection of pictures from Scottish life, but it was the book about which Benjamin Disraeli later on was able to say, "Are we authors, Madam?" because he had written dozens of novels and was a real author.

Queen Victoria was the first monarch to travel by train. While the Great Western Railroad had just been completed, she went from Windsor Castle, another of her residences, into London—it is only a matter of about 20 or 25 miles, on Brunel's Great Western Railway— and enjoyed it very much, although Albert thought the train went a bit too fast. He told the driver, "A little slower next time if you please, conductor." After that, she had her own private train built. It is still visible. You can go to the National Railway Museum in York and see Queen Victoria's train. Wherever the railway was going, that is how they traveled. The railway was by far the easiest way to get around. Her regular trips to Osborne in the Isle of Wight, to Sandringham in East Anglia, and to Balmoral in Scotland, she would go by train. Before each journey, her secretary would send a note to the railway company which would include this sentence: "The queen travels at 40 miles per hour." In other words, whatever you have scheduled, that was how fast the royal train was going to go.

A royal yacht was built in 1842 called the *Victoria and Albert,* and it used another brand-new technology, propellers. You probably remember that the earliest steamships had paddle wheels. Propellers were built in 1840, 1841. Straightaway, Victoria and Albert said, "Yes, let's try this new technology." They were very up to date. When we think about Victorian Britain, we think as though we are looking back on old stuff. What we have to do is to get into the frame of mind of the people that it was all new. The royal family was enthusiastic about new things.

In 1853, she was giving birth for the eighth time, to Prince Leopold, and she decided to experiment with anesthetics. She was given chloroform, which was just then being developed as an anesthetic, and successfully gave birth to Prince Leopold. She loved it. She called it "that blessed chloroform, soothing and delightful beyond measure." Some of the clergy, members of the church, were indignant about that because they said according to the book of *Genesis* women should suffer in giving birth. It is not right. It is deviating from our biblical duty to give birth in that way. She said, "Nonsense," and when she gave birth for the ninth time to Princess Beatrice she did it again. Incidentally, there is one prince, the eighth one, Prince Leopold, who was a hemophiliac. He suffered from uncontrollable bleeding and died early, having had a life of constant anxiety. There is no connection between the chloroform and the hemophilia.

She liked children, but she didn't like babies. This is a letter to one of her daughters, later on in life. "An ugly baby is a very nasty object, and even the prettiest is frightful when undressed, until about four months old; in short, as long as they have their big body and little limbs and that terrible frog-like action…"—clearly not the enthusiast for her own babies. She also suffered from what we now call post-partum depression. She became intensely depressed after giving birth, and it happened a lot. Sometimes she would fly into uncontrollable rages against Prince Albert, and, again, we have detailed written records of all their arguments. They have intense rows. They would fight verbally for a while, and then eventually he would withdraw and they would send letters to each other, many of which also still survive through which we can trace a documented course of their arguments.

His letters to her are rather condescending. He points out to her why it was that she lost her temper and where her faulty reasoning was, and eventually after a week or three she would feel better and they would get back together again and go off. So, in a way, it was a very intense and warm marriage on the whole. It certainly wasn't entirely trouble free. One of the anxieties that they shared was that their oldest son Bertie, who was due to become the next king, didn't live up to their standards. He wasn't as hard working as they would have liked. He wasn't as disciplined as they would have liked. He didn't seem particularly interested in serious matters, and he was a bit of a rogue. They worried chronically about Bertie.

In 1851, one of the highlights of their life together took place when the Great Exhibition opened in Hyde Park. This was one of the world's first trade fairs, world's fairs, in a beautiful building called the Crystal Palace, which I will talk more about later in the course. Albert had been a member of the planning committee which had brought it all together and made it happen. The queen opened it up on a spring morning in 1851, and at the end of the day wrote this letter to Uncle Leopold.

> "I wish you could have witnessed the 1st May 1851, the greatest day in our history, the most beautiful and imposing and touching spectacle ever seen, and the triumph of my beloved Albert. Truly it was astonishing, a fair scene. Many cried, and all felt touched and impressed with devotional feelings. It was the happiest, proudest day of my life and I can think of nothing else. Albert's name seems immortalized with the great conception, his own, and my dear country showed that she was worthy of it."

You can imagine that under these circumstances Prince Albert's death in 1861 came as an absolute catastrophe, a shattering blow from which she never fully recovered. In the short term, it sent her into a profound depression and withdrawal from society. Here is how it came about. Bertie, the prince, had a sexual affair with a musical actress, Nellie Clifton. It was common among the members of the upper classes to have flings with low-class women. Prince Albert found out about it. He was outraged, and he commanded repentance from his son. In fact, he did get a very penitent letter from Bertie.

Prince Albert feared all the possible consequences. There might be a baby. There might be revelations to the press. There might be a great public scandal. He himself would never had descended to such things and was horrified that his son, then about 18, had done so. He was already not well. He had a lot of anxious complaints, insomnia, rheumatism. Then when he went out to review some soldiers at Sandhurst, the British Military Academy, he became sick and got rheumatism because it was in the pouring rain. His condition got worse after he went up to Cambridge where Bertie was studying and had a long walk through the parks and Cambridge with Bertie, reproaching him and chastising him. It must have been an agonizingly embarrassing scene for both of them. When he got back to Windsor Castle, he collapsed. In the course of the next few days, he worsened and died.

Many things are striking about the scene, but one is that everything took place in public. As Albert's condition worsened, there were doctors and courtiers and members of the family, a big crowd in the room. In those days, death tended to be a very public matter. Here is a description of the deathbed scene.

> "I took his dear left had which was already cold...and knelt down by him...All, all was over...I stood up and kissed his dear heavenly forehead and called out in a bitter and agonizing cry "Oh, my dear darling," then I dropped on my knees in mute, distracted despair, unable to utter a word or shed a tear...Then, I lay down on the sofa in the red room and all the gentlemen came in and knelt down and kissed my hand, and I said a word to each."

She is surrounded by people as this is going on. Every day from then until the end of her own life, which lasted for another 40 years, she had Prince Albert's shaving gear brought in the morning. She had his bathrobe ready. They had a double desk where they had done their work. She had new paper and pens laid out on his side of the desk. She often used to go to bed with a plaster cast of one of his hands which she would hold when she went to sleep. In the early 1860s, she refused to attend public functions at all. She became more and more reclusive, with the result that her Prime Minister at that time, Lord Palmerston, was afraid that republicanism might start to gain ground in British politics as the queen had seemingly abdicated her responsibilities. The whole of the rest of her life, she wore black mourning clothes.

Nearly every public building in Britain that was made in the 1860s is named after Prince Albert—the Albert Hall, the Albert Memorial. As you go through Britain, you constantly see Albert Street. It is a fair guess that it was in the 1860s that they were put together.

Although they hadn't a trouble-free life, certainly Albert had been central to her existence. His death was an irreplaceable blot.

Lecture Three
The Industrial Revolution—1750–1830

Scope:

Britain was in the midst of a profound transformation when Victoria became queen. In the preceding 50 years, it had taken many of the steps necessary to become a primarily industrial nation. Agricultural enclosures and the beginning of scientific farming had raised crop yields. The nation had been politically stable since the Glorious Revolution of 1689, enabling it to develop a strong commercial infrastructure. The invention of cotton spinning machines and steam engines to drive them began the Industrial Revolution. Displaced farmers and a rising population provided the labor force and a growing demand for the goods factories could produce. Workers had to adapt to factory life and discipline rather than living according to daylight and the seasons. Transportation developments and pursuit of overseas markets accelerated the Industrial Revolution.

Outline

I. British farming was becoming more productive.

    A. British farming had historically been done on the open-field system.

        1. Each farmer had the right to plant crops on strips of land in the open fields.

        2. Each had the right to graze his animals on the village common and gather firewood in the local "waste."

        3. The squire was usually also the local magistrate.

        4. The Church of England vicar, usually appointed by the squire, was often the only other literate person in the community.

    B. The enclosure movement transformed rural Britain, more rapidly after 1750.

        1. Ambitious landlords realized that farming could be more profitable if farms were consolidated and fenced.

        2. They took advantage of developments in scientific agriculture and early farm machinery.

        3. Poor cottagers and smallholders lacked the money to enclose or lacked legal proof of their rights to do so.

        4. Many became landless farm laborers or migrated to the growing industrial cities.

II. Historians debate the reasons for Britain's industrialization, which began in the 18th century, but most agree on several main factors.

    A. Britain had enjoyed political stability since the Glorious Revolution of 1689; therefore, businessmen felt confident that their investments would not be destroyed by revolutionary mobs or invaders.

    B. Britain's commercial prosperity as a worldwide trader had led to the accumulation of capital that was available for investment.

    C. Britain had already developed sophisticated banking and insurance institutions to facilitate the high costs of industry.

    D. Britain's growing population at home provided potential customers, as did its growing empire and its aggressively mercantile foreign policy. England's population grew from about six million in 1750 to 13 million in 1830; the rate of growth accelerated after 1800.

    E. Rural depopulation, because of enclosure, also provided a labor force.

III. A series of inventions made factory production possible.

    A. Richard Arkwright's water frame, powered by the River Derwent at Cromford, enabled mass production of cotton thread in factories.

    B. Power looms after 1815 made machine weaving possible, too.

    C. The application of steam power to these textile processes meant that the makers would be less dependent on steady river levels.

IV. Steam power was crucial first in mining, later in textiles.

    A. Britain had been honeycombed with tin, iron, coal, clay, lead, and silver mines ever since the Roman era, but deep mines were chronically subject to flooding.

B. The first steam engines, invented by Thomas Savery and Thomas Newcomen in the early 18th century, were building-sized machines whose job was to pump water out of flooded mines.

    1. They can still be seen in operation at the Live Steam Museum in Kew, London.

    2. James Watt made crucial improvements in their efficiency.

C. Abundant coal supplies fueled the Industrial Revolution, already amounting to more than one million tons per year by 1800.

V. Iron and steel making were other key components of industrialization.

    A. The Darby family, father, son, and grandson, pioneered new iron founding and smelting techniques at Coalbrookdale, Shropshire.

        1. They learned how to replace limited charcoal resources with abundant hot-burning coke.

        2. They built the world's first iron bridge at a town now named Ironbridge.

    B. Their rival, John "Mad Iron" Wilkinson, built the world's first iron barge and proved that a metal vessel can float.

VI. The final component of early industrial improvements was the transportation revolution.

    A. Road transport was difficult before the mid-18th century.

        1. Roads were often swampy and rutted.

        2. Wagons could not carry heavy loads, were very slow, and had to stop for bad weather.

        3. Overland haulage, especially in winter, was often restricted to packhorses, which were slow and made transport costs high.

    B. River trade was hampered by waterfalls, rapids, and seasonal low flows. Coastal trade (such as coal from Newcastle to London) was vulnerable to rough seas.

    C. A generation of canal and road builders vastly improved and cheapened the safe transportation of bulk goods.

VII. Early industrialists not only had to overcome technical and financial problems, but they also had to teach a new way of life to the work force.

  A. Early factories often featured a clock tower (few workers owned clocks or watches), and employers taught their workers how to tell the time.

  B. Employers tried to convert erstwhile farm workers from living according to the daylight and seasons to an idea of punctuality based on clocks and factory whistles. Some religious, nonconformist employers tried to impose puritanical standards of sobriety on their workers.

  C. In textiles particularly, employers had more use for women than men as machine minders. The work was repetitive and monotonous rather than physically demanding.

  D. The low skill levels, along with the rapidly growing northern city populations, enabled manufacturers to pay meager wages.

  1. Their cold-hearted economic logic, parodied by Charles Dickens in *Hard Times* and elsewhere, ensured a hard life even for those who were in regular work.

  2. They were sowing the seeds for a later harvest of class bitterness and ugly industrial relations.

Essential Reading:

Harold Perkin, *The Origins of Modern English Society, 1780–1880*.

Eric Hobsbawm, *Industry and Empire*.

Supplementary Reading:

Peter Laslett, *The World We Have Lost*.

M. J. Daunton, *Progress and Poverty: An Economic and Social History of Britain: 1700–1850*.

Questions to Consider:

1. What changes in British life made the Industrial Revolution possible?

2. Did the benefits of industrialization outweigh the drawbacks?

Lecture Three—Transcript
The Industrial Revolution—1750-1830

Britain was in the middle of a great transformation when Victoria became queen. In the preceding 50 years, it had taken many of the steps necessary to become a primarily industrial nation. Agricultural enclosures and the beginning of scientific farming had raised crop yields, so now it was less necessary for as many people in the population to devote themselves to farming. Also, the nation had been politically stable ever since the Glorious Revolution back in 1689. This long period of peace and tranquility at home had enabled it to develop a strong commercial infrastructure.

The invention of cotton spinning machines and the steam engines to drive them is what really set off the industrial revolution. Displaced farm workers and a rising population created a labor force and a growing demand for the goods that the factories could now produce. People going from agriculture into factory life had to adapt in a way which for us is hard to realize, learning a new kind of attitude toward time, the seasons, and the discipline of industrial work by contrast of that of work in workshops or on the land. Finally, transport developments and the pursuit of overseas markets, particularly in the Empire, accelerated the industrial revolution by continually generating more stimulus.

Let's look first of all at the agricultural questions. Historically, British farming had been done mainly on the open field system. In many parts of Britain still today, when you look at fields, you can see an undulation, a wavering between shallow depressions and crests. This is because the fields had been broken up into strips. A typical parish, village, would have a series of large open fields divided into strips of land, and each of the farmers living in the village would have strips in each of the fields. It was a way of sharing out the better farmland. Each man had the right to graze his own animals on the village common, a piece of open land, the kind of common you can still see occasionally in American villages like Lexington. Each one had traditional rights to gather firewood in the village waste area where it was possible to graze animals and pick up wood.

These communities were very isolated and insular, especially in the days before the transportation revolution. In the late 1700s it was common for the only two literate people in the village to be the squire and the vicar, sometimes not even the squire, or he would have some elementary literacy. The squire was usually the local magistrate who resolved problems arising inside the little village. The vicar was the one to whom everyone would go to listen to preaching on Sundays and was also the person who would bring news into the community from the outside world. Britain was made up of hundreds of these little agricultural islands.

The enclosure movement was beginning to transform Britain. It had begun earlier, but had begun to accelerate after 1750. Ambitious landlords realized that farming could be much more profitable if, instead of having the fields broken up into these little strips and consolidated and fenced, it was possible to use some of the new farm machines which were just beginning to be invented, and it was going to be possible to do things like selective breeding of animals rather than have them mingling indiscriminately on the commons. In the late 1700s, agricultural chemistry was in its infancy; it was just beginning. But the idea of farming more scientifically was beginning to attract the attention of more ambitious farmers. So, there was selective breeding, intensive cultivation, the use of the first farm machines, and also the introduction of new crops which made different demands on the soil.

Usually what had happened was that a simple rotation system would take place. A different crop would be growing in the field each year, and then after two or three years it would be left fallow for a year to begin to recover some of its nutrients. They now have the possibility of using legumes which can actually introduce nitrogen compounds into the soil, and were starting to replace the old haphazard methods that had been used time out of mind. This enclosure system usually required an act of parliament. It was expensive and time consuming. Whereas only the more prosperous farmers could hope to participate, the ones who lived a marginal existence already, the poor cottagers or small holders, the ones who did not have a defendable legal title to any of the land were often unable to prove that they had a right to participate in this system. Some of them became either landless farm laborers—they worked for some of the enclosing farmers—or they migrated out to the new industrial towns. These are the people who actually provided the labor force which was going to make the industrial revolution work.

The depopulation of the British countryside was much remarked upon at the time in the mid and late 1700s. A famous poem by Oliver Goldsmith is called "The Deserted Village." It is a description of a village that once had a thriving farm life, but no longer, because one of their enclosing landlords has driven away the poor farmers who live there. A couple of lines from it, "Ill fares the land to hast'ning ills a prey, where wealth accumulates, and men decay."

One of the great debates among British historians is "Why did the industrial revolution take place and why did it take place first in Britain? It is an immensely complicated debate, and I can't hope to do justice to it in the course of this time. Just let me enumerate some of the principle factors on which all of the historians agree. First of all, there is the matter of political stability. It is very difficult to overestimate its importance. Nobody is going to take the risk of building a factory because of the enormous expenditure it entails if he isn't confident that it is going to stay there, if it is going to be burned down by an incendiary mob, or if a dramatic change of regime is going to lead to it being taken out of his hands. The businessmen had to feel confident that their investment was not going to be destroyed and that their right to it would be widely honored in this society.

Over the preceding hundred years, in the late 1600s and early and mid 1700s, Britain had already got a worldwide commercial interest. British traders had been sailing across the world. This is a time when India was being conquered and so on. These merchants and traders started accumulating capital. They had the money to put to work in big new projects; that is, the money itself was available. It had already developed the sophisticated banking and insurance institutions which are necessary if you are going to have an industrial society.

Insurance: At first it was regarded with horror particularly life insurance. The idea that you would bet against somebody's death seemed to be almost sacrilegious. It wasn't long before the pioneers of insurance, people like Lloyd's in London, had overcome that idea and started to make a regular business of it. Britain itself had a rapidly growing population. That itself meant that there were going to be more customers available for the produce of the new factories. The population of England was about six million in 1750. By 1830, it was about 13 million. It more than doubled in that 80-year period, with the rate of growth accelerating after 1800. The whole British population is rapidly getting much bigger.

That is another thing that is of much dispute among historians, is that there are so many conflicting factors. The population will rise if the death rate falls or life expectancy increases. There are other factors; for example, the falling age of marriage. More and more British women were marrying younger. That meant that they had more years of fertility and the possibility of giving birth to more children. More of these children tended to survive. It was still an extremely anxious prospect. There were slightly more. There were slight improvements in food. The yield of British agriculture was going up steadily in the face of these improvements.

There were also some primitive medical improvements, such as the introduction of smallpox inoculations at the end of the 18th century. About 16 percent of all the people who died in Britain in 1750 died of smallpox. By 1850, only about 1 percent did. Smallpox had traditionally been one of the great killers, and it was becoming decreasingly so. Certainly, the net effect was a rising population.

Obviously, industrialization presupposed certain machines, inventions; and generations of practical, industrious, ingenious men made the stuff which made it happen. Already, before mechanization, the subdivision of labor started to take place in workshops. The subdivision of labor is important. One of the books written in this period is Adam Smith's book *An Inquiry into the Wealth of Nations*, published in 1776. Think about the title for a second, *An Inquiry into the Wealth of Nations*. Adam Smith's great puzzle was this: Why are some nations wealthy? Where does wealth come from? We now live in a world where we say things like, "Why is there still so much poverty?" It is only because we are so very rich that we can even ask that question. Throughout the whole history of the world, poverty had been almost universal. It still is in many places, but now some nations were becoming wealthy, and Britain was first among them. That is what drew Smith's attention.

He pointed out that one of the ways that you became more efficient and more productive was through the subdivision of labor. If you have one man making a pair of shoes from start to finish, he will produce one shoe. If you have 20 men doing it, they will produce far more than 20 shoes in the same period that he has produced one.

Really, you get economies of scale doing it in that way. Smith had worked on this puzzle particularly with reference to the nail-making industry which is the example he uses.

Once work had been brought together in workshops, the next stage was to mechanize it. The very earliest factories relied on water power. For example, Richard Arkwright, who is one of the pioneers, built a water-powered factory in Cromford, in Derbyshire, which is very close to my home town. The water in the fast-flowing River Derwent turned water wheels which were connected to machinery inside the factory which made cotton thread at very high speed, where previously it had just been done individually, usually by ladies with spinning wheels. The cotton came from the British West Indies, and then, after the 1790s, it came mainly from the American south. It was in 1792 that Eli Whitney invented the cotton gin, which made it possible for American cotton to be used commercially in the development of cotton cloth. Very rapidly after the American Revolution, Britain and America resumed close commercial relations, particularly in this matter of cotton, because cotton was the commodity on which the industrial revolution developed, and it nearly all came from the American south, the slave south.

After the thread had been made, then hand loom weavers would turn it into cloth. The spinning machines were invented first. So, between 1780 and 1820, there is a great boom in hand loom weaving. Then, when machines were invented to do the weaving instead, the hand loom weavers went into a great depression because they could not compete adequately with the factories. There is a picture of a hand loom weaver in George Eliot's novel *Silas Marner*. It has been assigned to generations of American school children. It is a fabulous book if you don't read it too early in life. It is about a hand loom weaver, and he is a miser. It is about how his life is transformed by his discovery of a lovely orphan girl. Power looms developed after 1850 made machine weaving possible too.

Then, the application of steam power to these processes of spinning and weaving made it more dependable. The problem with relying on water power is that rivers flow at different rates depending on rainfall upstream. There are seasons when the river tends to flow high and be reliable, and then if it is dry for a long spell, especially in the summer and early fall, you can't get as much power. So, the factory would tend to slow down. Steam engines aren't constrained in the same way. They can run at whatever rate you set for them.

That means that, having begun in the countryside, the industrial revolution could then move to town. At first, the factories had to be sited beside fast-flowing rivers, usually in rural areas. Once they had become adapted to steam, they could move into town, where they had the advantage of being close together and near port authorities and so on. Manchester became the center of the cotton textile industry. This is in the northwest of England about 15 miles inland from the port of Liverpool. About 1830, Manchester contained hundreds of steam powered cotton factories, enough to make cotton cloth for the whole nation and plenty for export as well.

When historians talk about the Manchester School, what they are talking about is the economic theory of the Manchester cotton factory owners. They were people who were enthusiastic for free trade. They said, "Let's get rid of all the tariff barriers so that we can trade freely with our commodities throughout the world. That way, we are going to be far more profitable than if we are confined by customs and excise duties to having our product be expensive abroad." One of the most successful of these Lancashire cotton owners was Sir Robert Peel, who lived from 1750 to 1830. He was the father of the man who became Queen Victoria's second Prime Minister, Robert Peel, Jr. He made a fortune, primarily in cotton manufacture, and left his son about a million pounds. The son didn't have to go into business. The son could be a landowner, a gentleman, even join the Tory party and become Prime Minister in his generation.

Steam power is absolutely crucial, so a word about steam itself. Britain had already been a mining country for centuries, ever since it was part of the Roman Empire—tin mines, iron ore mines, coal, clay, lead, and silver. The main problem with mining in Britain is that you only have to dig down in the mine a few feet before the mine starts to flood. Underwater aquifers are constantly flooding the mines. The very first steam engines were developed to pump water out of mines. The first ones were developed by Thomas Savery and Thomas Newcomen in the early 18th century. They were absolutely vast. They were as big as a four-story building, huge great things. There are two or three of them still operating. One of the best places to go to visit in Britain, if you are interested in Victorian artifacts, is the

Live Steam Museum in Kew (near Kew Gardens.) It is a wonderful old water work where they have some of these old steam engines still operating. They only rotate about once or twice a minute. They're very, very slow. Each stroke of the engine with these colossal cylinders could bring up 100 or 200 gallons of water for draining the mines.

Crucial improvements to steam engines were made by James Watt. He is the man who is often credited with inventing the steam engine. That is not particularly true. He was perfecting a technology which already existed. He certainly made them much more efficient with the result that eventually they could be miniaturized to ultimately be placed on moving locomotives. The steam engines in turn needed a source of fuel, and coal was the fuel. There was lots of coal mining in Britain already, particularly in Newcastle-on-Tyne. This is in the northeast of England near the Scottish border. Already by 1800 a million tons a year of coal was being mined in the Northumberland coal fields. The result was that everything was covered in soot, at least everything in urban areas. Coal in huge quantities was shipped from Newcastle-on-Tyne down the east coast of Britain to the port of London. Remember the south was a massive importer of coal. Everyone had a coal fire for keeping warm, and that is how cooking was done as well. It was all very dirty.

Until 1952, London had awful fogs. The London pea soup fog was a famous and dangerous source of pollution. The fog would form around gross smoke particles in the air. There actually was legislation which was cast in the 1950s to get rid of the smoke. The fog disappeared as well. London hasn't been a foggy place since the 1950s. It certainly was all through the 19th century. There is an area near Birmingham called The Black Country. It is black because everything is covered in soot. Princess Victoria, when she was a 13-year-old, traveled through this area in a carriage. This is what she wrote in her journal then. This is the 13-year-old Victoria, before she became queen.

> "We just passed through a town where all coal mines are. You see the fire glimmer at a distance in the engines in many places. The men, women, children, country and houses are all black. But I cannot by any description give an idea of its strange and extraordinary experience. The country is very desolate everywhere; there are coals about, and the grass is

quite blasted and black. I just now see an extraordinary building flaming with fire. The country continues black, engines flaming, coals, in abundance, everywhere, smoking and burning coal heaps, intermingled with wretched huts and carts, and little children."

So, the early industrial revolution was water powered, but then it moved into the cities and, in doing so, concentrated a lot of fire in the same place to create levels of atmospheric pollution, which we would regard as absolutely intolerable, quite apart from all the other sanitary problems they had.

Another very important component of this industrialization was the iron and steel industry. Iron and steel have been made for several thousand years. We know that the Romans were good at iron technology. It was put onto a completely different scale in the 18th and early 19th centuries. One of the great pioneers here was a man called Abraham Darby. This is one of the few cases where there is a dynasty from father to son to grandson passing on the factory. This is in a place called Coalbrookdale, in Shropshire. It is near the border of England and Wales, and now the whole area has been converted into an area of industrial archeology. If you are minded to do such things when you are in Britain, go have a look at Coalbrookdale. It was there that the Darby family discovered how to smote iron with coke. This was a very important invention because until then the only way of making good iron and steel (particularly) was by burning charcoal. Britain had been so heavily populated for so long that there wasn't a lot of forest. You need a lot of wood to make charcoal. Wood is a scarce commodity.

Darby discovered that by preheating coal, you could drive off a lot of the sulfur compounds and actually convert it into coke, which could then be used for steel smelting. That discovery meant that the steel industry, far from being in danger of becoming extinct, as some people said it was in 1730, started to thrive as never before. It was there, in Coalbrookdale that the world's first iron bridge was built, and you can go to see it. It's still there now. The town where it was built has been renamed Ironbridge. It is lovely. It is a delicate span, a single span across the River Severn. Until about 20 years ago, cars were still driving across it after 200 years. It's been closed off, but it is still there.

One of the Darby family's great rivals was a man called John Wilkinson. His nickname was "Mad Iron" because he was keen on building everything out of iron. Apparently, he said to his wife, "Great news! I've got some new plates and, instead of being china, they are all made of iron," as were all the knives and forks. He was the first man in the history of the world to build a boat out of iron. All his friends thought this was a hilarious idea because they were familiar with the fact that if you take a piece of wood and throw it in the water, it will float. If you take a piece of iron and throw it in the water, it will sink. They all said this is bound to sink.

Wilkinson himself argued Archimedes' principle that the important matter was that if a boat is hollow the weight of the water displaced will be greater than the weight of the boat plus the air inside it combined. So, bets were held, and everyone was waiting for the great metal launching, and there were jokes, a carnival atmosphere. It was a barge—it wasn't an elegant boat—but it floated, and that had immense significance as well. From then on the superior qualities of an iron ship over a wooden one became clear. They rot much more slowly. They are less infested and so on. When he died, he was buried in an iron coffin. So, his whole life was dedicated to the possibilities of iron.

The final component of the early industrial revolution was transportation. Road transport was difficult before the mid 18th century, because the roads were so bad. There were no hard roads at all, which means that every time it rained they tended to get swampy and rutted. There were a handful of roads that the Romans had built. The Roman roads were still the best way of getting about, nearly two millennia later. Most of the roads were just what we call dirt tracks. There were very few bridges, which meant that every single little stream that you came to (We splash across them in cars in an instant and never think twice about them.) was a problem. You would go lurching down into the valley, wade across and up the other side. It meant that wagons couldn't carry very heavy loads. They would get bogged down. They would have to stop altogether for bad weather.

It also meant that long-distance haulage, which had to be done mainly by pack horses, was extremely expensive. If you carried a commodity a hundred miles, you could almost pay more for the transport costs than for the actual value of the device itself. There was some river traffic, but most of Britain's rivers aren't very navigable for long distances because of seasonal variations in the amount of water, waterfalls, and so on. There was a coastal trade like the coal trade from Newcastle down to London, but it was always vulnerable to rough seas.

The building of canals in Britain was the first great leap forward in industrial transport technology. It was vital. The production of lock technology, where you could actually take a canal over a hill, made it possible for a network of canals to be built throughout Britain. They all went into decay after the completion of the railway network, but at the end of the twentieth century they were restored, so now once again you can actually see Britain's canal network. It is now a pleasure boat complex, but it was one of the arteries along which the first industrial generation conducted its business.

The early industrialists had to overcome some psychological problems as well as some technical ones. Probably the hardest was to train people to become factory workers. Many people living on farm land weren't literate, and what they certainly didn't have was a clock. There weren't very many clocks. They were difficult and complicated to make and very expensive. If you look at the design of early factories, they nearly always have a clock tower as one of their central features. This is true of our Arkwright Mills in Derbyshire, for example. One of the first things the boss would do is to teach the workers to tell time. You have to get it into their heads that he wanted them to come to work at a certain clock time.

The rhythm of agricultural life is quite different than that. If you lived in farming country, especially then, you got up when it got light. You went to bed when it got dark, and you worked when it was light. Since Britain is farther north than most of the United States, then maybe you didn't work very much in the winter because it is mainly dark. Conversely, in the summer, when it gets light at four in the morning and is light until ten at night, you work very long hours. But there would be great differences. What the new industrialists were saying to their workers was, "You need to work for 12 hours a day, whether it is winter or summer." It sounds like a common sense idea for us, but to them it was a revolutionary idea. In fact, they found that if they said, "You report to work at six in the morning and you work until six at night," in the summer they would show up early. In the winter, you couldn't get them there. That was the thing. So, converting from seasonal time to clock time and saying whether it is light or dark doesn't matter any more. These were the pioneers of things like gas light illumination inside the factories.

They had to teach the workers how to tell time and give them some rudimentary sense of industrial discipline. Very often workers' housing would be close to the factory so the workers could walk there. There would be a series of whistles. There would be the getting up whistle, and then five minutes before the shift was due to start there would be the ready whistle, and five minutes later the start work whistle. They posted fines on people who were late. The fine had to be big or the workers wouldn't take it seriously. Certainly, when we look at the accounts and the annals of the early factories, it was a constant battle to try to get people to go there and work for the regulated number of hours. These early owners were very often non-conformists although they were members of the Church of England. If you were an Anglican, you tended not to be interested in these things. It is really the Congregationalists, the Quakers, and the Baptists who made the running in the early days of British industrialization. There were Puritans who were morally ascetic and severe who tried to impose a new discipline on their workers.

In the textile factories, the work wasn't particularly hard. It was mainly a matter of machine minding, watching to make sure that the threads didn't break in both spinning and weaving. They often had a greater need for female workers or even children than they did for men. This was a period where, the first half of the 19th century, there was an immense rise in the number of children working in factories, sometimes for very long hours and under very hard conditions. It was extremely monotonous and deadening work too.

The low levels of skill and the low wages meant for many of these industrial workers hardship and hard times. One of the most effective of Charles Dickens' novels is called *Hard Times,* where he parodies the hardhearted economic logic of this first generation of industrialists. Certainly, in their intolerance and zeal to transform these workers' way of life, they were laying the seeds for a harvest of great bitterness later in the century as the trade union movement developed and as workers and employers became more and more alienated from one another, each one thinking that the other one didn't take its needs sufficiently seriously.

There is a German businessman called Harcourt visiting Manchester factories, being astonished by what he sees, in about 1825.

"Mechanization and the incredibly elaborate division of labor diminish the strength and intelligence which is required among the masses, and competition diminishes their wages to a bare subsistence." He said, "Every time there is a slump, an economic recession, they're found temporarily out of work. Then a mass of miserable humanity is exposed to hunger and to all the tortures of want."

These are also the circumstances in which two famous revolutionaries were growing up, Karl Marx and Friedrich Engels. They were both German, but they both spent most of their lives in England, observing very closely. In fact, Engels himself was sent to England to be a factory manager for his father who was an industrialist. He became horrified by some of the sights he witnessed in some of the rapidly growing industrial cities. With the help of his friend Marx, the two of them together became outspoken critics of this new industrial system and foresaw the days when, as they thought, the workers would rise up and throw off the tyranny of the owners.

From our point of view, we know that Marx and Engels didn't get it right. They thought there was going to be a socialist revolution, which we know is not right. We have to take seriously both sides of the equation. Despite their hardheartedness, these early industrialists were very brilliant people. To work out the techniques of the devices— financial, mechanical, and psychological—was an astonishing achievement. They did lay the foundations for Victorian commercial greatness.

Lecture Four
Railways and Steamships

Scope:

Railways built on the early technological achievements of the Industrial Revolution and literally accelerated the nation's economic life. The earliest railways were primitive horse-drawn systems at Northumberland collieries, and it is no coincidence that the first great railway builder, George Stephenson, was a mine technician. Taking advantage of the miniaturization of steam engines, Stephenson and his son Robert proved, with the Liverpool and Manchester Railway (completed in 1829), that the new device was profitable as a carrier of both goods and passengers. Their great rival, Isambard K. Brunel, built the Great Western Railway in the 1830s, and by 1850 every major town in Britain was connected by rail with its neighbors and with London. Legislation ensured public access to trains, and the system proved an immense stimulus to further economic growth. Brunel went on to pioneer the building of oceangoing steamships. His *Great Western* was the first to cross the Atlantic. It, and its successors, *Great Britain* and *Great Eastern*, made ocean crossings far faster, safer, and more predictable than had ever been the case with sailing ships.

Outline

I. Britain's first railways predated steam locomotives.

    A. They were built in coal-mining areas, often with wooden rails and simple horse-drawn trucks, designed to take coal from the pithead to loading wharves.

    B. Miners were familiar with the fact that the reduced friction of a railway enabled horses to pull a greater weight than was possible on a road.

II. Cornish and Northumbrian mining engineers built steam engines that were small enough and powerful enough to create the first locomotives.

    A. Richard Trevithick, a Cornish mine-drainage engineer, experimented with the first locomotives.

        1. He built one on a bet, but its weight broke the Welsh colliery rails it ran on.

2. In London in 1808, Trevithick ran another, *Catch Me Who Can*, on a circle of track—as an amusement.

B. George Stephenson built the first viable steam-driven railway, the Stockton and Darlington, between 1821 and 1825, using iron rails.

    1. Wheezy early engines, such as *Locomotion*, had to pause sometimes to gather steam pressure but were far more powerful than horses.

    2. The coaches were simple open-air wagons—at first, passenger trains were drawn by horse and only coal trains by locomotive.

    3. The track gauge was four feet, eight-and-a-half inches, because that was the standard prevailing in the northern collieries.

C. Stephenson, learning from his experiences on the Stockton and Darlington and helped by his son Robert, built the superior Liverpool and Manchester Railway.

    1. At the Rainhill Trials in 1829, the *Rocket* proved the best locomotive. It could run at 30 miles per hour for long distances.

    2. The locomotive killed William Huskisson, President of the Board of Trade, at the grand opening, because he did not realize how quickly it was approaching him.

    3. The railway was an instant success, not only in goods, as the promoters had hoped, but as a passenger railway, carrying more than 1,000 people per day.

III. The Stephensons became northern Britain's premier railroad builders. Their great southern challenger was Isambard Kingdom Brunel.

A. Brunel was the son of a French immigrant, also an engineer and inventor, who tried to build the first tunnel under the River Thames.

    1. Isambard, chief engineer on the project before the age of 21, was nearly drowned when the tunnel flooded and had to be abandoned.

    2. He traveled around Britain in a custom-built stagecoach called a *britschka*, which included a bedroom and office, looking for work suitable to his talents.

3. He designed and built the Clifton suspension bridge in Bristol, which still stands.

B. Brunel competed for and won the contract to build the Great Western Railway, from Bristol to London.

1. The work was a battle against dubious directors, incompetent contractors, and a difficult landscape.

2. Land cost the railway nearly 7,000 pounds per mile.

3. Brunel believed that only he understood all the problems and how to solve them, sometimes cheated his contractors, and browbeat even his most loyal supporters, such as locomotive engineer Daniel Gooch.

4. Brunel built the railway to a seven-foot gauge after finding travel on the Liverpool and Manchester Railway uncomfortable. Stephenson and other rivals criticized this move as impractical, because it prevented exchanges onto other lines.

5. Nevertheless, the Great Western was the flattest, best engineered, and most comfortable railway in Britain when completed. It was capable of sustained high speeds and was eventually continued down to Exeter, Plymouth, and Cornwall, where it crossed Brunel's spectacular Royal Albert Bridge at Saltash.

6. The rails remained broad-gauge until all Britain's railways were standardized in 1892.

IV. The success of the main lines led to railway fever.

A. Each new railway needed its own act of Parliament, a time-consuming process but necessary to gain rights of eminent domain. The consent of some Members of Parliament (MPs) and lords could be gained only if they were assured of the lines' invisibility from their estates.

B. The early lines had to overcome farmers' fears that they would start neighborhood fires and frighten farm animals.

C. The success of the lines soon attracted speculators, and the belief that they were certain money-winners led to a speculative boom, "Railway Fever," in the 1840s. Lines planned in minor districts often went bankrupt and never lived up to the speculators' hopes.

D. The railroads had to overcome numerous critics.

1. Stagecoach owners and innkeepers foresaw ruin.

2. Canal companies also feared the competition and lobbied against the railways.

V. Government recognized that it should regulate railways but also that it could take advantage of their existence.

A. In 1838, the Royal Mail decided to use the railways.

B. In 1840, Rowland Hill invented the penny post, the world's first cheap bulk-mail system, all dependent on railways.

C. In 1842, Parliament passed a law requiring the Board of Trade to certify railways before they could open, and in 1844 it required all railways to run daily passenger trains that working people could afford, costing no more than a penny a mile (the "Parliamentary Trains").

D. By 1850, all the major British cities were linked, and the network was 6,500 miles long.

E. Collectively, the railways were an immense stimulus to the coal mining industry (for locomotive fuel) and to the iron industry.

VI. Experience gained in railway building was used in ships, too.

A. Brunel planned and built the *Great Western* steamer.

1. Admitting that he knew little about shipbuilding, he was willing to collaborate, and the project faced fewer problems than the Great Western Railway.

2. Brunel denied skeptics' claims that an oceangoing steamship would have to devote all its cargo space to coal. Instead, he showed that the ship, by virtue of the fact that it was larger than any sailing vessel, would be faster and more capacious.

3. The steamer caught fire after installation of the engines, when felt insulation near the funnel overheated.

B. Modified, the ship sailed from Bristol to New York in 1838 and just beat a rival ship, the *Sirius*, which went aground on the approach to New York Harbor when its captain failed to take a pilot onboard.

C. Early steamers had numerous problems with failing paddle wheels and propellers and were equipped with masts and sails for insurance.

D. Because he was more interested in fame and progress than wealth, Brunel wanted to make further technical advances with his next ship, the *Great Britain* (1840–1845).

  1. It was the first liner with propellers.

  2. It had an iron hull of 3,000 tons, in an age when the biggest iron ships were just 600.

  3. It was almost too big to launch.

  4. Its maiden voyage to New York in 1845 broke the record, arriving in just 14 days.

  5. Brunel salvaged the ship when it went severely aground in 1846.

E. His biggest ship of all, the *Great Eastern*, was designed to go directly from Britain to Australia without refueling.

  1. No other ship equaled it in size for the next 40 years.

  2. Brunel feuded ceaselessly with the builder, John Scott Russell.

  3. A first attempt to launch the ship, sideways into the river, in November 1857, failed, killing one man, wounding several others.

  4. Brunel died in 1859 before the *Eastern's* maiden voyage. He was fifty-three.

VII. Stephenson and Brunel were among the many larger-than-life engineers who left a vivid imprint on Victorian Britain, accomplishing massive technical advances through a combination of skill, daring, and personal force and taking full advantage of the maturing wealth and skills of an industrializing nation.

Essential Reading:

L. T. C. Rolt, *Victorian Engineering*.

Adrian Vaughan, *Isambard Brunel: Engineering Knight-Errant*.
Supplementary Reading:

Michael Freeman, *Railways and the Victorian Imagination*.

H. Perkin, *The Age of the Railway*.
Questions to Consider:

1. Why were railways so important to Victorian Britain?

2. How convincing were the critics of steam technology?

Lecture Four—Transcript
Railways and Steamships

Railways built on the early technological achievements of the industrial revolution and they literally accelerated the nation's economic life. The very early railways in the world were primitive horse-drawn systems in Northumberland in the coal fields. It is no coincidence that the first great railway builder should himself be a mining technologist, George Stephenson. He took advantage of the miniaturization of steam engines which had gone on during the preceding hundred years and with the help of his son Robert built two of the first great railways in the world: The Stockton and Darlington Railway and then the Liverpool and Manchester, which was finished in 1829. His railways proved conclusively that it was a viable technology and that it could be highly profitable, both as a carrier of people and as a carrier of goods.

The Stephensons were dominant particularly in the north of England, and their great rival, Isambard Kingdom Brunel, was perhaps the most prominent of the southern railway builders. He built the Great Western Railway in the 1830s, and by 1850 every major town in Britain was connected by a railway line and London had ready access to all points of the British provinces. The pace of transport all over the country had dramatically increased. Parliament legislated to make sure that there were some elementary safety rules on the early trains, though they were very dangerous, and to make sure that ordinary people had access to the trains. Together, this entrepreneurial ingenuity and political supervision ensured that the railways were going to be a great stimulus to further economic growth throughout the Victorian era.

Brunel, the southern railway builder, went on to create the first generation of oceangoing steamships. His first ship, the Great Western, was the first steam-powered ship to cross the Atlantic Ocean. Even its successors, the Great Britain and the Great Eastern had ocean crossings far faster, safer, and more predictable than they had ever been in the days of sailing ships.

Railways themselves predated steam technology. The very earliest ones were extremely simple devices built in mining areas where you had the problem of moving a bulk solid, coal, over short distances. The earliest ones had wooden rails and very simple horse-drawn wagons, designed to take the coal from the pithead where it was brought up out of the ground down to a loading wharf ready for shipment by sea. The miners were familiar with the fact that there is so much less friction involved in having the wagons run on a rail rather than on a road surface that it is possible for a horse to pull a much greater weight of coal if it is in rail wagons than if it is on the ground. That is the insight that they were taking advantage of. In Cornwall, another mining area of Britain, Cornwall and the extreme southwest, and Northumberland, the extreme northeast, mining engineers were constantly improving the quality of steam engines and building them smaller, until in the end it was possible to have them small enough that they could be loaded onto a trolley and become self-moving. That is what a locomotive is.

The first great name in this process is Richard Trevithick. He was a Cornish mine draining engineer, who experimented with these early locomotives. One of his friends bet him that he couldn't build a steam locomotive. He was confident that he could and finally built a self-moving locomotive which ran on a mine railway in south Wales. It was so heavy that it broke the rails. That is one of the early problems, before they learned how to miniaturize them. In 1808 he built a more effective one. The locomotive was called *Catch Me Who Can*. He went to an area of London called Uston (the place where Uston Station is today) and built a circle of track—the kind of thing you would have around a Christmas tree. He built a fence around that. The *Catch Me Who Can* just had two little wagons, and it went around in a circle. You had to pay a few pennies to go through the fence and have a ride in the train if you dared. It turned out as a great sensation.

Trevithick was an extremely capable technologist. He didn't really have the staying power to develop it into a practical technology. He spent most of his life wandering around the world working briefly in different mining projects in different places and died penniless. His northern contemporary, George Stephenson, was different than that. He was a mining engineer as well, and it was he to whom the credit usually goes for building the world's first viable railway, the Stockton and Darlington, begun in 1821 and finished in 1825. This was a railway which used iron rails throughout its distance. Stephenson himself was self-taught. This was in the days before there was any technical education in Britain. He had become an apprentice of the mine and had become familiar with how the engines worked. He would be in and out of the blacksmith's shop tinkering with metal devices. So, the early railway was built by trial and error. It was not a matter of engineering graduates putting it together. There was no such thing.

One of the locomotives on the Stockton and Darlington Railway was called the *Locomotion*. Its average speed was about two miles per hour. It was very slow and a great, ugly, hefty, wheezing thing pouring out smoke and sparks. Every now and again it would have to stop altogether to gather up its energy before it could carry on. It was no express. Nonetheless, it was very powerful. It could pull a long train of coal wagons. As you watched it, and as people who understood these things watched it, they recognized the possibilities inherent in the technology. The coaches at first were very simple, open air wagons. On this railway, the very first passenger trains weren't entrusted to the locomotives. They were given to the horses. The first passenger trains were with a horse going up and down the track. But, by 1826 or 1827, passengers were being pulled by the steam locomotive as well.

The gauge of the track, that is, the distance between the two actual rails, was four feet, eight-and-a-half inches. That was a standard gauge in the Northumberland collieries and it became the standard gauge on British railways, and indeed, it became the standard gauge throughout almost all the world. American railways have that gauge. Why? partly because a lot of the expertise was originally brought from England when Americans began building their own railways. They inherited a gauge which was familiar. The wagons were already done and the early locomotives. So from one place to the next, standard gauge was carried throughout most of the world.

When the Stockton and Darlington Railway opened in 1825, The Quarterly Review (this is a London journal) editorialized, "What could be more palpably absurd than the prospect held out by this railway of locomotives traveling twice as fast as stage coaches? Nonsense." Within five years, they were. The rate of improvement of the machines into the late '20s was astonishing. Stephenson learned a lot from his experience in building the Stockton and Darlington Railway, with the result that when he got his next nig commission which was to build the Liverpool and Manchester Railway, he was able to do it better.

Liverpool and Manchester were already important places, Manchester, because that is where the big cotton factories were, Liverpool, because that was the big port of which it thrived on the Atlantic trade. Cotton ships coming from Savannah or Charleston would come into Liverpool. In part, it was a slavery port. Ships would go out from Liverpool to Africa, then over to the West Indies and into the American south. The idea of linking Liverpool and Manchester by railway had enormous possibilities. It even crossed a swamp, which I have said was impossible until then, but the Stephensons worked out how to do it. This is George and his son working with him.

They decided to hold a competition to see who could build the best locomotive and then to give the contract for building more locomotives to the winner of the competition. It was Robert Stephenson himself who built the best of the locomotives. A trial was run, called the Rainhill Trials, along a section of this line, and the *Rocket*, which was the name of the locomotive that Robert Stephenson built, was able to run long distances at 30 miles per hour. The *Rocket* still exists. If you go to the National Railway Museum in York, one of the most interesting places in the whole of Britain, you can still see the *Rocket*. It is a wonderful little thing. Unfortunately, its early history was tainted by the fact that at the official opening of the railway it killed somebody. In Britain's first famous railway accident, it killed the president of the Board of Trade, a man called William Huskisson.

One thing it is hard for us to remember is this: If you are going at 30 in your car, you think of it as rather slow and restrained. We are familiar with much higher speeds than that. Then, 30 miles per hour was almost unimaginably fast. Can the fastest galloping horse go at 30? I'm not sure—maybe only just. Ordinary people certainly had never been that fast. It was a terrifying rate. We know from a lot of the history of early railway accidents that people didn't realize how quickly the train was coming toward them. Here is an account of what happened to poor old William Huskisson. It is taken from the *Biography of George Stephen's,* written by Samuel Smiles. He says:

> "The *Rocket* engine was observed rapidly coming up. At this moment, the Duke of Wellington (who was the Prime Minister), between whom and Mr. Huskisson some coolness had existed, made a sign of recognition and held out his

hand. A hurried but friendly grasp was given. But, before it was loosened, there was a general cry from the bystanders of "Get in! Get in!" Flurried and confused, Mr. Huskisson endeavored to get around the open door of the carriage, was projected over the opposite rail. In doing so, he was struck down by the *Rocket*, and falling, with his leg doubled across the rail, the limb was instantly crushed. His first words on being raised were "I have met my death," which unhappily proved too true, for he expired that same evening in the neighboring parsonage of Echols.

It was cited at the time as a remarkable fact that the *Northumbrian* (another locomotive) conveyed the wounded body of the unfortunate gentleman a distance of about 15 miles in 25 minutes, or at a rate of 36 miles per hour. This incredible speed burst upon the world with the effect of a new and unlooked-for phenomenon."

In other words, the ambulance train can go at 36 miles per hour. That was a real source of amazement. So, not surprising, the railway became an instant success and certainly contributed to the continuing development of Liverpool and Manchester. The promoters had in mind that it would carry goods, but they found it would carry passengers as well. Very quickly, a thousand people a day would be traveling back and forth on the line.

The Stephensons, father and son, were the premiere builders in the north. For the south, Isambard Brunel was the great figure. He was the son of a French immigrant. He was also an engineer and an inventor. It was Brunel senior who got the contracts to try to build the very first tunnel under the River Thames. He made his son Isambard, who wasn't yet 21, the project manager and on-the-spot engineer. Young Isambard was very nearly drowned when the tunnel caved in, flooded, and had to be abandoned.

The work had been very difficult, partly because the River Thames in those days was the only drain for the city of London. Everything was poured into the river. It became unbelievably filthy. So, the bed of the river was a great mass of slime and sewage 50 or 60 feet thick in some cases. Even so, they were making fairly good progress with the tunnel when they hit a place where underwater quarrying had taken place and the quarry manager tried to see where they could get gravel from the riverbed and had dug much more deeply into the riverbed, in effect making a deep spot which they didn't know about. When they encountered this place, water started pouring in under very high pressure. The builders just managed to get away in time to save their own lives.

Young Isambard, undeterred by this and many other escapades in his early engineering career, built for himself a special stagecoach called a *britschka*. It had built into it a bedroom and an office. It was a predecessor of the RV, something like that, a vehicle which could go around by horseback. He would look for work which he thought suitable to his talents. He is the most egotistical man in history. He was convinced that he was always right. He must have been very difficult to work with. But along with that was a great genius. One of his great projects was the Clifton suspension bridge in Bristol. Again, it is something which you can still see. It crosses a high gorge in a very precipitous place. It is a wonderful example of the daring and the beauty also of the Victorian building.

He competed for and won the contract of a railway from Bristol to London. Liverpool was the premiere port in the north of England, and Bristol was one of the premiere ports in the south of England. It is facing westward, and it had grown mighty on the American trade. The prospect of trains between London and Bristol would contribute to its further development. It was a great battle to get the Bristol and London railway built. He called it the Great Western Railway. That was his name for it. It was partly because there wasn't enough expertise in Britain in general for the undertaking of work of that magnitude.

Building a railway is awfully hard work. It needs a lot of capital, because you first have to acquire the land. Then you have to level the land. Trains come up or down steep hills. They can't really go on gradients more than about one in 50—in other words, one foot of rise for every 50 feet you've gone along. So if you are crossing ordinary hilly country, you have to make embankments and cuttings and sometimes tunnels to create a more or less level track bed all the way. Over every single stream you have to build a bridge. So, there is an enormous amount of elementary preparation of the track bed to be done. Brunel had endless difficulties with the subcontractors who didn't realize the scale of the work they had to do and very often went bankrupt trying to do it. To read his account of the difficulties he endured in getting the railway ready is very striking.

He budgeted about £2.5 million. He said the whole thing could be done for £2.5 million. In the end, it came to more than three times that much. We are all familiar with engineering cost overruns. The buying of the land itself was very difficult. The Great Western was spending £7,000 per mile just to buy the land. To get a comfortable contemporary figure, you'd have to multiply that by about a thousand to get a sense of what it was costing. Brunel sometimes made matters worse for himself by believing that he alone understood the problems that they were having to deal with. He didn't always treat his contractors or his assistants entirely fairly, and he would browbeat his most loyal supporters, such as his locomotive engineer.

The man who provided the locomotive is a man called Daniel Gooch, and he is credited as one of the great engineering railway builders. Gooch told him, "A moment, Mr. Brunel. You are planning locomotives which aren't powerful enough." Brunel said, "No, no, I know better," and actually created the first generation of underpowered locomotives for the railway even though Gooch could have told him that.

What really made the Great Western different than other lines was the fact that it was on a seven-foot gauge. He had been for a ride on the Liverpool and Manchester Railway, Stephenson's railway, and found it very uncomfortable. He said, "If we put the two pieces of line further apart, we will have broader carriages, they will be more luxurious inside, and the ride itself will be smoother." That proved to be true. Everybody who rode on both the Liverpool and Manchester and the Great Western agreed that the Great Western gave you a wonderful ride. It was extremely well-engineered track, very few steep bends, high speeds all the way. They were soon going 60 all the way from Bristol to London and so on. Seven-foot gauge was very impractical. It would be like building computers where your keyboard didn't conform to the standard keyboard.

The fact that everybody did use it made a great incentive for everyone to carry on using it. It meant that everything had to be specially built for the Great Western and couldn't be transferred onto any of the other lines. Eventually in the 1890s, they changed the gauge of the railway and had to gravely modify or abandon all of their equipment. For a long time it went on as the great anomaly in the whole system. Later on, Brunel also expanded the Great Western Railway, taking it further and further into the west country of England. This is the extreme southwest from Bristol down to Exeter and Plymouth and Cornwall. It crossed over the River Tamar on the Devon Cornwall border, over a wonderful bridge called the Royal Albert Bridge—as usual, named after Prince Albert.

The success of these early lines led to what was called "railway fever." The investors in these early lines made a great fortune, so the idea spread about, particularly in the city of London "Get into railways. Railways always make a profit." Unfortunately, failsafe schemes never are failsafe. They always do fail. Some lines were planned and built where they ought not to have been because they were between two minor places, where there wasn't any particular trading need. So, for every successful railway, there were quite a lot of failures. One of the things that made them so difficult to build was that they were being built through very heavily populated country, especially the urban areas. That meant that before you could begin building, you had to have an act of Parliament for each line because you had to get the right of eminent domain, that is, the right to compulsorily buy the land on which the railway was going to run. Parliament would grant these acts, but the lobbying was time consuming, and very often bribes changed hands to make sure that you would get the right combination of members of Parliament voting for your line.

Some members of the Houses of Commons, and, in particular, the House of Lords, would only vote for these lines, if they were going to go near to their home estates, if they were given a promise that they themselves would not be able to see the line. The place where I went to school, a village called Atwall in Derbyshire, my school was built on the estate of a local gentleman called Sir John Port (It was called The John Port School.) A railway line ran near to the school. Between the school playing fields, which had once been part of the lord's park, there was a big embankment. It didn't go anywhere. It just went up one side and down the other. I learned that the reason that it was there was so that Sir John Port, looking out his window, would not have to see the trains. He would see a column of smoke, but that would be it. This kind of deal had to be made. It was one of the many difficulties in getting them done.

Farmers were terrified that having a great locomotive rush past, the sparks would set fire to the crops or that the cows would be so traumatized that they would no longer give milk. This sort of anxiety had to be overcome by the first generation. Lines in minor countryside districts very often never did make any money. They went bankrupt and didn't live up to the speculators' hopes. Here is a description by Charles Dickens of a bankrupt railway. He was the editor of a journal called *Household Words*. This is from a story written in 1858 about a bankrupt railway.

> "The long-silent panorama of the Direct Barrygold Railway passes before me, the whole line in Chancery, choked and stiffened by the icy, relentless hand of legal death. The Barrygold station, once so full of life, is now an echoing and deserted cavern. Its crystal roof is an arch of broken glass, its rails torn away. Its rooms, offices, are empty and boarded up and its walls are defaced with old ghastly time bills, the mocking records of its former wealth and activity."

The railways had to overcome numerous critics, the farmers, sometimes the gentry. There was also the people who were going to be put out of business by them, the stagecoach operators. The stage owners battled as hard as they could to prevent these things from being built; so did the people who had invested heavily in canals. Between 1780 and about 1830, that was the golden age of the canal operators. Now they could see that although their technology worked, it was much slower. The canal boats went at one or two miles per hour. The trains were going at 30. They lobbied hard against railways. Nevertheless, the sheer potency of the technology meant that very quickly it displaced all of its rivals.

The government recognized that it should regulate railways to make sure they had some elementary degree of safety. It also quickly saw that it could take advantage of the railway for its own uses. In 1838, the post office, The Royal Mail, decided that it would send its letters on the trains. That had the effect of greatly accelerating the postal service. In 1840, one of the post office's senior officers, Roland Hill, decided that they were going to experiment with a revolutionary new way of sending mail, that is, that the sender was going to pay for it. Until then, it was the recipient who paid for the letter. What could be more sensible than that? You are the person getting the letter, and you should pay for it.

Apparently there are stories that the letter would be brought and presented, and the person would read it and say, "No, I don't want this," and decline to pay for it. Ronald Hill said, "Let's make it much cheaper than it has ever been before and let's make the sender pay." So, he introduced what is really the first modern postage stamp. It cost one penny. It was begun in 1840, and you could send it that way. Sure enough, he was right. Bulk mailing began at exactly that time. A businessman could start writing to people working for his concern all over the country, cheaply and quickly. A letter could get anywhere in Britain in one day already in the 1850s.

In 1842, the Houses of Parliament passed a law requiring that the Board of Trade should certify railways before they opened. The safety standards weren't very strict, and accidents were still very common. Nevertheless, it was elementary regulation there. In 1844 Parliament specified that all railways had to run at least one train a day for passengers and that the price of traveling on that train could not be more than one penny per mile. That had the effect of opening up railway travel to large sections of the population. It was still a lot of money for many people who were very poor. Nevertheless, it created circumstances in which vacations by railway could become popular for ordinary people, could become possible. These were called the "Parliamentary Trains." Some of the companies resented it. They didn't like the idea of having intrusions from the government. This is also the period of intense belief in laissez faire: The businessmen should be left alone to run their business however they wanted.

By 1850, a network 6,500 miles long had been completed linking up all major places in Britain. That made possible all sorts of things. It made nationwide marketing possible. It created national professional sports leagues. It meant businessmen could travel from one place to the next while keeping in touch with their headquarters. In effect, it shrank the nation. It made places which had once been weeks away (the north of Scotland) a day or a day and a half away. They were an immense stimulus to other business—iron and steel—for the actual building of the trains, and the coal mining industry, because the fuel which fueled the trains was also in great demand.

The experience which Brunel got in railway building, he put to use in building ships as well. He built the Great Western in 1838—that was his first great steamer—so the ship was named after the railway company. For once in his life he admitted that he didn't know very much about this technology, so he was perfectly willing to take help, and the project benefited from it because it was better for his collaboration. Skeptics said it is hopeless to try to build a steam-powered ship to go across the ocean. There were already boats which would go up and down rivers, like Robert Fulton's boats on the Hudson earlier that century. People said to go 3,000 miles across the ocean needs such a lot of fuel that the whole cargo space of the ship will be full of the fuel to get you there. Brunel said that was not true. He said with iron building, we are no longer confined in the size the ships can be. They can be immensely bigger than the biggest wooden ships. We can build them as long as we want, and the longer a ship is the faster it can go. I don't know the physics of this. I just know it to be true. So, he said we will build long ships which will have plenty of storage capacity in addition to their fuel, and they will be faster. They will make the crossing more quickly.

The Great Western was built in 1838 and caught fire on its trial cruise, so at first there were some difficulties, and Brunel was almost killed in the fire on the Great Western's trials. He was running down a ladder into the engine room to help put out the fire when he fell through the rungs of a ladder which had burned through, and he crashed down 20 feet on top of another man and then fell face down unconscious in the water there. Luckily, the other man wasn't knocked out and was able to pick him up and drag him back to the deck. Again, his life was providentially saved to carry on working.

The Great Western was launched and set sail from Bristol to New York in 1838, and it got there just ahead of another steamship which was also trying to get the honor of being the first one. This is a ship called the *Serious,* a much smaller ship, which had the misfortune of running aground as it approached New York because it hadn't taken a pilot on board. So, it was the Great Western which finally steamed in and has the honor of being the first Transatlantic Steamer.

They had endless problems with the paddle wheels. They were constantly failing, and most of the other steamers had masts as well so if the paddle wheels broke down, they would revert to sailing in the old way. Even so, they were a massive advance on sailing ships, because so long as you were sailing, you are completely at the mercy of the winds and the currents. A good Atlantic crossing by sailing ships took six weeks, but the steamers were doing it in three or four— much less. They could go direct. If you wanted to do it by sailing ship, you had to begin by sailing southwest to pick up the prevailing winds blowing east to west across the Atlantic. When you were coming back, you had to go far to the north to pick up the trade winds going home again. That was no longer necessary with a steamship. It could go directly back and forth. It became possible to actually schedule the times that they would leave and arrive, and they would do so with increasing degrees of reliability so that regular emigration ships, steerage ships, became possible in the '50s and '60s and so on. There were all sorts of advantages to the steam technology.

Brunel made another series of advances with his next ship, the Great Britain. It was the first liner built with propellers instead of paddle wheels. Propeller technology was perfected about 1840. He said, "We should use that. It is going to be better." It started originally as a paddle-wheeler commissioned to a man called Francis Humphries to build the engines. He said to Humphries when the job was half done, "We are switching the entire thing. We are going over to propeller screws instead of paddle screws." Humphries was so horrified after doing all this work for this dreadful boss that he collapsed and died.

Just to give you an idea of the changing scale of these ships, the Great Britain had a hull of 3,000 tons at a time when the biggest sailing ships were about 600. There is an enormous leap in magnitude in the scale of the ship itself. It was so big it could not even get out of Bristol dockyards except on the day of the highest tide of the year, the great spring tide, and they had to dismantle the locks to get the ship out into the estuary. On its maiden voyage to New York in 1845, it broke the record by arriving in just 14 days. When it ran aground a year later, everyone said it was lost and they would never get it up. Brunel also worked out some ingenious salvage techniques to get it back afloat and carry on working.

The biggest ship Brunel built was called the Great Eastern. This was designed to go all the way from England to Australia without refueling, again, an apparently impossible task. That is something like 8,000 miles. It was so big that no other ship was built of similar scale for the next 40 years. That is how far ahead of its time it was. It was built entirely in watertight sections, which becomes the standard way of building ships from then up to the present. Brunel, as usual, made difficulties for himself. He feuded ceaselessly with the builder,

Russell, who was a brilliant marine technologist and finally forced Russell out of the business altogether even though he ought to have been kept. The first attempt to launch the ship failed and it had to be done again. A man was killed on the slipways and so on. Finally, in 1859, Brunel himself became sick. He witnessed the ship itself and he witnessed its first cruises but never saw it go on its maiden voyage because he died in 1859, having worked himself to death. He was still a young man but had worn himself down. There was incredible daring and ingenuity—so there we are.

The Stephensons and Brunels were a generation of incredibly brilliant, adventurous and daring, ingenious, larger-than-life figures who left a very vivid imprint on Victorian Britain by creating these great technical advances on which the whole society was going to continue to build for the rest of the century.

Lecture Five
Parliamentary Reform and Chartism

Scope:

Britain was not a democracy in the 1830s. Supreme power rested with the prime minister rather than the monarch, and he led a parliamentary majority. Only about five percent of the British people voted for Members of Parliament (MPs) and they did it in public rather than by secret ballot, which made intimidation and bribery a regular part of every election campaign. Constituencies no longer corresponded with actual population clusters, and the big, new, industrial cities had no representation at all. In 1832, the Whig government under Lord Grey introduced the Reform Act. In the face of bitter Tory opposition, it abolished many of the old constituencies, created new ones for new cities, and cautiously expanded the franchise. Working-class and propertyless men (not to mention all women) were still excluded. They became recruits for the Chartist movement. Led by Fergus O'Connor and William Lovett, Chartists campaigned for much broader and more democratic political rights. Their great rallies were unable to win the support of the establishment, which continued to believe that property ownership was a necessary condition for participation in politics.

Outline

I. The British Constitution has never been a written document but a system that has evolved over generations.

   A. Parliament began as a council of advisers to the medieval kings.

      1. At first, the House of Lords was its most important branch, because the lords were the king's equals as landowners and warriors.

      2. The House of Commons became more important in the 17th century and tried to assure for itself a permanent role in government during the Civil Wars of the 1640s.

      3. The Glorious Revolution of 1688–1689 established the supremacy of the Commons and the subordination of the monarchy to Parliament.

   B. By the early 19th century, shifts in population and sources of national wealth meant that seats in Parliament did not represent the citizenry.

1. "Rotten boroughs" were depopulated places that still had two seats in Parliament but few electors.
2. "Pocket boroughs" were seats to which landowners could appoint their chosen candidates unopposed.
3. The big new manufacturing towns had no MPs.
4. No general franchise principle applied.
5. There was no secret ballot.

C. This eccentric system had defenders and detractors.
1. Edmund Burke (1729–1793) defended it as an "organic growth," ensuring stability.
2. Radicals, such as William Cobbett (1763–1835), condemned "Old Corruption."
3. The new manufacturers wanted political representation commensurate with their new wealth.

II. Lord Grey's Ministry of 1830 recognized the need for reform.

A. Grey was a Whig, a member of the political faction that combined wealthy aristocrats with the merchant elite.

B. Their opponents, the Tories, represented the smaller aristocrats and landlords. The Duke of Wellington led them. (The future prime minister, Robert Peel, was also a Tory.)

C. The governing classes feared that a revolution might sweep them away.

D. A second French Revolution in 1830 revived fears that the common people might try to seize power if they were not mollified by judicious reforms.

E. Grey persuaded King William IV that it was better to offer moderate reform first than be forced into violent reform later.

III. The attempt to pass the Reform Act in 1831–1832 witnessed chaotic scenes in Parliament.

A. Tories jeered at the 60 rotten boroughs Grey proposed to abolish.

B. Grey resigned and called for a general election when Parliament rejected the bill.

C. A pro-reform majority was elected.

D. The new Commons again passed the act, but the Lords still refused.

1. News of the Lords' refusal led to rioting.
2. Grey asked the king to create new lords if necessary, to outnumber the current members.
3. The king refused at first, but gave way when Grey threatened to resign.
4. Grey and the Duke of Wellington persuaded the Anglican bishops to change their votes.
5. The Duke of Wellington, a Tory leader, persuaded reluctant lords that defeat of reform would be dangerous.

IV. The reforms were relatively mild.

   A. Many rotten and pocket boroughs were abolished.

   B. Industrial cities got MPs for the first time. Northern industrialists with strong links to their constituencies replaced wealthy, absentee merchant MPs.

   C. Voting criteria were standardized throughout the nation, specifying ownership of property or tenancy that required 40 shillings of annual rent.
      1. The ballot was still not secret (until 1872).
      2. In Scotland, previously very unrepresentative, the electorate rose from 4,000 to 64,000.

   D. Landowners continued to dominate Parliament but with a larger mix of commercial MPs. Observers noticed a rise in the quality of debates and parliamentary reports on important issues (the "blue books").

   E. The Reform Act established the principle that reform is possible and can be done without revolution. It paved the way for further reforms.

V. The limits to reform provoked the Chartist movement.

   A. Its manifesto, the People's Charter, demanded six reforms, most of which already obtained in democratic America. The demands were for:
      1. Universal manhood suffrage.
      2. Election by secret ballot.
      3. Payment of MPs.
      4. Annual parliaments.
      5. Abolition of property qualifications for MPs.
      6. Equal-sized electoral districts.

B. Vast assemblies of Chartists, led by Fergus O'Connor and William Lovett, unsuccessfully petitioned Parliament in 1839 and again in 1842.

   1. Parliament refused to accept the charter as the basis of new legislation.

   2. A minority of Chartists advocated violence, and one, John Frost, led an uprising in Newport but was easily defeated.

   3. The government's lack of violence is conspicuous, however, especially by comparison with contemporaneous events in Europe.

   4. The government seized railways and telegraph lines to coordinate its response to the threat of Chartist uprisings and denied these means of communication to the Chartists.

C. Divided leadership and lack of an economic program (more important to most working-class people) contributed to the movement's decline.

D. Over the next century, however, five of the six points of the charter were achieved—but never annual parliaments.

VI. Further extensions of the vote did not come until 1867, and the secret ballot was not introduced until 1872. These reforms, and further electoral reform in 1884, laid the foundations for the rise of the Labour Party, which in the 20th century would become one of the two permanent parties in the British system.

Essential Reading:

W. D. Rubinstein, *Britain's Century*, chapter 3.

T. A. Jenkins, *The Liberal Ascendancy, 1830–1864*.

Supplementary Reading:

Michael Brock, *The Great Reform Act*.

Ian Newbould, *Whiggery and Reform, 1830–1841: The Politics of Government*.

Questions to Consider:

1. Was parliamentary reform really necessary to prevent revolution?

2. Why did the Lords finally accept the Reform Act of 1832?

Lecture Five—Transcript
Parliamentary Reform and Chartism

Britain was not a democracy in the 1830s. Supreme power rested with the prime minister rather than the monarch and the prime minister was the leader of the Parliamentary majority. Only about five percent of the British people voted for Members of Parliament (MPs), and they did this in public rather than by secret ballot, which meant that very election day was an opportunity for intimidation and bribery, which had become an integral part of public political life. Constituencies for the Members of Parliament no longer corresponded with actual clusters of population in Britain because so many changes had taken place over the last 200 years. The big industrial cities had no representation at all.

To correct that situation, in 1832 a Whig government under Lord Grey introduced the Reform Act. In the face of bitter opposition from the Tory party, it abolished many of the old constituencies, created some new ones (particularly for the industrial cities), and guardedly expanded the franchise. Working-class men were still excluded from the vote as were all women. Nonetheless, there was an expansion in the scope and size of the political nation.

Working-class people, disgruntled at being excluded, became recruits for the Chartist movement under the leadership of William Lovett and Fergus O'Conner. A series of great rallies by the Chartists enabled them to win a lot of support among the working classes, although they were never able to convert the people's charter, their plan, for a more democratic political society into a political reality.

The British Constitution had never been a written document. It is very unlike the American Constitution. Instead, it is a system which has evolved over the generations.

Parliament had its origins back in the Middle Ages as a council of advisers to the medieval kings. At first, the House of Lords was the senior of the two branches because the Lords were more nearly the king's equals as landowners and warriors. The House of Commons became progressively more important, and in the 17th century asserted itself, particularly during the civil wars of the 1640s, trying to assure for itself a permanent place in the British Constitution. Its members comprised the wealthy merchants from the city of London, the smaller landowners, who in the localities were essential because their cooperation with the king made it possible for taxes to be raised.

The Glorious Revolution of 1699–'89 had established the supremacy of the Commons and the subordination of the monarchy to Commons. It was after 1689 that Parliament was always meant to have a permanent role in the constitution and in fact, the dominant role. By the early 19th century, so many shifts in population had taken place and so many shifts in the nature of wealth and influence that representation in Parliament didn't represent the actual condition of the British nation.

There were various notorious inequities. One of them was called the "rotten boroughs." Rotten boroughs were depopulated places, places whose populations had dwindled over the last 200 years. They each still had two seats in Parliament. A famous example was a place called old Saran outside the city of Salisbury. It only had seven electors by 1832, yet it had two members of Parliament. Another abuse, or what was perceived to be abuse, was the "pocket boroughs," because no real election took place. The local big landowner was able, in effect, to nominate a candidate of his own and say, "I'll give you this seat in Parliament." In other words, the constituency was in his pocket. It wasn't really open to a free election of any kind.

The big new manufacturing cities, particularly in the north of England, Manchester, Liverpool, Birmingham, and Sheffield, had very large populations but no members of Parliament at all. There was an enormous patchwork of local custom dictating who got to vote and who did not. There was no standard principle governing the whole country. For example, in the constituency of Preston in Lancashire, all the men could vote. It was a very unusual constituency. In many others, hardly anyone was allowed to vote, and there were usually particular property qualifications. In any case, there was a wide variety of rules governing who got to vote. As I said in the beginning, nobody had a secret vote. When county elections took place, it was usually in the counties that the ballots were most fiercely contested. The candidates would have to bribe the vote, sometimes just by giving them drinks or dinners or treats. If the voters were the tenant farmers of a landlord and that landlord or his nominee was running for office, you would be very rash not to vote for your clear landlord's candidates.

Let me read you a passage from George Eliot's novel *Felix Holt*, where she describes an election and the way it used to go on in the days before the reform act. Mr. Transome is one of the landowners. Mr. Transome and the tenants come together to vote, and his opponent is called Debarry. Debarry's supporters have created a kind of gauntlet that the voters have to run at as they approach the balloting place. Of one of Mr. Transome's tenants, a rather simple-minded man, here is what she says:

> "Mr. Goff was cut off from his companions and hemmed in, asked by voices with hot breath close to his ear how many horses he had, how many cows, how many fat pigs, then jostled from one to another who made trumpets with their hands and deafened him by telling him to vote for Debarry. In this way, the melancholy Goff was hustled on 'til he was at the polling booth filled with confused alarms, the immediate alarm being that of having to go back in still worse fashion than he had come. Arriving in this way after the other tenants had left, he astonished all hearers who knew him for a tenant of the Transomes by saying "Debarry" and was jostled back, trembling, to shouts of laughter." (In other words, he was so rattled he votes for the wrong man.)

This eccentric system did have its defenders. One of them was Edmund Burke, the late 18th-century theorist and one of the great conservative theorists, who said, "It may be true that in the abstract, this system has got imperfections. Nevertheless, it is an organic growth. It has developed naturally over the course of centuries. And it is far better to keep it than to wrench it asunder on behalf of some new abstraction."

Other people, like the radical writer William Cobbett, "It's a disgraceful system, and it is corrupt from top to bottom." He called it "old corruption," and he argued for a rationalized, representative alternative in which the various groups of the population of Britain really were properly represented in Parliament. Another group of critics were the new industrial manufacturers because they were now in a situation where their wealth was growing very rapidly, but they still didn't have political representation commensurate with it.

The pioneer from the early 1830s was Lord Grey, and he recognized that reform of Parliament was necessary. He was subjected to more and more pressure from around the country, particularly from clubs called political unions which were arguing that political reform was necessary. Grey himself was a Whig, a member of a political faction which combined very wealthy aristocrats (the Whig aristocracy) with the merchant elite and most of the political intellectuals of the day. They claimed to be the adherents of a far more enlightened and rational approach to political life, although sometimes it was a slightly hollow claim.

Let me read you a very sharp remark about that from Karl Marx, who lived in Britain from the 1840s onwards and was a very shrewd observer of British political life. Marx says:

> "The historian of the Whigs, Mr. Cooke, with great naiveté, confesses in his history of parties that it is indeed a certain number of liberal, moral, and enlightened principles which constitute the Whig party. But that it is greatly to be regretted that during more than a century and half the Whigs have existed, they have been when in office always prevented from carrying out their principles.
>
> So that in the reality, according to the confession of their own historian, the Whigs are in the same position as the drunkard brought up before the Lord Mayor. He declared that he represented the temperance principle but through some accident or other always got drunk on Sundays."

I think that is an accurate summary of the paradoxical quality of the Whig party.

Their opponents, the Tories represented the smaller aristocrats and landlords, the country gentry, the backwoods gentlemen. They were opposed to the idea of reforming Parliament because they sensed that they would be weakened by it. They brought into their ranks some very influential and effective men. One was the Duke of Wellington, a hero of the Napoleonic Wars, and another was Robert Peel, whom I have mentioned at various occasions already in the course, who was the son of a manufacturer who had gone over to the Tories interests.

It is impossible to overestimate the fact that the members of the British governing classes were afraid that something like the French Revolution might happen in Britain as well. The French Revolution guillotined the aristocracy and the king and had raised up Napoleon, against whom Britain had fought a desperate war for 20 years. In 1830, there was a new French Revolution, and it revived fears among the gentry and aristocracy that the common people might try to seize power if they weren't mollified by judicious reforms first. I'd like to give you a fragment of a speech made by Thomas Babington Macaulay in Parliament during the great debate which took place over whether Parliament should be reformed. He said, "We need to give more Parliamentary representation to London, which is one of the underrepresented places. The city," he said, "is in more danger of mob rule if it is not politically represented than if it is." Listen to what he says:

> "By refusing to let eight or nine hundred thousand people express their opinions and wishes in a legal and constitutional way, you increase the risk of disaffection and tumult. Why is it that the population of unrepresented London, though physically far more powerful than the population of Madrid or Constantinople, has been far more peaceable? It may be because they have other means of giving vent to their feelings, because they enjoy the liberty of unlicensed printing and the liberty of holding public meetings. Just as the people of unrepresented London are more orderly than the people of Constantinople and Madrid, so are the people of represented London more orderly than the people of unrepresented London."

(In other words, give a legitimate outlet in addition to freedom of meeting and freedom of the press; give them proper political representation; draw them into the nation rather than freeze them out.) Debates over the Reform Act aroused intense interest around Britain. For example, William Gladstone, who was later to be a Liberal Prime Minister himself, was then an undergraduate at Oxford. He took five days off from his studies, went down to London and listened to the debate in the House of Lords, 50 hours of debate. When he got back to Oxford, he gave a speech at the Oxford Union, the student debating society at Oxford, and spoke so eloquently against the Reform Act (in those days, he was a young Tory) that the Duke of Newcastle at once offered him one of his pocket boroughs. He said, "As soon as you leave Oxford, we would be glad to have you representing our interests in Parliament." That was his first seat, in fact, for the city of Newark.

Lord Grey, the Prime Minister, was able to persuade the King, William IV (This is all just before Victoria became queen.) that it was better to offer moderate reforms first than to be forced into violent reforms later. When the legislation was introduced, there were chaotic scenes in Parliament. This is in 1831 and 1832. When the first bill was read aloud for the first time, the Tory members of the House hooted and jeered as each of the 60 rotten boroughs which they proposed to abolish was read out. There were cries of dismay and shout of horror from the Tories. The House of Commons refused to pass the bill. Some of the Whigs also were reluctant to go along with changes of this kind.

So the Prime Minister, Lord Grey, resigned and asked for the holding of a general election. The way it worked in those days was that there had to be an election at least once in every seven years—the Septennial Act governed that—but there could be a reform more frequently. The system is similar today, incidentally. Now there has to be an election every five years, but there can be one more frequently if in the judgment of the Prime Minister he is well placed to win a victory or if a vote of no confidence has led to the Prime Minister being defeated inside Parliament itself. Grey dissolved Parliament and called for an election. Again, there was a very vigorous campaign with intense interest all around Britain—in places, demonstrations too. The Duke of Wellington, who was one of the Tory leaders, had the windows of his house smashed in the center of London.

Grey had been right in his estimate, and there was widespread public support for reforming the nation. The result was that in the ensuing election a pro-reform majority was elected. The new House of Commons passed the act, but the House of Lords, through which legislation also had to pass, still refused to do it. When news got around England that the House of Lords had rejected the Reform Act, again there was a wave of rioting. Derby and Nottingham, there were great riots in the streets. In the city of Bristol, the jail was burned to the ground. In some cities newspapers with black edges were published to say "The nation itself is in mourning over the rejection of this legislation."

Lord Grey asked the king to create some new Lords if necessary to outnumber the current members. This is one of the interesting aspects of British political life. The king has the right to create peerages, to make new people lords. So, periodically, when the House of Lords had felt threatened in one of its most intimate interests, the Prime Minister has been able to say to the king or queen, "We would like you to make more people into Lords," and then listing whom they want to be ennobled. In the end you have to have a majority of lords made who will then pass the legislation.

That is the kind of action which is likely to make the current lords rethink. If suddenly a lot of people get made into lords, the title itself loses some of its prestige. If you are a lord, you probably want to have less other lords in the nation than more. So, this is the threat that is going to be held over the heads of the currently sitting lords. At first, the king refused to do it. This was at the time, although the king's prerogatives were clearly declining, if he refuses to cooperate, a political deadlock can ensue. When the king refused to make more lords, Lord Grey resigned. The king said to the Duke of Wellington, "Will you make a ministry which will carry on according to the old system?" The Duke of Wellington had a good grasp of certain realities, and he said, "It is impossible for us to continue to hold out in the face of this kind of popular enthusiasm for reform."

Briefly, for about a week between May 8 and May 15 of 1832, Britain didn't really have a government. Meanwhile, the Duke of Wellington was trying to persuade the king and various of his colleagues in the House of Lords that they had got to make the necessary concessions. He was able to persuade the Anglican bishops who sat in the House of Lords that they should vote for the legislation rather than against it. Otherwise, they would put the church itself as seeming to be opposed to what were widely being construed as necessary national reforms. Finally, he was able to persuade all the necessary sitting lords either to abstain from voting altogether or to vote for the Reform Act. Finally, only 22 of the lords went to the wall right to the bitter end and refused to endorse the act.

From our vantage point, when we look back on the Great Reform Act, what strikes us is how mild and incremental the reforms really were. They don't have a particularly radical look from our vantage point. Obviously, we are looking at it from the point of view of a universal democracy. Many of the rotten and pocket boroughs were abolished. Many of the industrial cities got members of Parliament for the first time. Forty-one new towns, boroughs, were given members of Parliament for the first time. This meant that the northern industrialists in particular were now given the opportunity to have direct representation in Parliament. In the ensuing decades between the '30s and '70s, a great many of the industrialists actually became members of Parliament.

They had come to have very strong links with the constituencies from which they had come, so that the interests of Manchester, Liverpool, and Sheffield could be directly represented in Parliament rather than simply virtually as previously. Even so, they were still relatively underrepresented. As the urbanization of Britain continued, and as the industrialization of the nation intensified, there was still a relative overrepresentation of the rural counties and a relative under-representation of the cities.

The criterion for voting was standardized throughout the nation. In places, there is a great hodge-podge of qualifications which had existed previously. Now, a uniform system was established specifying ownership of property which was either 40 shillings annual rent in the countryside or £10 in town. Even after the Reform Act, only about 20 percent of the British male population could vote, about one man in five. The rise in the electorate was still less than 100 percent. Voting also was biased toward the south of England, because in the south the property values were higher and therefore it was more likely that you would qualify for the 40 shilling free vote. One of the reforms which didn't take place was the idea of the secret ballot. Balloting remained public, and therefore it remained subject to all the abuses which had beset it previously. A lot of representatives of both parties thought that a public ballot was right. They thought that if you were going to vote for somebody, you should be fully willing to say in public who you were going to vote for.

Here is Lord John Russell, who himself was Prime Minister: "What pitiful figures we should cut sneaking up to the ballot box, looking with fear to the right and to the left, and dropping in our paper, the contents of which we are afraid or ashamed to acknowledge." In other words, how dreadful it would be to vote secretly. Secret voting was already taking place in America, but regularly news came from America about ballot-box stuffing. In fact, when it is done secretly, it is very easy to get control of the balloting machinery and vote for your own candidate. So the English defenders of the old system said, "It is much better to do it our way, much less abuse." The place where the Reform Act had the biggest effect was probably in Scotland. There, the total number of voters rose from about 4,000 in the whole country to about 64,000, a big increase.

After 1832, landowners and landowner's retainers continued to dominate Parliament. Now, they did have a larger mix of commercial members than previously. Observers noticed a rise in the quality of debate in Parliament in the ensuing decades. Particularly, there was a rise in the quality of what were called the Blue Books, the reports that the members of Parliament wrote about various pressing issues of social equity, urban reform, reform of the church, and so on. Of course, the Reform Act established the principle that reforms of Parliament can be undertaken. This is always the case. Once a reform had been undertaken well, it establishes the principle that reform is something that Parliament does, and it is much more likely that subsequent reforms were going to take place thereafter, which has remained true right up to the present to, the very beginning of the 21st century. The House of Lords is again going through a period of reform.

Lord John Russell, whom I mentioned a moment ago, was nicknamed "Finality John" because he said, quite wrongly, that these reforms were going to be the very last reforms ever to take place in Parliament. The *London Times* editorialized very enthusiastically about the Reform Act. (This is an editorial.)

> "The race of usurpers has been ousted from the field of their usurpation and a great empire reconquered by its own people without the shedding of one drop of blood or disturbance of any one right of person or property which the common consent of civilized men holds certain."

They are congratulating themselves for having done it peacefully rather than through the violence which was endemic in France.

The limits to these reforms were enraging to working-class advocates of a much wider franchise. Working-class people were the principle recruits for the Chartist Movement, which in the late '30s and early '40s was the biggest expression of working-class dissatisfaction with political life as it was. They gained nothing from the act at all, and some working class said, "We are now in a weaker position than before, because now our industrial bosses are in Parliament our interests are much less likely to be represented even than before. Their two leaders were William Lovett, a cabinetmaker, and Fergus O'Conner, a barrister and a newspaper editor, both very talented orators.

The Chartists had a manifesto, The People's Charter, and it had six reforms, most of which were already obtained in America. America, to the Chartists, was an inspiring example. It showed that democracy was possible and that its principles could operate. It had already been going for about 50 years. Here is what they wanted: first of all, universal suffrage, one man one vote no matter whether he owned property or not; second, election by secret ballot; third, the payment of members of Parliament. (This is important. At this time the members of Parliament weren't paid. It was more of a service to the nation. But that meant that if you didn't have an income of your own, a fortune, you couldn't afford to be an MP.) One of the things the Chartists hoped for was salaried politicians so that working men could go into Parliament and manage to keep body and soul together while they were there.

They also wanted annual Parliaments (this is another of their reforms) so that as the interests and ideas of the population changed, so would the composition of Parliament be more representative of those changes. They wanted an abolition of property qualifications for MPs. Again, this was so that workingmen could go to Parliament, and they wanted equal-sized electoral districts so that the same number of people were voting in every constituency.

Recurrently, in the late '30s and early '40s, there were vast assemblies of Chartists, big political demonstrations, particularly in 1839, and again in 1842. Parliament itself refused to accept The People's Charter as the basis for a new round of political reforms.

I read to you previously one of Thomas Macaulay's speeches on behalf of the Reform Act. Now let me read you one of his speeches opposing The People's Charter. He said he was opposed to it because of the universal suffrage clause. He could not justify giving the vote to uneducated men. Many of the working-class people were very undereducated. It seemed to him madness for men of property to give the vote to unpropertied men because, he said, the first thing that will happen is that they will vote to take away the property from those who had got it. Here is what he said:

> "The chances of being taken in by demagogues who say it is not the fault of the laborer that he is not well educated, most true. It is not his fault. Though he has no share in the fault, he will, if you are foolish enough to give him supreme power in the state, have a very large share in the punishment. You stated if the government had not culpably omitted to establish a good system of public education, the petitioners would have been fit to   the elective franchise. Is that the reason for giving them the franchise when their own petition proves that they are not fit for it, when they give us fair notice that if we let them have it they will use it to their own ruin and ours?"

In other words, it will be bad for everybody. That is why we must reject it. Surely enough, Parliament did reject it each time these great petitions were presented.

A minority of Chartists actually favored revolutionary action under the leadership of a man called John Frost in Newport in South Wales. There was an uprising, but it was very easily defeated because the government had mobilized the army. However, this is at the time when the railway system is gradually being extended over the nation, and the telegraph system, so that the government can take control of both the railways and the telegraph and send rapid messages back and forth to coordinate its response to the perceived threat of Chartist uprisings. The Chartists themselves didn't have access to this kind of advantageous communication, and therefore could be isolated and relatively easily confined or repressed.

What is so striking, some of the historians who've studied it have said, is that what we should be particularly attentive to is the restraint which the British government showed in putting down the Chartist demonstrations and uprisings. Demonstrations of this kind in continental Europe often lead to the killing of a hundred or more people. In Britain, it was very restrained. That is partly a measure of the government's confidence that it is not going to lose control of the situation altogether.

Perhaps one of the great problems that the Chartist movement suffered—not only was it undereducated and mostly very poor—it wasn't clear to most workingmen that what they most needed was a change in the political system. If you could get the vote and if you vote for a sympathetic candidate and if that candidate lobbies for sympathetic legislation, it is all going to take a very long time. An enormous amount of energy can be devoted to a very slight return. What most working people needed was job security and higher pay. There were much more simple and direct things to which they tended to devote their energy. The alumni of the Chartist movement often became leaders of the trade union movement because it was more directly relevant to the things that seemed to concern them most. There was a Chartist revival in 1848 which coincided with the outbreak of new revolutions in Europe. Once again, the army was called out in case the threat got out of hand. What the governing class thought was a providential thunderstorm, a torrential rain, broke up the big demonstration in the center of London and it fizzled out without any great harm being done.

Over the next century, five out of the six points on The People's Charter were brought about. The only one which wasn't was the annual Parliaments. The British shifted to a system of five-year Parliaments but has never moved to an annual Parliament system. The principle of Parliamentary reform had been established, and there were to be further reform acts. In 1867, the vote was expanded further, and again in 1884. In 1872, the secret ballot was introduced for the first time. When those reforms had come about, the working class was more fully represented, and that lays the foundations for the creation of the Labour Party which was to play such a big role in 20th-century British politics.

Lecture Six
The Upper- and Middle-Class Woman

Scope:

Today, we emphasize the similarities of men and women. The Victorians emphasized the differences between them and believed that they had distinct and complementary roles to play. Men, according to the Victorian ideal, were physical, rational, and sexually domineering, the opposite of emotional, spiritual, and sexually passive women. For upper- and middle-class women who did not work, courtship, marriage, and motherhood were the central issues of life. Marriage contracts, while not excluding love, often contained a distinct business element too, as families jockeyed for financially advantageous matches. The London "season" became highly formalized in the Victorian era, offering debutantes maximum opportunities to locate suitable husbands.

Once married, women faced the hazards of childbirth, which was often fatal. Middle- and upper-class women eager for careers found it difficult to overcome traditional rules of exclusion but those with sufficient determination showed the possibilities: Florence Nightingale in nursing, the Bronte sisters and George Eliot as novelists, Ada Lovelace as a mathematician.

Outline

I. Ideas about gender relations and the nature of women, published by men and women, emphasized women's inferiority.

    A. Popular writers, male and female, emphasized women's natural inferiority and submissiveness.

        1. They said that women were physically and mentally inferior.

        2. They added that the inferiority was biological.

        3. These writers asserted that women's inferiority was underlined by biblical texts.

    B. They treated home as a sanctuary away from the rough world and woman as morally and religiously elevated.

II. The upper- and middle-class woman's principal interests were courtship, marriage, and motherhood.

    A. Marriage contracts specified the details of the union, which was a business transaction, as well as a personal one.

        1. Dowries, allowances, and pin money ensured the financial security of the wife.

        2. The husband gained control of the wife's property and legal interests.

        3. The "banns of marriage" and the request for "just cause or impediment" publicized forthcoming weddings in the Church of England.

        4. Dissenters, Catholics, and Jews needed a civil license for their weddings outside the state religion.

    B. A well-organized and closely policed marriage market was based on the London "season" and the debutante ritual. Debutantes, usually 17 or 18 years old, were officially presented at court to the queen and declared to be of marriageable age.

    C. Women were expected to be virgins at marriage and to have little knowledge of sex but to be sexually available at their husbands' demand thereafter.

        1. Lack of knowledge about contraceptives meant that frequent pregnancies and regular childbearing were common.

        2. Death in childbirth was also common.

    D. Victorian writers attributed great moral and spiritual power to mothers and sanctified the role of motherhood.

    E. Women were more attentive to religion than men, despite their lack of leadership roles, and were expected to create a religious home atmosphere.

    F. Divorce was extremely rare and required an individual act of Parliament until 1857.

III. The designs of clothes for upper- and middle-class women emphasized the fact that they could not be worn without the help of servants and that their owners did not work.

    A. Elaborate dresses, crinolines, and bustles were deliberately impractical.

B. To keep out of the mud and horse manure in the streets, women wore "pattens," miniature stilts attached to their shoes.

IV. Women with middle-class careers were exceptional but not unknown.

    A. The classic career for an educated but impoverished young woman was that of governess. Emily Bronte's Jane Eyre is the most famous example.

    B. Several eminent Victorian writers were women.
        1. Mary Ann Evans wrote as George Eliot.
        2. The Bronte sisters also used male pen names.
        3. Rachel Beer was editor of the *Sunday Times* and the *Observer* in the 1890s.
        4. Mary Somerville (after whom one of the first Oxford colleges for women was named) published a series of books on astronomy and the interconnections of the physical sciences.
        5. Ada Lovelace, Lord Byron's daughter, was an outstanding theoretical mathematician.

    C. Women played an important role in reform projects.
        1. Florence Nightingale made nursing a respectable profession for young women.
        2. After the 1867 Second Reform Act expanded the vote for men, women began to campaign for the vote and for enhanced legal rights.
        3. Two widows, Millicent Fawcett and Emmeline Pankhurst, led the moderate and radical wings of the suffrage movement later in the century.

    D. An intellectually ambitious minority complained about the lack of better education and career opportunities for women. Harriet Martineau, Charlotte Bronte, and many others lamented their stifling upbringings and laid the foundations for feminist reform.

Essential Reading:

Joan Perkin, *Victorian Women*.

W. D. Rubinstein, *Britain's Century: A Political and Social History*, chapter 19.

Supplementary Reading:

Gertrude Himmelfarb, *Marriage and Morals among the Victorians*.

Penny Kane, *Victorian Families in Fact and Fiction*.

Questions to Consider:

1. How did social and economic changes contribute to changing gender relations in Britain between 1830 and 1900?

2. How did ambitious women find ways to overcome restrictions to their careers?

Lecture Six—Transcript
The Upper- and Middle-Class Woman

Today, we emphasize the similarities of men and women. The Victorians emphasized the differences between them, and literally the men and women have different and complementary roles to play. According to the Victorian ideal, men were physical, rational, and sexually domineering, the very opposite of the emotional, spiritual and sexually passive woman. For upper- and middle-class women who are the subject of this lecture, most of them didn't work, so the center of their principal interest was courtship, marriage, and motherhood.

Marriage was a business. There were marriage contracts. Love wasn't excluded from marriage, but there was often a very distinct business element involved in marriages as well, especially the higher up in society you got as families jockeyed for prestige and for financially advantageous matches. The marriage of the upper classes was arranged through an annual event called the London Season, which was an environment in which eligible young women and men were brought together in chaperoned settings in which their marriages might take place. Debutante season was designed to make sure that the women got appropriate husbands.

Once they were married, women had to face the hazard of childbirth (and it was very hazardous) and the few middling upper-class women who wanted to have careers found it very difficult to get them, because they had to overcome large principal social objections to the idea that women should work. Nonetheless, there were clearly some working women who had very interesting careers in Victorian Britain. The queen herself is obviously one, but there are also people like Florence Nightingale, who created nursing as a respectable career for women, the Bronte sisters and George Eliot, great novelists, and even Lord Byron's daughter, Eva Lovelace, who was a theoretical mathematician.

There are always books being written about men and women and the proper relation between the two sexes and how they ought to be. Most of the Victorian books about gender relations emphasized the inferiority of women—this is true of books written by men and women—women's inferiority and submissiveness. For example, a clergyman's wife, called Sarah Ellis, who wrote a great string of these advice books about what men and women are like, a typical quotation from her would be: "The first thing of importance is to be content to be inferior to men, inferior in mental power, in the same proportion that you are inferior in bodily strength."

It was widely believed by both men and women that this inferiority was not just a social or cultural thing; it was biological. It was rooted in nature itself. Here is an influential physiologist and writer called Alexander Walker, writing in 1840:

> "It is evident that the man, possessing reasoning faculties, muscular power, and the coach to employ it, is qualified for being the protector. Woman, being little capable of reasoning, feeble and timid, requires protection. Under such circumstances, the man naturally governs; the woman as naturally obeys."

This kind of dichotomy was underlined by a rabid use of biblical texts. Eve was an afterthought. She was made out of Adam's Rib. St. Paul's letters constantly emphasize the theme: wives, submit to your husbands. The idea of submission and inferiority was abroad in the land, and it was being emphasized by both men and women. On the other hand, women had a very special and dignified role to play. They were the guardians of the home, and the home was idealized in Victorian literature as an almost religious place in its own right. That is an area which is morally more elevated and more dignified than the harsh outside world.

Another advice writer, Sarah Lewis, wrote a book called *Woman's Mission* in 1839, and it says, "The woman's job is to make the home into a sanctuary, and she must take the man, who is naturally a kind of wild beast, and learn how to tame, domesticate, and subordinate him." Of all the ways she is inferior, in another way she is clearly superior. She is naturally more religious. She is the one who has naturally got more moral qualities and the job to tame the tiger. As I said, the upper- and middle-class women who could afford not to work were intensely preoccupied with the question of getting the right husband. One of the earliest English feminists, a woman called Mona Caird remembered her own girlhood as a period of great stress and misery because of this assumption which was foisted upon her. She said:

"People think women who do not want to marry unfeminine. People find women who do want to marry immodest. People combine both opinions by regarding it as unfeminine for women not to look forward longingly to wifehood as the hope and purpose of their lives, and ridiculing and condemning any individual woman of their acquaintance whom they suspect of entertaining such a longing. They must wish and not wish. They must by no means give, and they must certainly not withhold encouragement. And so it goes on, each precept canceling the last, and most of them negative."

When it came time for a marriage to be arranged, very often a contract was drawn up. We call it a prenuptial agreement. It was a business transaction as well as a personal one, and it was quite common for the bride's father to give an allowance to the bridegroom. Very often what would happen is that for families which had made money in trade, one of the ways in which they would get enhanced social status was to marry their daughters to impoverished members of the aristocracy. They had the titles and the prestige but no longer had the money. So, each half got something out of this deal. The wife would be given sometimes an allowance, pin money, so that her own financial security would be assured even in the event that her husband turned out to be a complete wastrel, or if the husband died suddenly or became a drunk. Then she would have some residual property which would protect her against destitution. That is why in these upper classes, if a young man wanted to marry, the protocol was not for him to ask the girl but to ask the girl's father, to go first to her father to ask for permission. If he granted it, then haggle over the terms. Then he could present the suit to the daughter herself. There are lots of scenes in Victorian literature underlining that point.

Once the marriage had taken place, the husband gained control of all the wife's assets and property and even her legal interests. Here is another of those advice booklets. This one is called *The Ladies Handbook*, and it was published in 1859.

"Once a woman has accepted an offer of marriage, all she has or expects to have becomes the property, becomes virtually the property of the man she has accepted as her husband. No gift or deed executed by her is held to be valid.

Were she permitted to give away or otherwise settle her property between the period of acceptance and the marriage, he might be disappointed in the wealth he looked to in making the offer." (They are very frank about this.)

Under these circumstances, an heiress—that is, women who have access to large sums of money were intensely sought after on the London marriage market. The most famous of the Victorian heiresses was a woman called Angela Burdett Coutts, because she had inherited £2 million from her father, a banker, when he died in 1837. You need to multiply that by something like a thousand to get a sense of what a gigantic fortune £2 million was then. She kept diaries and wrote letters—she was a great friend of Charles Dickens—and she received dozens of marriage proposals. Nearly every young man in London had a go at proposing to Angela Burdett Coutts. There is a famous example of a bankrupt Irish lawyer, named Richard Dunn, who proposed to her repeatedly. Every few months he would be after her constantly. In fact, he was something like a stalker. For 18 years, he constantly renewed his suit, always unsuccessfully.

Lord Houghton, a gentleman in London, wrote to one of his friends: "This Coutts likes me because I have never proposed to her. Almost all the young men of family did. Those who did their duty by their families always did." A little later in 1872, Anthony Trollope wrote a magnificent novel called *The Way We Live Now*. It is a thousand-page masterpiece in my opinion, and one of the central issues in the story is that of the daughter of a rather disreputable businessman called Melmotte—Marie Melmotte, she is herself rather plain and unprepossessing, but all the young degenerate aristocrats have gambled away their fortunes at competing with one another to try to get her to marry them.

Because the wife's property became legally the husband's, wives tended to be in a very vulnerable legal position. When things went wrong in the marriage, the wife didn't have very much independent legal recourse against the husband. It was even legal for a husband to have his wife locked up or put into an asylum if in his judgment she was disobedient. He could elect that she was mad. A legal reform in 1882 finally allowed women to maintain control of their own property after marriage.

When a marriage was being prepared, the bands of marriage would be read out in the parish church to which she belonged and to which he belonged. The rector or the vicar would say, "I publish the vows of marriage between Jane Smith of this parish and Robert Bloggs of the parish of St. Jude. If any of you know any just cause or impediment why these persons should not be joined together in the bonds of holy matrimony, you may now declare it. When the actual marriage service itself was taking place, he would renew this request. This was a safeguard against bigamy. There is a famous example of this in literature as well. When Jane Eyre goes to the altar with Mr. Rochester, there is an impediment. He is already married. In fact, his other wife is locked up in the attic, the mad woman in the attic. It is one of the most dramatic scenes of *Jane Eyre*.

If you weren't a member of the state church, you weren't an Anglican; that is, if you belonged to one of the dissenting protestant sects or were Catholic or a Jew, you could get a civil license from the government and be married outside of the state religion.

The marriage market in London was organized around the London "season." As a young girl from these classes, when you were 17 or 18, you were brought out of the schoolroom and had a debut. This was an official meeting with the queen. There were rules governing exactly what would happen at the royal levy where you met the queen. You had to wear a dress which had bare neck and shoulders. It had to have a train at least three feet long. When the moment came, you went to the royal palace, were introduced to the queen and kissed her hand, unless you were yourself the holder of a title, in which case the queen kissed you on the forehead. As you retreated from the queen's presence, you did so walking backwards while continuing to hold her in view. It was highly ritualized.

These levies would take place usually early in the year, March, April and May. The beginning of the London season coincided with the beginning of the Parliamentary session, because very often the girls' fathers were members of Parliament, so they would come to London in December or January. The climax of the season came between April and July with a series of spring events, some of which would be outdoors if the weather was good enough, culminating in horse race meetings like Royal Ascot. The language then was this: coming out. Now if you say it, it is a reference to being publicly homosexual. Then, it meant coming out of the schoolroom, having had your debut with the queen and therefore being eligible to be proposed to in marriage.

A series of very well-chaperoned parties would take place where the young men of the season and the young ladies would mingle together. Ideally, a young girl would make a brilliant match in her first season or her second season. As British prosperity increased and more and more commercial families made the money to buy their way into landed society, the London "season" swelled, and by the mid and late Victorian period, about 4,000 families were involved, so there is still only a tiny minority of the British population but far bigger than it had been at the beginning of the century. If you failed to get married, if you had your debut and went through one season after the next and failed to get a proposal of marriage you regarded as appropriate, you would be regarded as one of the great losers in this game and become the maiden aunt or the lifelong spinster, a figure of sorrow and sometimes a figure of jokes.

Women from this class were expected to be virgins when they got married and to have very little knowledge of sex. They were also, by law, required to be sexually available at their husband's demand thereafter. This was an ideal which was very tenaciously adhered to. Clearly, the loss of virginity was a catastrophic event, particularly if it became public for a girl who was not married.

Here is a letter written by a woman called Mrs. Layton in the 1870s. She said that the man to whom she had been engaged had made improper suggestions to her (presumably that they should have sex before they were married). They had been engaged for two years. She wrote: "From that moment, I lost all respect for him and, in spite of all his protestations of regret and promises that it should not occur again, I told him I would never forgive him and broke off the engagement there and then." Later on, she married somebody else, Mr. Layton.

The ladies of this class would have very little knowledge of contraception and very often would have a religious or moral exception to contraceptives in any case. That meant that childbearing was extremely common. It was quite normal for a Victorian lady to have 10 or 15 children. There were people who recognized that the switch from being a maidenly girl to suddenly being a wife was going to be a jarring shock and change. Some people actually anticipated or looked for ways to make it a little less of a surprise. For example, Charles Kingsley was one of the most delightful Victorian writers and a social reformer and clergyman. He got married to a woman called Frances Grenfeld. They planned their wedding night ahead of time. They planned to have it as a tribute to God himself. In their view, there wasn't just the two of them in the bedroom. There would be three, the two of them and God, and it would be an act of collective prayer. It was a celibate wedding night. Here is a letter that she wrote to him outlining her idea of what they ought to do that evening when they were alone.

> "After dinner I shall perhaps feel worn out, so I shall just lie on your bosom and say nothing but feel a great deal. You will be very loving and call me your poor child. Then you will perhaps show me your lives of St. Elizabeth, your wedding gift. After tea, we will go up and rest. We will undress and bathe, and then you will come to my room, and we will kiss and love very much and read the psalms together. Then, we will kneel down and pray in our nightdresses. Oh, what solemn bliss. How hallowing. Then, you will take me up in your arms, will you not? and lay me down in bed. Then you will extinguish our light and come to me. How I will open my arms to you and sink into yours. You will kiss me and clasp me and we will praise God alone in the dark night with his eyes shining down upon us and his love enclosing us. After a time, we shall sleep. Yet, I fear you will yearn so for fuller communion that you will not be so happy as me, and I too perhaps will yearn, frightened as I am, but every yearning will remind me of our self-denial, your sorrow for your sin, your strength of repentance. I shall glory in my yearning, please God."

It is a loving letter, isn't it? in which she confesses her hopes and fears for the night. Apparently, this is more or less of what they did do that evening.

Now, death in childbirth was very common in every class, including the highest. You have only got to go to visit an English country churchyard to see that the graves of women who died in childbirth are very common. I have a friend called Geoffrey Clarke who has written a history of the British insurance industry. At first glance, that doesn't sound too promising, but actually it is fascinating. One of the things he discovered is this: Today, when you get an insurance policy, the older you are when you get the policy, the higher the premium you have to pay. In those days, for men that was true but for women it wasn't. Women paid high premiums in their 20s and 30s; then the premiums began to fall off because the insurance companies were familiar with the fact that a woman was more likely to die in childbirth in her mid 20s or early 30s than she was to die in her 40s from other causes. So, when she reached menopause, the premiums went down. She was more likely to live after that.

Victorian writers in fiction and in non-fiction, as I said earlier, attributed great moral and spiritual power to mothers and sanctified the role of motherhood. They constantly say, although you are inferior to your husband, subordinate to him, behind the scenes you are the one with the real power. It certainly is true that women played a more active role in religious life than men. On almost any Sunday morning more women than men would be in church, although women were denied leadership roles. Divorce was extremely unusual. Before 1857, any divorce required an act of Parliament and therefore was very singly unlikely to come about.

Women in the elite classes were dressed in such a way as to underline the point that they did not work. If you think of paintings or drawings of Victorian women, there are incredibly elaborate dresses with the whale bone corsets and the great crinolines and a little bit later the bustles and so on. These were all clothes which demonstrated by their appearance that they belonged to people who did not work. It was a sign of high status because leisure was a more high-status thing than work, especially for a woman. The cage-crinolines, the ones which had a massive train both to the side and to the front and back, were very difficult to live with apparently. As you were walking around with tiny steps, very slowly, the whole thing would begin to bounce up and down like an immense balloon, so ladies had to learn how to walk when wearing a cage-crinoline. Of course, they were very likely to sweep objects off tables. Victorian tables would be covered in knick-knacks, so you had to walk very delicately and carefully to do it. It was hard to sit down wearing one and even harder to get through doorways. Eventually, they became so massive they were dysfunctional in the very best way. Of course, by wearing clothes of this kind, you were declaring "I've got servants," for you could not put on such clothes without the help of a team of servants.

They had numbers of cartoons and jokes about them even at the time. *Punch,* which was a London humorist magazine, had crinoline jokes.

Even in their own day they were regarded as a bit ridiculous. There were elaborate rituals governing who could wear what under what circumstances. Ladies out of doors would always wear a hat or bonnet and always wear gloves. On formal occasions, they would even wear gloves inside. There were elaborate rituals governing mourning after a death, the wearing of black clothes and so on.

When women were out in the streets, particularly the town streets, they were vulnerable to enormous quantities of horse manure which was very common in the streets then because transportation was run by horses. So, they wore special things called "pattens," which were like wooden stilts, to elevate them up above the level of the street to keep them out of the muck in the roads.

Periodically, there were attempts at dress reform. One of the most famous was undertaken by an American lady named Amelia Bloomer that was early trousers for women, nicknamed Bloomers. They also were ruthlessly parodied at the time they first appeared in the middle of the century. As I said, careers for women were not unknown, but they were difficult to achieve, because for a woman who didn't need the work—she could be supported by her own income or her husband's—it was regarded as degrading to the man to have his wife at work.

The Victorian women were hemmed in by social expectations. On the other hand, they were far less hemmed in than women in many other parts of the world, in a way even than some women are today. British upper-class women have always had an imperious manner and plenty of self-assurance, and, if you look at the life of Queen Victoria or Florence Nightingale, there is nothing shy and retiring about them at all. They are big, powerful, and capable and effective people.

If you came from a genteel family or were impoverished, the classic career would be as a governess. Again, Jane Eyre is the obvious example of that. The governess did not quite become a member of the family, but she was clearly a big step above the servants in the family where she went. Most governesses weren't expected to be particularly intellectually rigorous. Again, *Punch* gives us a lovely insight into that. There is a *Punch* cartoon which shows a governess reproaching her young pupil, a little girl. The governess says, "I wonder what your mother would say if she knew how backward you are in geography." The little girl answers, "My mother said she never learned any geography, and she is married." A young child says she never learned any geography and she is married, and you did and you ain't. In other words, this is education for a girl. She has to learn some accomplishments, some French and drawing and playing at the piano and so on, but whether she learned geography or not didn't particularly matter.

Some of the greatest of the Victorian novelists were women: the three Bronte sisters, Charlotte, Anne, and Emily. Mary Ann Evans wrote under the name George Eliot. She is perhaps the greatest of all the Victorian novelists. A woman called Rachel Beer was the editor of two London Sunday newspapers in the 1890s, *The Sunday Times* and *The Observer*. Admittedly, her husband was the owner, so it wasn't as if she went on a conventional career path to get to that point. Nonetheless, she was a very effective journalist. It was she who broke the story that the documents convicting Dreyfus in the great Dreyfus scandal were forged. Mary Somerville, after whom one of the Oxford colleges for women is named, was an astronomer and the author of several books on the sciences, particularly in pointing out the connections between the various sciences. Ada Lovelace, Lord Byron's daughter, was an outstanding theoretical mathematician whose work anticipated in various ways binary numbers theory. There were scattered examples of women having responsible and intellectually stimulating careers. Woman played an informed part in reform projects. Florence Nightingale created nursing as a respectable option for young women.

A few women in the later Victorian period began to campaign for women's votes. In 1865, a woman called Barbara Bodichon gave a speech on votes for women to a few of her friends. She knew John Stuart Mill, who himself wrote the book called *On the Subjection of Women*, in 1869, criticizing the legal asymmetry of the British system whereby a wife could so easily be tyrannized by her husband. Harriet Martineau and this woman I mentioned a second ago, Mary Somerville signed petitions in favor of votes for women, but when John Stuart Mill introduced the idea in Parliament the legislation was laughed down almost at once. There was no serious attempt to introduce it. In 1867, the Second Reform Act had expanded the electorate to a lot of working-class men. Upper-class women said "It is outrageous that these men should have the vote when we, much more highly educated, don't have the vote. It is inappropriate." The same kind of thing was going on in America at the same time.

Elizabeth Cady Stanton and Susan B. Anthony were saying just then, "The free slaves are being given the vote, even though many of them can't read and write, through no fault of their own, but we are highly educated women. We ought to be part of the political nation as well." So, on both sides of the Atlantic, there is the beginning of a women's suffrage movement. It was the leadership of two widows, Millicent Fawcett and Emmeline Pankhurst who intensified the campaign and the work to get women the vote. Millicent Fawcett was studiously moderate, and Emmeline Pankhurst later on became the leader of the suffragettes, the most militant of the pro-suffrage groups.

Millicent Fawcett began speaking on the issue in 1869, and she saw the vote as a way of bringing the feminine virtues out into the world. She said in other words, "It is true that we are morally and religiously more superior, so, if we can bring these virtues into the public world, how much better and elevated it will be." She was supported by Bertram Russell's mother, Lady Amberley, but most of the members of Parliament thought this was all nonsense. One liberal MP said that according to the common view, "We regard women as something to admire, to reverence, to love, and while we share with her the happiness of life, we will shield her as far as possible from its harsher and sterner duties." The radical MP, Henry Labouchere says, "Intellectually women have not the gifts which fit them to being elected. They have got a certain amount of what I might call instinct, rather than reason, but they are impulsive, emotional, and they have absolutely no sense of proportion."

Nobody was more emphatic in their rejection of votes for women then Queen Victoria herself. Here she is talking about herself in the third person again. "The queen is anxious to enlist everyone who can speak or write to join in checking this mad wicked folly of women's rights with all its attendant horrors, on which her poor, feeble sex is bent, forgetting every sense of womanly feeling and propriety. Lady Amberley ought to get a good whipping." That is the queen, so carried away, it makes you wonder when you hear her speak, maybe there is something to this. Certainly in her own life, she was leading a very active political career.

We can imagine that for the intellectually ambitious minority women, it was galling to be so constricted. Here is what Harriet Martineau said, another writer of the time.

> "When I was young, it was not thought proper for ladies to study very conspicuously and especially with pen in hand. Young ladies, at least in the provincial towns, were expected to sit down in the parlor and to sew, herein which reading aloud was permitted, or to practice their music. They were supposed to be fit to receive callers without any sign of Bluestockingism." (A blue stocking is a studious lady. It was a slur.)

Martineau goes on to say:

> "Jane Austen herself, the queen of novelists, was compelled by the feelings of her family to cover up her manuscripts with a piece of muslin work kept on the table for that purpose whenever any genteel people came in. So it was with other young ladies. Thus, my first studies in philosophy were carried on with great care and reserve."

You can see from these examples that it would be wrong to say that middle-class and upper-class women had no opportunities. If they wanted to pursue opportunities, they had to be very tough minded indeed and had to overcome the expectations of their families and friends which collectively could be a great moral pressure. When you read about the minority women who did break into careers and, for example, in the 1870s, the very first women doctors in Britain, in almost every case they had an intense struggle against the expectations and the shocked sense of disappointment of their own menfolk. Many of them even took the further step of saying "Because I want to have a career, I want never to marry," and in many cases never did.

Lecture Seven
The Working-Class Woman

Scope:

The vast contrasts in Victorian life are apparent when we move from the privileged minority to consider the lives of working-class women, the majority. These women were often aware of the ideal woman's existence, to which the middle and upper classes could aspire, but they were unable to live according to it, because they, and their families, lacked the money. Instead, they were forced to work from an early age, nearly always at the worst jobs. Pay for working-class women was always lower than men's (even when the work was identical), and they suffered an array of diseases from overwork, malnutrition, too-frequent childbirth, and contaminated work places. Their home lives were usually scenes of hard domestic work, overcrowding, and poor diet. No wonder some working-class women joined the ranks of prostitutes, of whom there were thousands throughout the Victorian era. They could earn more money, more easily, than their laboring sisters. Some took to the life from choice; others, from economic necessity. Moral reformers, including Liberal Prime Minister William Gladstone, tried to "rescue" these "fallen women" and, by the end of the 19th century, purity crusaders, such as William Stead and Josephine Butler, had begun to drive the prostitutes' world out of sight.

Outline

I. Economic necessity forced many working-class women to work outside the home; such work began when they were very young.

   A. Large numbers of women worked as domestic servants.

   B. Women and children comprised a large part of the landless agricultural work force.

   C. Girls and women worked hard in the "sweated trades" too, doing textile piecework at home.

   D. In the industrial cities, women were in high demand for factory work.

   1. The hours were long; the unskilled work, monotonous.

   2. Conditions were often unhealthy.

   3. Women would be paid less than men, even for identical work.

  4. Men often resented women working in factories, because it weakened their bargaining positions.

E. Mid-century legislation prohibited women from working in coal mines and restricted their hours in some factories.

F. Some working-class women became small-scale entrepreneurs.

G. Work that is easy today, such as laundry, was then physically exhausting.

H. In the later 19th century, many new job opportunities for upper working-class women developed.

  1. Florence Nightingale made nursing a respectable option.

  2. Growing numbers of unmarried women became schoolteachers when universal preliminary education was required after the 1870s.

  3. Shop assistants, secretaries, librarians, and typists were mainly women by 1900.

II. Working-class women faced challenges at each stage of the life cycle.

A. Family poverty often made work a necessity.

B. Overcrowding and dependency on parents made work or marriage seem attractive alternatives.

C. Factory work sometimes provided young working women with comradeship and fun.

  1. They enjoyed practical jokes.

  2. They had a limited social life in pubs and clubs.

D. Working-class marriages often followed, rather than preceded, pregnancy.

  1. Parish guardians sometimes forced reluctant swains to wed.

  2. Abandoned pregnant women often faced social censure and acute poverty.

  3. Infanticide was widespread.

E. Combining motherhood with work created child-care challenges.

F. Poor and adulterated food added to working women's difficulties.

III. Prostitution was common, as a job or as a supplement to low wages in other work.

    A. We know a great deal about Victorian prostitution from the anonymous *My Secret Life*.

    B. Some skillful young women chose the life as a route to riches.

        1. King William IV had ten children by his mistress.

        2. Catherine "Skittles" Walters was a famous and beautiful courtesan.

    C. Others were forced into the life if abandoned or widowed or if sickness prevented the family breadwinner from working.

        1. Prostitution paid better than any other working-class occupation.

        2. It was hazardous to women's health and safety.

    D. Brothels were common, and many cafes and pubs provided beds. A survey from 1838 estimated that there were 5,000 brothels in London alone.

    E. The government experimented with legal regulation of prostitution, but a purity crusade tried to prevent it.

        1. In 1864, Parliament passed the Contagious Diseases Act, to ensure regular VD inspection of prostitutes in military towns.

        2. Josephine Butler led a protest campaign against the act.

        3. Parliament condemned brothels in 1885 and repealed the Contagious Diseases Act in 1886.

        4. The Salvation Army tried to rescue "fallen" women.

        5. Religiously motivated individuals, including William Gladstone, also sought to rescue "fallen" women; he flagellated himself when he realized that he enjoyed the work.

Essential Reading:

Trevor Fisher, *Prostitution and the Victorians*.

Joan Perkin, *Victorian Women*.

Supplementary Reading:

John Benson, *The Working Class in Britain*.

Stephen Marcus, *The Other Victorians*.

Questions to Consider:

1. What were the most difficult aspects of Victorian working-class women's lives?

2. Why was prostitution so widespread in Victorian Britain?

Lecture Seven—Transcript
The Working-Class Woman

The vast contrasts in Victorian life become apparent immediately when we switch from looking at this elite of women to the great majority of British women, those in the working classes. They were often aware of the existence led by the privileged minority, and it was a way of life to which they aspired. Economic realities made it essential in their case that they must work. Why? because they lacked money. Very often, they had to start working at an early age and to work at the most menial jobs. Their pay was lower than that of men even when the work was identical. And they suffered all the hazards which work brought, particularly contaminated work places, the characteristic diseases which tended to afflict people in certain jobs. In addition, they had to suffer from too frequent childbirth and poverty in their home lives.

Their home lives were usually scenes of great overcrowding, extreme hard work, and very poor diet. No wonder so many women joined the ranks of prostitutes in Victorian London, of whom there were thousands. It was one of the commonest forms of women's work. As a prostitute, you could earn money more easily from less work than your honest laboring sisters. Some people took to the life from choice, others from economic necessity. Eventually, prostitution among working-class Victorian women became so widespread that it became a source of national concern and legislation, and several people in prominent public life, such as William Gladstone, the liberal Prime Minister, took it as a personal job to try to rescue fallen women.

As I said, economic necessity was the primary reason most working-class women had to work outside the home and to begin when they were very young. The biggest source of women's work was as domestic servants. It was such a big and complicated thing that I am going to devote a whole lecture to that a little later in the course. For the moment, I will shelve that and put it to one side. It is important to remember that in every generation, tens of thousands of young girls were going out as domestic servants. Second, women and children comprised a large part of the agricultural work force, the landless farm workers. A Parliamentary committee which was investigating women's work talked to a girl who said that she came from the county of Lincolnshire in the east of England. She said she left school when she was eight years old and joined a traveling farm work gang that worked 14 hours per day.

> "For four years, summer and winter, I worked in these gangs, no holiday of any sort, with the exception of very wet days and Sundays. At the end of that time, I felt it was like heaven to me when I was taken to the town of Leeds and put to work in a cotton factory."

A lot of girls worked in what were called the sweated trades. That is usually textile piecework, which was done at home. They would go to a master clothier and take the work home to their houses. Here it was very hard and grinding work, very low piecework rates with lots of regional variation depending on where in the country they lived. Some places it was straw plaiting to make hats. Some places it was lace making or knitting or glove stitching, this kind of trade which was still often done outside of the factories well into the Victorian period.

Becky Usedale was a child knitter in Yorkshire, and she said, "We knit as hard as we can because the one who knits the slowest gets well thumped." Very often their parents would drive them to do this work from knowledge that the family could not do without the income that it would bring in, the sweated trades. This has remained true in sweatshops right up to the present. It is still common in the third world today. It required working very long hours in very overcrowded conditions. One of the early working class radical writers we have access to is Francis Place. He was a tailor interested in reform projects of the time. He said: "Nothing conduces so much to the degradation of the woman than her having to eat and drink and cook and iron and transact all her domestic concerns in the room in which she and her family also work and in which they sleep."

It was common for working-class families to occupy just one room. Overcrowding was very widespread. Home piecework of this kind, working at home on textiles, was sometimes subject to regional fluctuations. In the lead up to Christmas, there was often an intense rush as members of society were getting their ball gowns ready. Then there would be other slack times in the trade when being out of work was even more dreadful than being in work, when you really had to work very long hours—when you were out, you lost the necessary income.

As the industrial factory system spread, more and more women went to work in the factories partly because in many trades, particularly factory textile trades, it wasn't really hard work. It was mainly machine minding, very dull, monotonous, often terribly noisy as well. The conditions tended to be unhealthy. Each occupation tended to have its own illness. You have probably heard the phrase "mad as a hatter." This is because the hatters, making hats, used mercury compounds which actually did have a physiological effect and produced a very high level of madness among hat workers. Girls who made matches, who had the job of dipping little match sticks into the phosphorous compounds which made the igniting match heads, were required to sit at the benches for 12 hours per day, although they had a few minutes off for lunch. They had to stay at the benches and didn't have the opportunity to wash up properly before they ate, so they were actually taking into their bodies these phosphorous compounds which often led to a kind of degenerative disease of the jaw. There is an illness called "phosey jaw" which the match girls tended to suffer from.

The people who worked in Staffordshire in a district called "The Potteries," where pottery was made by companies like Wedgwood, tended to suffer from lead poisoning because of the lead that they used in the glazes. Cotton factory girls often suffered from tuberculosis because the inside of the cotton factory was damp and full of lint, which would tend to aggravate lung complaints. The lace makers who worked their whole lives often with poor illumination and doing very tiny detail work suffered from blindness or severely deteriorating eyesight because of the great eye strain from which they suffered. There are all these ways; different types of work had characteristic distinctive forms of suffering.

Even when men and women, who were doing exactly the same work, the women were paid less for it. It was widely assumed that this was an appropriate thing to do, not among the women, but certainly among the men. Men themselves often resented the fact that women were working in the factories because they understood that it weakened their own bargaining position. If only the women could have been taken out of the factories, which they wanted to do from the point of view of their pride as husbands and providers, it would also strengthen their bargaining position with their employers. The employers knew all about this.

Here is an unscrupulous Lancashire textile boss giving evidence to a Parliamentary commission in 1844. He says, "I have a decided preference for married females, especially those who have families at home dependent on them for support. They are attendant, docile (more so than unmarried females), and are compelled to use their utmost exertions to procure the necessities of life." In other words, he deliberately employed married women because he knew that they were going to have to put up with the worst conditions and the lowest pay without kicking about it too much.

In the middle of the Victorian period, gradually reforms started to limit the number of hours that women and children could work in the factories, and particularly the number of hours they could work in the coal mines. This was partly in reaction to a sense of the degradation involved, but it was also often a matter of sexual anxiety. For example, a lot of women worked in the coal mines where the heat meant that they often worked almost naked. The assumption was, on the part of the Parliamentary reformers, there was probably a great deal of promiscuity in the coal mines when the nearly naked men and women were working there together. That seems to have dominated the debates about whether women should be excluded from the coal mines, more than the fact that these women were often being required to drag heavy wagons of coal to the pithead from the actual face where the coal was cut.

Some working-class women became entrepreneurs, little shopkeepers for example, or laundresses. The laundry business was widespread. This was in the days before the invention of electric washing machines. Laundry work was an incredibly hard job to do. It would require usually that the laundress would have to go to her customer and carry the laundry back to her own place, then scrub the clothes without any of the detergents that we have today or any of the labor-saving devices which now surround the doing of laundry. It is still a pain, but compared to how it used to be it is nothing. Most working-class people didn't have running water in their houses. You would have to go out to the well, fill up copper kettles and bring them inside and put the water over the fire to warm up, then boil all the clothes which you were going to launder—and the starching and bluing process was long and complicated—and then when they dried, you would have to do the long ironing process. There were no wrinkle- free fabrics, so the ironing was much more difficult than it is today, especially with elaborate clothes.

Before the days of electric irons, you would simply have two or three pound irons, just blocks of iron with a handle which you would place on the hot stove, take one off and iron with it until it began to cool down, put it back on the stove and take another one and carry on. All in all it was a very hard job, and people who became laundresses had a reputation of becoming very muscular because of the sheer hard work it entailed.

Some women became street vendors, peddlers. Descriptions of working class life in London talk about the fact that the streets were full of people selling things, very small, what is called penny capitalists, small-scale entrepreneurs, half of whom were women.

Toward the end of the 19th century, slightly more job opportunities began to open up for working-class women. I should pause here to say that it is important to assume that the working class is one thing; it is clearly not one entity. It is subdivided into dozens of groups. There is all the world between respectable people at the top end of the working class, the so-called aristocracy of labor, that is, people who come from families with the most dependable and most highly paying working jobs, and those at the bottom of the working class, with far less opportunities to aspire to respectability. I mentioned *Pygmalion,* and I should mention it again here. Remember that Eliza Doolittle's father is a dustman. He says, when he comes to see Henry Higgins, "I belong to the undeserving poor." He makes his own progressive puns about his low status within the working class.

Nursing became a decent profession for working-class girls toward the end of the century, and, once universal education became specified at the end of the 1870s, more and more young women, particularly from the upper working class, could be drawn into school teaching if they themselves had done well in school. By 1900, girls were working as shop assistants, as secretaries, as librarians, and as typists, so gradually a wider array of work began to open up to them.

They faced challenges and difficulties at every stage of the life cycle. They had to go to work often because of economic necessity. It is easy to imagine that many girls would have wanted to go to work because if they were dependent on their parents, living in terribly overcrowded conditions, going out to the factory must have seemed like a liberating alternative. A Mrs. Layton told a Parliamentary inquiry, in her family the parents and 14 children lived in three little rooms. They lived in a place which was chronically vulnerable to epidemics of typhoid and cholera. They shared the privies with 20 other families (This is the non-flushing toilets in the back yards.). They had no running water, and they lived in a great cloud of smoke and soot all the time. Imagine that just to get away from such conditions was an attractive option.

Factory work provided young girls with the companionship of others like them. Sometimes they enjoyed some fun and practical jokes. It could be very rough, too. The man who became the leader of the English Communist Party in the early 20th century was a man called Harry Pollitt. He remembered that when he was a lad he went to work as an apprentice in a Lancashire cotton factory. He said the first day a group of the factory women, teenage girls, grabbed hold of him, pulled his trousers down, and "daubed my unmentionable parts with oil," then packed me up in cotton waste, so it was rough horseplay on the part of the factory girl.

They often had social clubs of their own, really pubs, places where they could drink and smoke, and these places shocked middle-class reformists. Lord Ashley, who was one of the most severe and upright of the Victorian evangelical reformers, told Parliament in 1844, "Fifty or 60 females, married and single, form themselves into clubs, ostensibly for protection, but in fact they meet together to drink, sing, and smoke. They use, it is stated, the lowest, most brutal, and most disgusting language imaginable."

Marriage customs among the working classes were very different from those among the upper classes, as we looked at before. There were regional variations in this as in everything. It was quite common for the marriage to follow the announcement of a pregnancy rather than to precede it. We know that premarital sexual activity was quite common. For example, historian Joan Perkin recounts a Cumberland girl getting pregnant and realizing that now she is pregnant she has to get married and she has this conversation with her aunt. The aunt says "Anna, that has been tasting the soup before it was ready." Anna says, "Yes, and I found a carrot in it."

If the man refused to marry his pregnant girlfriend, that was a source of alarm to the parish poverty officials. They became aware that if a girl had a baby without being married, they would become dependent on the parish. Sometimes the overseers of the poor house would coerce the young man to marry the girl. Working-class cohabitation without marriage was also quite common. Certainly in the cities, very often a working-class boy and girl, teenagers, would get together, some said have children, but never would marry. Investigators found that the incidence of wife beating was less among couples who weren't married than those who were. You might have been tempted as a working-class girl not to marry the man from knowledge that you would probably be treated worse if you did.

The people who suffered most in these situations were working-class girls who'd had affairs with upper-class men and then were abandoned by them. Abandonment could be catastrophic. There are two good literary examples here. One is Hetty Sorel, the farm girl in George Eliot's novel *Adam Bede,* who has an affair with a young gentleman who then abandons her and goes off with his army regiment. She has a child and doesn't know what to do with herself. She finally kills the child and is then convicted of infanticide. In Thomas Hardy's *Far From the Madding Crowd*, one of the girls, Fanny, has an affair with Sergeant Troy, but he abandons her and goes off to marry Bathsheba Everdene, and she has to drag herself to the workhouse where she dies giving birth, and she and the child both die in the workhouse in desperate poverty.

Infanticide, the killing of children, was widespread, particularly when the children were very young—giving birth to a child who you couldn't possibly afford to keep. Juries, when women were put on trial for infanticide, tended to be lenient. Unless the evidence was incontrovertible that they really had killed the child, they tended to give the woman the benefit of the doubt. Very often the woman would say that the baby had smothered in the bedclothes. In places where people are living three, four, and five to a bed, it is possible to imagine that children were sometimes smothered. So, often that would be a successful defense against a prosecution for infanticide.

As I said, there were regional variations, particularly in the north of England, where a woman would get pregnant but decide that rather than marry the father of the child she would stay with her own family and carry on contributing to its income, especially if the man in question was willing to pay a certain amount of money for the upkeep of the child even though they weren't marrying. Women would give birth, and very often they had to go straight back to work immediately. Then, as now, child care was an immediate and very pressing concern. Often it was a matter of networks of neighbors and grandmothers and younger sisters, all the women in the locality. Because people tended to stay in the same place, they tended to have a lot of relatives living nearby. That way they could work out informal child care arrangements with one another.

In the Potteries, the area of Staffordshire where the ceramics were made, very often a new mother would go back to work within two or three days of giving birth, but she would get one of her slightly older daughters to bring the baby in so she could breast feed it during her breaks from work. It was also extremely common to use pacifiers for babies. That included what we mean by a pacifier, but it could also include bread soaked in alcohol, gin, or even opium, which was legally on sale in the stores, as a way of calming the baby down and making it less troublesome. As if all these problems weren't enough, women also had to suffer from very poor quality adulterated food, milk that was watered down, lime in the flour, elm leaves in the tea. There are everlastingly complaints about poor quality food. It wasn't until 1872 that Parliament began to legislate to make it illegal to sell adulterated food and also to prosecute people who did.

As I said at the beginning, this is the background to a situation in which a lot of women turned to prostitution either as their primary source of income or as a supplement to very low wages in other work. The Victorian middle classes had an extremely strong taboo about the open discussion of sex. They would be horrified to think that somebody like me, a hundred years later, was actually lecturing about sexual matters, publicly. It would be regarded as absolutely disgraceful. At the same time, a weird double standard operated. Everybody knew that there were thousands of women out there who were making their livings as prostitutes for various reasons, usually economic need, but occasionally the sense that it was actually a desirable career option because you could make rapid upward strides in society with it.

The thing to emphasize is how common it was. Here is an early Victorian visitor from Germany describing what it is like at the London theaters.

> "The higher classes rarely visit their national theater. The reason for the absence of decent families is the attendance of several thousand *filles de joie* (in other words, prostitutes)

from the kept lady who devours six thousand pounds sterling a year, and has her own box at the theater, down to those who bivouac on the streets under the open sky. During the intermissions they crowd the fairly large and elaborate foyer where they put on all air of effrontery, unrestrainedly on show. It goes on to such an extent that often in the theater one can hardly ward off these repellant priestesses of Venus, especially when they are drunk, which is not infrequently the case, at which time they always beg in the most shameless fashion."

One of the places which we know a lot about the prostitute's subculture is through an amazing book called *My Secret Life*. It is a multi-volume book, published anonymously, and there are still competing theories about exactly who it was who wrote it. A recent historian called Stephen Marcus read the whole book and published his own study of it called *The Other Victorians*. It is about the great Victorian sexual underworld. This man himself, the author of *My Secret Life*, had sufficient income that he could devote his whole life to sex, and he traveled around Europe and all over Britain and had sex with literally hundreds of different women and wrote a lot. Not only are they erotic books, but they are also great books of social commentary, because he talked to the girls he had affairs with and they described to him the sort of circumstances which had led them to go into this life.

He often has flings with servants or casually picks girls up on the street and finds that they are factory workers or working as seamstresses, and this is for them an opportunity to earn a little bit more money from him. Here is a little passage from his book on the advantages of having an occasional love or sexual affair with a servant. He gets tired of the prostitutes for a while and says, "I am going to try a servant instead."

> "I was tired of the prostitutes' lies, their tricks and the dissatisfied money-grabbing, money-begging style. I wanted a change. So I began to look out for a nice fresh servant. I have now had many servants in my time and know no better companions in amorous amusements. They have rarely lost all modesty. A new lover is a treat and a fresh experience to them, even when they have had several, and few have had that. They only get a chance of copulating once a week or so.

They are clean, well fed, full blooded, and when they come out to meet their friend or give way with a chance man on the sly, they are ready. So, I longed for a servant and soon found my chance. I suppose all men do if they set their mind upon a woman."

Anyway, there are about nine volumes of this. It is a rich and interesting source.

Some young women clearly chose to become the mistresses of upper-class men as an avenue to gaining wealth of their own. The luckiest ones were definitely those who could get themselves kept, and it was like a kept mistress of a man who was in the highest ranks of society. In the early period, this was very common. I mentioned earlier that King William IV, although his legitimate children died, had ten children by his mistress, an actress called Dorothy Jordan, and most of them survived.

In the mid-Victorian period, a few mistresses were great public celebrities. One of them was a woman called Catherine Walters, and her nickname was Skittles. When she went riding in Hyde Park, crowds would gather to actually watch her putting on a magnificent show. She was very beautiful, brilliantly well-dressed, and had a flock of admirers around her all the time. She was friends with the Prince of Wales, one of his many indiscretions, and the Prime Minister Gladstone knew her very well.

The Marquis of Hartington (This is a man who was going to become the Duke of Devonshire after his father's death, one of the richest and grandest of the aristocrats in the land.) was madly in love with her and wanted to marry her, but his father squashed that plan. Finally, the Marquis of Hartington gave to her capital sufficient to generate an income of £2,000 per year. In other words, he made her a rich woman, even though they weren't allowed to marry. She lived to the ripe old age of 81 and had a fascinating and varied career.

In Victorian melodrama, there were fallen women, and in the plays they always come to a bad end. Any woman who loses her virtue in the literature tends to suffer for it. In reality, many of them made enough money that they could set up legitimate businesses of their own. Some women were forced into prostitution if they were abandoned by their husbands or if they were widowed or if sickness prevented the family breadwinner from going to work. In the days before there was any sort of welfare system, all kinds of contingencies could suddenly make a family penniless and women sometimes turned to prostitution as a way of overcoming it.

I don't mean to diminish the fact that there was a very great social stigma attaching to it. Respectable people always hated and dreaded and feared this possibility. But, you can see the temptation when you hear this evidence: A London investigator called Henry Mayhew was talking to a girl and she said that she used to work making shirts and would earn four pence in a day. As a prostitute she could get five shillings a day. That is something like 15 times as much, even though she was just a very poor streetwalker.

The lower down the social scale you went, the greater the dangers—venereal disease was extremely widespread—the danger of predatory pimps, non-payment by clients, and pregnancy, because contraception was so bad in those days. Brothels were very common all through the cities. A survey in 1838 estimated that there were 5,000 brothels in London alone. When Jack the Ripper committed his famous murders in 1858, police said they knew of 62 brothels just in that area, Whitechapel, where the murders took place.

Eventually the government got involved in the attempt to regulate prostitution, and they passed a law in 1864 called The Contagious Diseases Act. The idea was, in towns where there was an army barracks or a navy base, they wanted to try to prevent the soldiers and sailors from getting venereal disease. Their way of doing it was to give regular inspections to women they suspected of being prostitutes. If the women were found to be suffering of the disease, they were sequestered in a locked hospital until they could be treated with various mercury medicines and make a recovery.

The legislation was bitterly controversial and the campaign to repeal it was lead by a middle-class woman called Josephine Butler. She said that she was campaigning for its repeal on the grounds of the double standard. It was unreasonable that the women should be locked up in hospital, but that their clients, the men, should be exempt from the force of the law. Many other middle-class women gathered her. A woman could be suspected of prostitution wrongly. Once she had been arrested and brought in, the stigma of having been a prostitute would attach to her even if it was false. Here is Josephine Butler speaking to a royal commission in 1871.

"We claim that laws should not be made which teach in an indirect but subtle, most effectual manner that impurity of life is not a sin, but a necessity. Neither can our moral objections to these acts be met by assurances that a certain number of women are reclaimed by their operations. I ask, where are the men who are reclaimed by them? As the mothers of sons, we demand to know what the influence of these acts is on young men. It is vain to restore fallen women to virtue on the one hand while on the other you stimulate the demand for these victims. Prove to us if you can that these acts promote chastity among men. That is what we are concerned about."

In other words, don't have this legislation regulating it, because the legislation is predicated upon the assumption that it is going to continue to happen. She is aspiring for a higher sexual ideal in which the people of both sexes will achieve the condition of chastity.

She goes on.

"Men of every class go to the prostitutes and they ought not to. All legislation hitherto had been directed against one sex only, but we insist that it should be directed against both sexes. Whereas it has been directed only against the poor, we insist, and the working men insist, that it also apply to the rich profligate. It cannot be said that there is no such thing as seduction of young girls by gentlemen of the upper classes. It cannot be said that there is no such thing as patronage of houses of ill fame by rich profligate men."

Finally, under this kind of pressure, Parliament decided to act. In 1886, it repealed the Contagious Diseases Act and by legislation in 1885 tried to stamp out the operation of brothels. It was a very difficult thing to do because they were so widespread. Progressively, more and more people in the middle classes became convinced that this was the right thing to do, to try to stamp it out or force it more and more underground. The early work of the Salvation Army was dedicated to this.

One of the most quixotic examples we have is of William Gladstone. Throughout his life and even when he was Prime Minister, he would go out onto the streets and accost prostitutes and try to persuade them to give up the life. He would say, "I can find a place for you to live and stay, and I can find you some honest work to do." Some of them even went to live on his own estate in North Wales, Hawarden. His diaries show us that sometimes he was aware that he was sexually attracted to them. On those occasions he would draw a little whip in the corner of his diary which we think means that he flagellates himself as a way of trying to repress these sexual demons which taunted even him.

You can see from all this there was an enormous contrast between the lives of the upper- and middle-class women on the one hand and the lives of working-class women on the other.

Lecture Eight
The State Church and Evangelical Revival

Scope:

Britain had an established church, the Anglican Church, or Church of England, to which the majority of the population nominally belonged. The church ministered to the respectable every Sunday and to nearly everyone during such rites of passage as christening, marriage, and burial. It was run by a hierarchy of officials, stretching from the archbishops and bishops at the top, appointed by the prime minister, down to the vicars and curates at the bottom. The right to appoint vicars often lay in the hands of landlords, who usually favored their younger sons. The early Victorian era witnessed the reform of many old church abuses, including plural livings and inequalities of church incomes. Meanwhile, an evangelical revival, gathering force from the late 18th century, created a new mood of zeal and moral Puritanism. Its advocates worked to abolish slavery and brutal working conditions in factories, but they also tried to stamp out all forms of nonreligious Sunday entertainment. The working classes stayed away from church in growing numbers until such groups as the Salvation Army set out to "rescue" them for Christianity.

Outline

I. Most British people were Christians, at least nominally, and most belonged to the Church of England, a branch of the state.

   A. They assumed that the Bible contained God's revealed truth and that by living virtuous lives they would eventually go to heaven.

      1. The *Book of Common Prayer* ensured a standard liturgy over the whole country.

      2. The Church of England subscribed to the "Thirty-Nine Articles."

   B. Bishops were appointed by the prime minister and governed a hierarchy of lesser clergy in their dioceses.

   C. Tithe exactions made the church wealthy but unpopular.

   D. Twenty-four bishops and the two archbishops (of Canterbury and York) were members of the House of Lords.

   E. The ministry was a highly respectable profession.

1. It was an avenue of upward mobility for middle-class men, giving them leisure and time for intellectual interests.
2. It provided places for younger sons of the gentry and aristocracy.

F. Landowners often had the right of appointment to "livings."
   1. They could sell livings, too, and sometimes advertised them in the *Times*.
   2. A new rector or curate would "read himself in" to his living by reciting the Thirty-Nine Articles from the pulpit.
   3. The holding of plural livings was still common in the early 19th century.

G. Cathedral chapters were often rich from ancient bequests.

H. Reform of obvious inequalities and abuses began in the 1830s by the creation of a permanent Ecclesiastical Commission.
   1. Bishops' incomes were standardized at 4,000 pounds.
   2. Plural livings were abolished by Parliament in 1838.

II. The evangelical movement in the established church emphasized personal conversion, emotional commitment to Jesus, exacting moral standards, and Biblical literalism.

A. It originated largely with John Wesley and the Methodists.

B. George Whitefield, who was known for his unusual practice of preaching outdoors, advocated a religion of personal transformation.

C. Evangelicalism became socially influential inside the Church of England through the Clapham sect.
   1. William Wilberforce led the campaign for abolishing the slave trade (1807) and slavery (1833) in the British Empire, against the West India lobby's opposition.
   2. Lord Shaftesbury campaigned for improved conditions in factories and mines.

D. Evangelicals campaigned for sabbatarianism and temperance.
   1. John Henderson, a Scottish evangelical, bought the Glasgow and Edinburgh railway to prevent it from running trains on the Sabbath.

2. The high level of consumption of alcoholic beverages was partly attributable to the fact that urban water supplies were not safe to drink.

E. Evangelicals were willing to cooperate with Dissenters to spread Bible-reading and Sunday schools.

F. Evangelicals encouraged a religious seriousness that became popular among Victorian artists, even those who were not themselves evangelicals.

1. Pre-Raphaelites took up religious themes, as we see in Holman Hunt's *The Light of the World* and Rossetti's *The Annunciation*.

2. Henry Alexander Bowler's *The Doubt: Can These Dry Bones Live?* shows a young woman meditating by a grave.

G. Evangelicals were often satirized and parodied by Victorian novelists for their zeal and intolerance. Reverend Obadiah Slope in Trollope's *Barchester Towers* is the classic example.

III. The working classes were increasingly alienated from organized religion, especially working-class men.

A. Many felt that the church represented forces of surveillance and repression.

B. They had distinctive religious ideas of their own.

1. They thought that christening, marriage, and burial services were essential.

2. Otherwise, they believed more in good works than in justification by faith.

C. William Booth founded the Salvation Army in 1878 in an attempt to regain working-class people to Christianity through clever use of popular idioms.

Essential Reading:

W. B. Rubinstein, *Britain's Century*, chapter 18.

Owen Chadwick, *The Victorian Church: 1829–1901*.

Supplementary Reading:

David Bebbington, *Evangelicalism in Modern Britain: A History from the 1730s to the 1980s*.

Alec Vidler, *The Church in an Age of Revolution.*

Questions to Consider:

1. Why was the Church of England vulnerable to criticism in the Victorian era?

2. What were the attractions of evangelicalism?

Lecture Eight—Transcript
The State Church and Evangelical Revival

Britain had an established church, the Anglican Church, or Church of England, to which the majority of the people nominally belonged. It administered to respectable people every Sunday and to nearly everybody at crucial moments of the life cycle, birth, marriage, and death. It was run by a hierarchy of officials, stretching from the Archbishops of Canterbury and York, at the very top, all the way down to the humblest vicars and curates at the bottom. The right to appoint a man to become the vicar, parson, or curate of a parish church often lay not in the hands of other church officials but in the hands of a local landlord. Very often landlords favored members of their own families or the families of their friends to become the members of the clergy, who tended to be younger sons of gentry families.

The Victorian period witnessed a series of reforms of some of the most glaring abuses of the Church of England, because just as the political system had become corrupt and inappropriate with age, so had the church in many ways. A great evangelical revival was sweeping through the Church of England, gathering force in the 18th century, particularly with the influence of Methodism. They are entering the Church of England itself with great force in the first three or four decades of the 19th century. Its advocates were people who had worked hard to abolish slavery in the British Empire and who tried to abolish brutal working conditions in the factories and coal mines. They also tried to stamp out what they regarded as unpardonable breaches of the Sabbath. There were Sabbatarians who wanted Sunday to be devoted solely to religious worship.

The working-class people, who often only had Sunday off as the only day of the week they didn't have to work, reacted by abandoning the church in large numbers until eventually evangelical groups like the Salvation Army began to look for new ways to try to keep people living active religious lives even if they were working-class people.

Because it was a state church, you were assumed to be a member unless you specified that you were not. In those days, if you joined the British Army, and you were asked, What is your religion? and you said none, they would write down "CofE," Church of England.

Most British people were at least nominally Christian. They assumed that the Bible contained God's revealed truth, and that by living virtuous lives eventually they would go to heaven. Queen Victoria, like most respectable people, went to church every Sunday.

The liturgy was governed by the Book of Common Prayer. This was a book that enshrined the standard liturgy for the whole country, and it had Sunday services for Holy Communion, for Matins, and for Evensong, the three standard Sunday services. It also contained the Baptism ceremony, the marriage service, and the funeral service.

The Church of England was based upon the Thirty-Nine Articles. These were 39 principles which had been drawn up when Queen Elizabeth I came to the throne back in the late 1550s, when she decisively separated the English church from Roman Catholicism. The history of the English Reformation in the 1500s is itself very complicated. Her father, Henry VIII, had first separated the church from Rome. Elizabeth's older sister Mary had tried to reintegrate Britain into the Catholic Christendom. Elizabeth once again took it out. From Elizabeth's accession right up into the 19th century, the English church was distinct from Rome. The Thirty-Nine Articles were the basis of Anglicanism, and they blended conventional Christian assertions, which Catholics could agree with, with various declarations condemning the papacy and the Catholic practices.

Queen Victoria is a good example; she is a typical Christian of her time in some ways. She comforted herself after Albert's death with the thought that she was going to meet him again in heaven. And later on in life, she told one of her granddaughters: "You know, my dear, when I die, I shall be just a little bit nervous about meeting grandpapa, as I have taken to doing a good many things that he would not quite approve of." It was a very literal and direct sense of her destiny in heaven. Her biographer, Christopher Hibbert, has some lovely passages where she talks about who she is going to meet in heaven—King David for one—other kings from throughout the ages. She didn't quite like the idea of meeting King David because he treated Uriah so badly. This is the man whom he sent off into the army to be killed so that he could seduce Bathsheba, Uriah's wife. She disapproved of that and didn't think it was quite right to meet him. She flatly refused to meet Abraham. She thought that Abraham wasn't up to the mark. She had ideas about what post-life was going to be like in heaven.

The bishops, the senior churchmen, were appointed by the prime minister, again because it is a state church. They governed a hierarchy of lesser officials in their own area; it was called a diocese. The very top of the pyramid were the two Archbishops—of Canterbury (the senior one) and the Archbishop of York (who was the junior one)— then a series of bishop ranks below them. There was a great variation in the quality of the income you would get from being a bishop. If you were the Bishop of Durham, you could enjoy an income of £19,000 per year. It was a very wealthy diocese. By contrast, if you were the Bishop of Landath, in Wales, you could look forward to making only £900. It is an enormous difference there.

The cathedrals themselves, which are the seats of the bishops had a whole succession of staff positions, arch-deacons, deans, canons, prebendaries, and parochial clergy, each one fulfilling various positions and functions within the administration of the diocese. All this was paid for through tithes, and a tithe was a tenth of the income which every subject of the queen was expected to give to the church. These tithing actions made the church wealthy but also made it unpopular. It is a heavy tax to pay a tenth of your income to the church.

It also meant that depending on the economic prosperity of the parish, your income as the minister would vary widely. If you lived in a wealthy parish, particularly in the southeastern counties of Britain, which tended to be very prosperous areas, you could get a very good living from the tithes coming in from all the wealthy farms in the area. By contrast, if you lived in a remote hill farm district, the tithes might not amount to very much. Traditionally, they had always been paid in kind. You would actually give wheat, chickens, and pigs to the minister. As Britain was becoming a more and more commercial society, in 1840, a commutation of tithes to a cash payment was commuted, so it became more of a money transaction.

Most parish churches also carried with them what was called a glebe. A glebe was farm land, and the right to farm this land went to the holder of the living, that is, to the man who was the vicar. In many cases, the vicar, rather than do his own farming, would rent it out to a local farmer. It would give that farmer more land on which to do his own work.

Twenty-four senior bishops and the Archbishops of Canterbury and York were themselves members of the House of Lords. They had a direct role in the political life of the nation. The bishops' switch in their votes in 1832 was one of the moments which lead to the Reform Act being passed.

To become a man of the cloth, as it was called, was a highly respectable profession. If you came from the middle classes, it was an avenue of upward social mobility because it was one of the very few jobs you could do which actually had a great deal of leisure time. You had duties on Sundays and you were certainly expected to visit members of your parish, but there was plenty of time left over for intellectual pursuits. A great many of early mid 19th-century British intellectuals were clergy who had the time to do it.

The church also provided a berth for younger sons of the gentry and aristocracy. The land-owing classes had the principle of primary geniture, which is that the oldest son inherits the whole estate. That meant that the youngest son had to find an alternative occupation. It was quite common for the oldest to inherit the title, for the second to become an army or navy officer, and for the third son to go into the church.

Landowners themselves often had the right of appointments to the living. When the old minister died, the landlord could decide whom he wanted next. It was common for him to choose his own third son. William Gladstone—we have mentioned him many times—appointed his own son to the living of Hawarden. That meant that the members of the clergy often were closely connected to the landowning families. Think of the novels of Jane Austen for a moment. Very often the only eligible man in the area that one of the young ladies can marry, apart from the gentry, is the vicar. In *Emma,* for example, Mr. Elton is not quite good enough, but he is half suitable to be a good husband, or Mr. Collins in *Pride and Prejudice*, the man who is going to inherit the Bennett family house, at the moment is working as the minister for Lady Catherine de Bourgh. The same is true if you think of the novels of Anthony Trollope or Mrs. Gaskell or the Brontes. It recurs again and again. The clergyman, the local parish priest, is a gentleman.

Some appointees to these livings only got a minority of the tithes. If you are the rector, you get all of the tithe income from the parish.

You get only part if you were the curate. The Bronte sisters' father was a curate for Haworth in Yorkshire. Some curates were desperately poor because the income attached to the curacy wasn't sufficient. In Anthony Trollope's *Barchester Tower,* there is a very poor curate, Mr. Quiverful, a lovely name because he says he has 13 children living and his income is tiny. He was desperate to get a better income if he can find it somewhere.

The right to appoint a clergyman to the parish church (or what was called a living) was actually a commodity which could be traded. Sometimes you would see advertisements in the *Times* where a gentleman was selling the right of appointment to a parish church. When a new rector or curate was chosen, he would read himself into the parish. He would man the pulpit and recite the Thirty-Nine Articles, the principles according to which the church was conducted. In the early 19th century, it was still quite common for plural livings to be held, that is, for one clergyman to have more than one parish church in his control. You can imagine that if you were appointed to five or six and got the tithes from all of them, that again could make you very prosperous. People who were well connected in the aristocracy and slated as bishops of the future could often enjoy plural livings of this kind.

The cathedrals themselves, which were the centers of the diocese, were very rich, sometimes enjoying profits from ancient bequests. Probably the single best place to study the emotional mood of it all is in the fiction of Anthony Trollope. The Chronicles of Barchester is a marvelous series of novels he wrote about clergy life in one of the county towns. It is based on probably Salisbury or Winchester, one of the southwest towns of England with a prosperous cathedral.

The first of this series, *The Warden*, is all about an old man called Mr. Harding who is the beneficiary of a medieval bequest. He takes care of Alms House in which some old gentlemen live. They are all men who had been disabled, had accidents of various kinds, or are too old to work. Mr. Harding, the warden, looks after them. They get a little income, but they are secure. Mr. Harding enjoys a very big income. He is the man who overlooks them. He is a member of the gentry, and they are not. Eventually, a reformer comes to town, a man called Mr. Bold. He is in love with Mr. Harding's daughter, which provides the romantic interest for the book. Mr. Bold starts investigating this bequest and says the land wasn't left to the welfare of the warden. It was left to the welfare of the poor broken-down men who lived there. They are the ones who are entitled to this money. With the passage of the centuries, the value of this thing has accumulated, so Mr. Harding gets a good living from it. Bold says the old men should be getting that. He stirs up the old men and tells them "This should be yours, you know."

Then, they start clamoring for this income. Poor Mr. Harding is a good man and is stricken in conscience and realizes "I am taking away good things that they should have." The point is that it is catastrophically wrong. Trollope's point is that sometimes you do an act which in the abstract is good but which has horrible practical consequences. Trollope has a rather conservative outlook on life and doesn't like intemperate reforms to take place.

There were many cases where the inequities were genuine, and the 1830s is a period of vigorous reform within the Church of England. An ecclesiastical commission was founded, at first temporary but then becoming permanent, which, for example, abolished plural livings. After 1838, you weren't able to hold more than one living. You had to live and work in the parish to which you were appointed, and only one each. The income of the bishops was standardized at £4,000 each, still a very handsome sum, but no longer the enormous disparities which had existed previously.

Part of the energy for reforms of this kind came from the great Evangelical Revival. The evangelical movement took place on both sides of the Atlantic Ocean. The early 19th century is a period of enormous evangelical vigor in America and so it is in Britain as well. It emphasized personal conversion, an individual turning away from a life of sin toward putting one's trust in Jesus and with that adherence to very exacting moral standards and a biblical literalism, a belief that the Bible is an absolutely trustworthy guide in all your life, what these days we call Fundamentalism, although that term didn't begin until the 20th century.

A lot of the energy for the evangelical revival came from John Wesley and the Methodists, who were a 19th-century reform movement within the Church of England. One of the most famous preachers in England and America was George Whitefield, a galvanizing speaker who electrified audiences on both sides of the Atlantic, and very charismatic. He preached a religion of personal transformation, turning to Jesus from fear that if you don't you are threatened with eternal hellfire. One of the things which made Whitefield so extraordinary was his willingness to hold open air services. Rather than confining religious life just into the church, it would be taken outside.

The Methodists, the only Wesleyans, made the most progress in the new industrial towns. As they grew very rapidly, the Methodists were better keeping pace than the Church of England itself was, which tended to move at a slightly more stately pace. Wesley himself never was a Wesleyan. He always remained within the Church of England, and he was politically very conservative. So he was horrified at what he regarded as the emotional excesses of some of his own followers. When he transformed their lives in this absolute turning to faith in Jesus, for some of them it brought with it a political message. Wesley wanted none of that. He was socially very conservative, and some historians speculate that the reason Britain didn't have a revolutionary tradition in the late 18th and early 19th centuries was because of the wide spread of socially and politically conservative Methodism.

Evangelicalism became very influential within the Church of England as well as outside its doors, particularly through the influence of a group called the Clapham Sect. Clapham then was a village (It is now a suburb of London.). A group of prosperous men living there got together to practice austere religious habits and methodical bible reading. They pledged themselves to a series of good works, the abolition of slavery in the British Empire, the improvement of education, and the elimination of brutal public spectacles like sports in which animals were killed and public executions.

The most famous representative of the Clapham Sect was William Wilberforce, and it was he who led the campaign for the abolition first of the slave trade, which was achieved by legislation in 1807, and then for the abolition of slavery in the British Empire. There was no slavery in Britain itself, but slavery was practiced in the West Indies. Many West Indian islands were British colonies, sugar plantations for the most part. Slaves worked there just as they worked on the cotton plantations in the American south. In 1833, Wilberforce was able to accomplish legislation to outlaw slavery in the British Empire. It was a very big moment because it meant that for the American slave owners, suddenly they became more exposed. They were now slaveholders in a world, much of whose opinion was turning against slaveholding.

The second generation of these evangelical reformers was best represented by Lord Shaftsbury. I mentioned before he was the man who condemned the working-class girls' social clubs. He was a great campaigner for improvement of conditions in factories and coal mines and for ending child labor. Under his enthusiastic lobbying, Parliament did begin to pass acts intervening to prevent abusive child labor in factories.

He came from a long line of English aristocrats. He had a miserable childhood, neglected by his parents, and went through a traumatic religious conversion period when he was in his early twenties. Like many evangelicals, he believed very strongly in what were called "special providences," that is, nothing happened without God particularly intending it. If there was a particular thunderstorm, he wouldn't regard it as a naturalistic occurrence. He would say "God sent this thunderstorm to me as a reminder of my sins." So, he would speculate on the exact meaning of events which were taking place around him. He certainly believed in the reality of hellfire and the reality of an angry god.

At the same time, he was a devoted family man. He had a very sympathetic wife called Minnie, and they had 10 children together. He attempted to embody the benevolent, high-minded Victorian father, a little bit comparable to Prince Albert, but home grown. Most of the Church of England was rather suspicious of outdoor preaching, but Lord Shaftsbury thought it was okay, especially if you could bring together large numbers of people who weren't members of the church, working-class people particularly, and by using revival techniques generate the enthusiasm which would bring them back into religious life.

He approved the hiring of theaters or musicals, things usually given up to secular entertainment, and said "Let's have religious worship in these places." Sometimes he would become so carried away by religious raptures that his wife used to urge him to calm down, and she would mock him in a very good-natured way. I am going to read you an entry from his diary. This is in 1843 and he and his wife Minnie and the children have gone to the seaside. "Minnie and I, through God's mercy, took the sacrament together and afterwards, towards evening, a solitary walk on the seashore while our blessed children ran about the sands, and recalled the past and anticipated the future in faith and fear and fervent prayer." That is the way his diary runs.

He and many of his evangelical contemporaries campaigned hard for temperance, that is, the abolition of alcoholic drinks, and also for sabbatarianism. In the early days of the temperance movement, beer was regarded as a temperance drink because it was so much less alcoholic than gin. Later on, especially in America but also in Britain, beer became regarded as part of the problem rather than part of the solution. It is an important issue, because in those days there were so few uncontaminated drinking water sources that drinking water wasn't even safe. It is no wonder that the consumption of alcohol is so high.

Sabbatarianism is devoting the day, Sunday, exclusively to worship. The idea was that you would go to church in the morning, then again in the afternoon and early evening, and at both of these services you would listen to a long sermon, serious, elevated preaching taking biblical text with great seriousness, and elucidating their significance for everyday life. In addition to two services on Sunday, there was a long lecture, usually on Wednesday evening. One Scottish evangelical, a man called John Henderson, bought the Glasgow and Edinburgh railway, the busiest railway in Scotland, so that he could close it on Sundays. He was shocked by the fact that the trains continued to run, and he tried to prevent it.

A visitor from Switzerland in London in 1851 was astonished to find everything closed down on Sunday. He says,

> "I walked down Cheapside, which is quite a long street. I would have liked to go into a coffee house for a glass of ale or claret. But all the shops were hermetically sealed. Even the front door of my hotel was locked. On returning there, I asked for my bill because I had been accustomed to settle my account every day. The innkeeper politely asked me to wait until Monday. He didn't like to do business on the Lord's day."

There were also evangelicals inside and outside the Church of England who were instrumental in suppressing some of the rougher rural amusements. Here is one William Howard, writing in 1838.

> "In the manufacturing districts where the Methodists have gained most influence, it is true enough that they have helped to expel an immense quantity of dog fighting, cock fighting, bull bating, badger bating, and other such blackguard amusements, rough blood sports."

The evangelicals were shocked at the idea that people would take pleasure from witnessing such scenes.

As I said earlier, the queen herself was a regular churchgoer, although her diary is full of comments about how dull and tedious and long the sermons were. She was opposed to sabbatarianism. She never really did become fully converted to the evangelical enthusiasm of the day. She said on one occasion, "I am not at all an admirer or an approver of our very dull Sundays for I think the absence of innocent amusements for the poor people a misfortune and an encouragement of vice." That was the respectable argument against sabbatarianism. If people had nothing to do, they were more likely to become involved in vicious activities.

Throughout the 19th century, as we will see later on in one of the later lectures in the course, there was a movement to spread education, to get more and more of the working-class people literate. It was always compromised and complicated by the fact that people disagreed on exactly what sort of religious education was going to take place within the schools. Many of the evangelicals thought the purpose of education is to enable people to study their own Bibles. That is what education is for. Therefore, they didn't regard the religious component of the education as peripheral; they regarded it as central, so they set up Sunday schools to try to get more working class children at least some elementary literacy.

They also did things like this: They went to railway stations and would put up little lecterns with a Bible on, so that as you were waiting for the train you could browse the Bible to make the Bible more and more central to everyday life. They encouraged a religious seriousness which became very popular among Victorian artists, even those who were themselves not members of the Evangelical Church. You can see that very clearly by looking at the paintings of the Pre-Raphaelite artists. Some of the greatest of their paintings are themselves of religious themes, Holman Hunt's *Jesus the Light of the World*, a picture of Jesus holding a lantern, or Dante Gabriel Rossetti's *The Annunciation* where the Virgin Mary is told by the angel that she is going to bear the messiah, or one of my favorites, Henry Alexander Bowler's *The Doubt: Can These Dry Bones Live?* It is a wonderful painting, rather sentimental, and it shows a young woman in a graveyard beside the church looking down at the grave of someone she loves and meditating about the possibility of the resurrection. There are various iconographic clues in the painting. There is a skull with a butterfly resting on it. The butterfly represents the generation of new life out of something dead. That is supposed to be a clue for the audience, that the answer about the resurrection is, yes, it is possible.

The evangelicals certainly didn't go unopposed. A lot of the working class would have little to do with them, and they were widely satirized and parodied by Victorian novelists, particularly for their zeal and intolerance. Once again, Anthony Trollope gives us absolutely the classic example. This is in *Barchester Towers,* and it is the Reverend Obadiah Slope. Here is a little description of what the Reverend Slope is like.

> "He is gifted with a certain kind of pulpit eloquence, not likely indeed to be persuasive with men but powerful with the softer sex. In his sermons, he deals greatly in denunciations, excites the minds of his weaker hearers with a not unpleasant terror and leaves an impression on their minds that all mankind are in a perilous state, and all womankind too, except those who attend regularly to the evening lectures in Baker Street. His looks and tones are extremely severe, so much so that one cannot but fancy that he regards the greater part of the world as being infinitely too bad for his care. As he walks through the streets, his very face denotes his horror of the world's wickedness, and there is always an anathema lurking in the corner of his eye."

Charles Dickens also was very scornful about evangelical excesses, and he was another critic of sabbatarianism. He found legislation that was proposed in 1836, to make all work and all recreation on Sundays legally punishable offenses, this is what Dickens wrote about it.

"The constables are invested with arbitrary, extensive and vexacious powers. And all version a bill which sets out with a hypocritical and counting declaration that 'Nothing is more acceptable to God than the true and sincere worship of him according to his holy will, and that it is the bound duty of Parliament to promote the observance of the Lord's day by protecting every class of society against being required to sacrifice their comfort, health, religious privileges, and conscience for the convenience, enjoyment, or proposed advantage of any other class on the Lord's day.' "

Dickens says: "The idea of making a man truly moral through the ministry of constables and sincerely religious under the influence of penalties! That is worthy of the mind which could form such a massive, monstrous absurdity as this bill is composed of." So, although there were Sunday closing laws and limitations on Sunday activities, particularly Sunday business activities, the sabbatarians were never successful in completely closing down all forms of entertainment on the weekend. The other hostile depictions in the literature would be somebody like Mr. Brocklehurst, the horrible man who runs the schooling in *Jane Eyre*, or David Copperfield's step- father, the man who woos David's mother and, in effect, turns David out—humorless, zealous evangelicals.

As I mentioned earlier, the Evangelical Movement did have working-class recruits, but not all that many. Increasingly, members of the working class were staying away from church altogether. By 1850, only about half the British population went to any kind of church every week. More particularly, the working class was staying away completely, partly because they felt that the church represented the state, and sometimes it represented the state in its most odious aspect as the forces of surveillance and repression. Charles Kingsley himself, a sympathizer with many aspects of the evangelical revival, himself, said, "We have used the Bible as if it were a mere special constable's handbook or an opium dose for keeping beasts of burden patient while they were being overloaded, a mere book to keep the poor in order." He understood. It has got to be more than that to attract working-class people.

Meanwhile, ordinary working people had religious ideas of their own. They certainly believed that it was important to be christened in church and to be married in church and to be buried with a proper funeral service. Otherwise, their theology was much more heterodoxy. They didn't believe in salvation by faith alone. Their view was a much more pragmatic one. If you act right and live a decent and generous life and are kind to your family and friends, that is what your salvation depends upon. These are the kinds of insights upon which William Booth built when he created the Salvation Army in the 1870s. It was an attempt to dress up evangelical religion in a bright uniform and attach a brass band to it and make it joyful and celebratory rather than oppressive, narrow, and puritanical, as it had so often been in the early part of the evangelical revival.

Lecture Nine
The Oxford Movement and Catholicism

Scope:

The Oxford movement of the 1830s and 1840s tried to emphasize the supernatural as opposed to the political character of the Church of England. The defection of two of its most luminous members, Newman and Manning, to Roman Catholicism, damaged its reputation in the 1840s; however, the Oxford movement, like the evangelical revival, animated Christianity in many parts of Britain. Meanwhile, the Roman Catholic Church, made up mainly of Irish immigrants and old "recusants," newly leavened with a group of energetic converts, weathered a storm of prejudice and criticism as it created its own diocesan structure. British Christianity was also under intellectual pressure from scientific developments, especially Darwinian evolution, and from German methods of biblical criticism. Successive controversies in the mid-Victorian era indicated anxiety and doubt on the part of influential men; Thomas Huxley, a leading scientist, invented the term "agnosticism" to describe his own religious situation between faith and doubt.

Outline

I. The Oxford movement emphasized the catholic and supernatural aspects of Anglicanism.

   A. Like the evangelical movement, with which it was contemporaneous, the Oxford movement focused on the importance of warmth and vitality in the individual's relationship with God and Jesus.

   B. It was culturally richer and less puritanical than the evangelical movement.

   C. One of its hallmarks was an emphasis on the "beauty of holiness"—the idea that religious life should be beautified and that worship should take place in glorious surroundings.

   D. While the evangelical movement preached the importance of the individual's direct encounter with God, the Oxford movement saw the church itself as a crucial institution, responsible for mediating the relationship between God and the individual.

II. Oxford University divines (the "Tractarians") John Henry Newman, Richard Hurrell Froude, and John Keble, issued a series of tracts (the "Tracts for the Times," 1833–1841) deploring the sleepiness of the Anglican Church and its subservience to the state.

A. They opposed the Irish Church Temporalities Bill (1833) and the Catholic Emancipation legislation of 1829, whereby Catholics were permitted to sit in Parliament, because it meant that political expediency, rather than divine truth, would affect the governance of the Church of England.

B. They emphasized the concept of apostolic succession.
   1. Jesus had entrusted Saint Peter with the keys of the faith and charged him to create the church.
   2. Saint Peter had created bishops, and each new generation of bishops had passed on the succession from Jesus's apostles.

C. John Henry Newman's respect for the 16th-century Protestant reformers declined, while his appreciation for the early Church fathers (such as St. Augustine and St. Ambrose) increased.

D. Of the "Tracts for the Times," Tract 90 was the most controversial; in it, Newman argued for the compatibility of the Thirty-Nine Articles of the Church of England with Catholic doctrine, despite their original anti-Catholic animus.

E. Newman tried to argue for Anglicanism as the *via media*, the middle way, between Catholic and Protestant errors.

III. Newman's intensive study of the Church fathers—he strongly believed that it was crucial to get the doctrines right to be a good Christian—led him toward Catholicism, and he converted in 1845. The Oxford movement then fell under a cloud.

A. Henry Manning also became a Roman Catholic in 1851 after the Gorham Decision emphasized the Erastianism of the Anglican Church.

B. Some Anglicans were horrified by Catholic (and later, Jewish) emancipation because it meant that, conceivably, a Roman Catholic could become prime minister and would have the responsibility for appointing the Anglican bishops.

IV. The other leaders of the Oxford movement remained ostentatiously loyal to the state church; Anglo-Catholicism—or "High Church," as the Oxford movement came to be known—began to reach out to urban slum dwellers, with growing success toward 1900.

A. The mid-Victorian era saw vigorous restoration of old churches and the building of many new ones.

    1. Between 1840 and 1876, the Anglicans built 1,700 new churches, mainly in the industrial towns, and restored about 7,000 more.

    2. Some of these churches were beautiful, in the neo-Gothic style.

B. The High Church emphasized display: elaborate decoration, sumptuous vestments, and ritual embellishments, such as choral music, candles, bells, and incense.

C. It de-emphasized preaching (which was so essential to the evangelical movement).

V. The Roman Catholic Church in Britain gained recruits from Ireland and by conversion.

A. Anti-Catholicism had a long post-Reformation history.

    1. To many Britons, Catholicism was synonymous with treason.

    2. The Catholicism of Queen Mary I and Guy Fawkes was remembered as cruel and repressive.

    3. Foxe's *Book of Martyrs* (1559) was staple fare for Protestant children.

    4. Many Protestants believed that to be Roman Catholic implied allegiance to a foreign monarch.

B. Recusant families (those not attending Church of England services) included the Earls of Shrewsbury and the Dukes of Norfolk.

C. The Catholic population of Britain swelled rapidly after the Irish famine. East London, Glasgow, and the Lancashire textile towns developed Catholic ghettoes.

D. Converts were a source of pleasure and concern to the Catholic bishops.

    1. Their intellectual adventurousness dismayed Cardinal Wiseman.

2. St. George Mivart and George Tyrrell were both censured by the hierarchy.

3. Newman's *Apologia Pro Vita Sua*, written in answer to Charles Kingsley, who did not believe Newman had converted in good faith, was recognized as a masterpiece by Anglicans and Catholics alike.

E. The re-establishment of the Catholic hierarchy in 1850 led to an outburst of anti-popery.

1. Prime Minister Lord John Russell protested against "papal aggression."

2. Parliament legislated against Catholic use of Anglican titles.

F. Henry Manning succeeded Nicholas Wiseman as Archbishop of Westminster and became a hero to working-class people in London.

1. He arbitrated the dockers' strike of 1889.

2. Londoners lined the streets for his funeral in 1892.

VI. New intellectual trends disturbed the Christian sense of assurance.

A. Darwinian evolution challenged the biblical creation story and the uniqueness of humanity.

B. Critical methods of biblical study led to new ideas about the nature of Christianity; publication of *Essays and Reviews* set off a furor in 1861, including some heresy trials.

C. Thomas Huxley, a champion of Darwin, gave a name to agnosticism.

D. Growing numbers of Victorians (including George Eliot and Thomas Huxley) had become doubtful about Christianity, not only because of the Darwinian revolution and the new critical revelations about the Bible but also for ethical reasons: When they reread the Old Testament, they were horrified by accounts of God's brutality.

E. As the British Empire increased its reach throughout the world, small numbers of Britons began to adapt to exotic religions.

VII. The Church of England was shocked by the results of a survey in 1851 that tried to record who actually went to church and to which one.

    A. The church discovered that only about a quarter of the population went to its services, another quarter attended nonconformist or Catholic services, and half the people attended no services at all.

    B. The church worked through the second half of the century to build new churches, train more ministers, and regain its central role in national life. Membership figures did rise, but intellectual challenges, particularly Darwinian biology and historical-critical methods, created new problems.

Essential Reading:

E. Norman, *The English Catholic Church in the Nineteenth Century.*

Theodore Hoppen, *The Mid-Victorian Generation*, chapters 12 and 13.

Supplementary Reading:

Patrick Allitt, *Catholic Converts: British and American Intellectuals Turn to Rome.*

M. A. Crowther, *Church Embattled: Religious Controversy in Mid-Victorian England.*

Questions to Consider:

1. Why did comparatively few Oxford movement Anglicans follow Newman when he converted to Catholicism?

2. How severe were the new intellectual challenges to conventional Christian belief in the mid 19th century?

Lecture Nine—Transcript
The Oxford Movement and Catholicism

The Oxford Movement of the 1830s and '40s tried to emphasize the supernatural as opposed to the political character of the Church of England. The defection of two of its most luminous members, John Henry Newman and Henry Manning, to the Roman Catholic Church damaged its reputation in the late '40s and early '50s. The Oxford Movement, like the Evangelical revival, had the effect of reviving the vigor of Christianity in England. Meanwhile, the Roman Catholic Church itself, made up mainly of Irish immigrants but also consisting of a handful of families which never converted to Anglicanism, the Church of England, weathered the storm of criticism as it began to recover its energy in English and British life more generally.

British Christianity of all forms, Evangelical, Anglican, Catholic, and nonconformist alike, all the churches were under pressure from new developments in science, particularly the revolution in scientific thought which was carried out by Darwin in biology and Charles Lyell in geology, also from new developments in German biblical criticism. So, the new Victorian period witnessed a whole succession of religious crises. One man affected by all this was Thomas Huxley, himself a leading scientist, who invented the term agnosticism to describe his own condition, one of increasing religious doubt and uncertainty.

The Oxford Movement wanted to emphasize the supernatural aspects of the Church of England. Like the Evangelical Movement, with which it was contemporaneous, or a little bit late, it emphasized the importance of the liveliness, vitality, and warmth of the individual's relationship with God and with Jesus. It was also culturally richer and tended to be a little bit less puritanical. One of the great phrases that comes from the Oxford Movement is the beauty of holiness, the idea that religion should be beautified and that worship should take place in glorious surroundings. In this version of Christianity, the church itself is a very important institution. Evangelicals tended to emphasize the individual's relationship with God, that it is a direct encounter. The Oxford Movement's view is that the church itself is a mediating institution, that the individual belongs to the church and through the church receives God's blessings.

It was called The Oxford Movement because a series of Oxford dons, scholars, began the work. In the early 1830s, John Henry Newman, Hurrell Froude, and John Keble, all talented writers, began to write a series called the *Tracts of the Times*, pamphlets about religious controversy. Another of the names of this movement is The Tractarians, because other people's names were associated with the tracts. Between 1833 and 1841, they published a long succession of these things, critical of the condition of the Anglican Church. One of the things that they particularly deplored was the fact that it was too obvious. The Church of England was subordinate to the state. Because it was an established religion, it was very often political motives which led to church actions.

They were opposed to Catholic emancipation, the legislation of 1829 whereby Roman Catholics were permitted to sit in Parliament. This made it all too obvious that political consideration rather than religious truth had been the decisive factor. Political expediency was going to guide the church rather than divine truth. The Tractarians wanted to emphasize that the church itself was a supernatural society. It had been founded by Jesus, and one of the Christian doctrines they emphasized particularly powerfully was the idea of apostolic succession, that is, that Jesus had entrusted St. Peter with the keys of the faith and charged him to create the church, that St. Peter had created bishops, and that each generation of bishops right down through the history of the church had passed on the succession right from the apostles. There was a direct lineage from Jesus right down to the church leaders of the 19th century, apostolic succession. This was the kind of question which the evangelicals were less interested in.

The Church of England, according to the Tractarians, was founded by Jesus himself, a paradoxical claim on the face of it, one that they tried very hard to assert. The church historian Alec Vidler writes this: "It was as if the Tractarians were declaring that on the drab, dirty, distempered walls within which English churchmen were accustomed to worship or doze, there were wonderful pictures that when uncovered would transform the whole building into something mysterious and sublime."

Newman, in particular of these three writers, found that his respect for the 16th-century reformers was diminishing. Everybody attached to Protestantism tended to think very highly of the great protestant reformers of the 1500s. Newman, the more he studied them and thought about it, the more he became inclined to see them as rather crude and iconoclastic. He began to develop a greater appreciation for the church fathers, that is, the very early Christian writers, people like St. Augustine and St. Ambrose, and to recognize continuity in their work more than a sharp fracture at the time of the Reformation.

The really explosive tract was Tract 90, when Newman argued that it was possible to read the Thirty-Nine Articles, the principles upon which the Church of England was based, in a way which was compatible with Catholic doctrine. When you read the Thirty-Nine Articles and then read Tract 90, it is very hard to be convinced by the tract, because some of the Thirty-Nine Articles are very explicitly anti-Popish. Nevertheless, that is the direction of Newman's argumentation. He was interested in working out what exactly was the druidical status of the Anglican Church? He argued in the late 1830s and early '40s for what he called the *via media*, the middle way. As he said, the Church of England is the one Christian group which has steered a middle course between the errors of the Catholic Church on the one side (errors which were notorious at the time of the Reformation,) and the equal errors of the radical protestant churches on the other side. For a while this was Newman's position.

He read a rejoinder which had been made by Nicholas Wiseman, the leader of the Catholics in England, and Wiseman said "Is it really likely that God would single out this one little offshore island of England and make it alone the repository of Christian truth?" Many British people, especially the English, were sufficiently xenophobic to think this was a reasonable proposition. Newman himself gradually became reconciled to the idea that probably it was not. Wiseman, the Catholic apologist's point was that the Catholic Church appears all over—this is logic confined to Europe. Nevertheless, it is far less parochial than England. Newman, in the early 1840s, studied the church fathers very intensely. Finally, after three or four years of intense anguish, during which period he would retire from many of his public services at Oxford University, he converted to Roman Catholicism. He had reached the conclusion that the Catholics were right after all.

He was a morbid and obsessive man, deeply troubled by the problems of faith, agonizing over the question of whether his soul is going to be saved, and he certainly believed, as all the members of the Oxford Movement did, that you have got to get the doctrines right. The doctrines really matter. It isn't sufficient to have a good mood, attitude, or a loving relationship with Jesus; you have got to get the details right. His very last work as an Anglican was a book called *An Essay on the Development of Doctrine* in which he worried about the question of whether the Catholic church in its claim always to be right, infallible, was justifiable. He concluded that it was, because he said:

> "Although the church teaches things today which it didn't teach in the first of the early Christians, nevertheless, the seeds of those doctrines were already embedded in the work of the early church and have just flowered. Just as a seed contains the material from which the flower will come, so did the early church contain the implicit doctrines which it is now making explicit."

There was an enormous scandal at Oxford University and throughout the whole nation because Newman had been regarded as one of the most promising divines, writers, in the whole country. The movement as a whole suddenly fell under a great cloud because its other leaders, those who were trying to reinvigorate Anglicanism, didn't want to be vulnerable to the accusation that they were latently Roman Catholics as well. They certainly tried to bring out some of the catholic qualities in Anglicanism, but they were emphatic that The Oxford Movement was an Anglican movement.

The name given to this movement from then onward is the Anglo-Catholics, or The High Churchmen. One of the Anglicans that was horrified by Newman's conversion to Rome was Henry Manning. He preached against Newman's conversion very sharply, saying that he'd been seduced by the papists. He was now Archdeacon of Chichester Cathedral, a rising star of the Anglican Church also. Five or six years later, he also converted to Roman Catholicism. The trigger for his conversion was the Gorham Decision.

It is interesting to follow through what happened in the case of G.C. Gorham. He was the man who was appointed to be the parish vicar in a village called Bramford-Speke. The local bishop, Bishop Philpotts of Exeter, refused to accept Gorham on a doctrinal point. He said Gorham is a Calvinist who believes in absolute human depravity and denies the regeneration of the soul in baptism. The bishop said, "I refuse to have him installed in this parish church." In those days, the Church of England had an elaborate structure of church courts, and so the case was taken to the church courts to arbitrate. Was Gorham entitled to the living at Bramford-Speke, or should the bishop's view prevail?

The church upheld the bishop and said yes the bishop was justified in rejecting Gorham from the living. Then, Gorham appealed to the Privy Council, that is, to a political body. The Privy Council, after hearing the case, overturned the bishop and overturned the church courts, with the result that Gorham was installed after all.

Henry Manning, hearing news of this, was horrified because once again it showed all too clearly that the Church of England was not a supernatural society; it was a branch of the state. It came to the point that politicians were going to decide. One of the reasons that some Anglicans were so horrified by Catholic emancipation was that it meant that conceivably a Roman Catholic could become Prime Minister, and then he'd have the responsibility for appointing the Anglican bishops. You see that kind of paradox. Again, when Jewish emancipation was brought into Parliament in the late '50s, the same question came up again. Are we really going to have Catholic and Jewish people deciding who are the nominees of the Church of England?

So, Manning also converted to Roman Catholicism. These two men, Newman and Manning had a transformative effect on Roman Catholicism in Britain for the rest of the century, as we will see in a minute. The other leaders of the movement remained ostentatiously loyal to the state church. Anglo-Catholicism, the High Church movement, began to reach out, particularly to urban slum districts, in hopes of being able to recapture the working people. Many of them weren't going to church at all.

The mid-Victorian period was a very vigorous era of church building, between 1840 and 1876. The Church of England built 1,700 new churches, mainly in the industrial towns, and they restored about 7,000 more, so an enormous quantity of resources were devoted to improving church buildings. Some of the ones they made, nearly all of which are still there, were very beautiful. They were built according to the principles of neo-Gothic architecture, made to look as if they were much older, emphasizing the continuity between the Middle Ages and their own day. They were much more beautifully decked out than had been the tradition for the previous 300, years ever since the Reformation. They tended to be elaborately painted inside.

The pulpit would be moved to one side, and the congregation's attention focused on the altar. There was an emphasis on sacraments, on the clothes you were wearing—brilliant liturgical clothes—introduction of church choirs, the singing of great hymns, vestments, rituals, candles, genuflection before the altar, even the sprinkling of holy water in some cases, these activities, which might be construed as Catholic, taking place within the Anglican church. There was a de-emphasis on preaching, which was so central to the evangelical side of the Anglican Church. The dismissive word for all these kinds of things is "smells and bells." There was the idea that all this ritual activity was going on inside the church.

The High Churchmen were right to think that they would get a bigger working class audience with this kind of display than they would have got if they were going to have two-hour sermons on theological points and biblical exigencies. It is not that they weren't interested in biblical matters, they were. The relative emphasis had moved over to these more liturgical and sacramental activities.

Now, let's look at what was happening in the Catholic Church in Britain. It gained its recruits mainly from Ireland, and there was a steady stream of Irish immigration into Britain all through the 19th century but intensified after the terrible Irish famine of 1846 to 1848. A smaller supply of people was coming in for conversions, people like Newman and Manning and people who were influenced by them.

It is important to understand just how intense anti-Catholic prejudice was among the Anglican majority. Ever since the Reformation, the ordinary British view had been that Catholicism was practically synonymous with treason. Certainly, all through the 16th and 17th centuries, Britain's enemies had been Catholic nations—Spain, the time of the Armada; France, through generations of wars. The assumption was that if you were a Catholic you might be an enemy spy or agent and that you secretly hoped that the Catholic enemy was going to prevail and overthrow the rights of Protestant England. One of the annual festivals in England, every November 5, which still persists right up to the present, was Guy Fawkes Day. This is the day in England when the children have fireworks to commemorate a time when a conspiracy to blow up the Houses of Parliament by a group of Catholics was discovered just in time. So, kids right up to the present burn a martyred figure called a "Guy" on a bonfire and let off fireworks. It is an anti-Catholic festival and rejoicing. In my day, the Catholic kids loved it just as much as everybody else. By then, its origins had largely been forgotten.

One of the great books read by the members of the Church of England was Foxe's *Book of Martyrs,* published in 1559 to commemorate the suffering of the early Protestant bishops in the face of Queen Mary of England, who tried to drag England back into the Catholic hold. There was the idea that to be a Catholic meant that you were a follower of a foreign monarch, an Italian king in Rome, that you had necessarily divided loyalties between Britain and Italy. There were lots of stories about how convents were really brothels in which the priests and the nuns had frenzied sex, flagellation, infanticide, all sorts of lurid stories. There were even some ex-priests, a man called Giacinto Achille, an ex-Dominican priest who was on the English lecture circuit, and they'd pay a few pennies to go and listen to him and he would describe the horrors of Catholic life. It provided the same kind of function then that the tabloid newspapers do now.

There were a handful of traditionally Catholic families in Britain who were recusants. Recusancy meant not going to the Church of England. Catholics wouldn't. They would have to pay recusancy fines throughout the centuries since the Reformation. The Catholic population is swelling because of Catholic immigration from Ireland. There were about 500 Catholic priests in England in 1840 but about 2,500 by 1890, so a very rapid growth. The Catholics were even more successful in keeping the loyalty of working-class members than the Anglican Church was. At the same time, converts are coming in, people like Newman. They were a source of pleasure to the Catholic bishops. Obviously, it would please them to see that some Anglicans were finally waking up to the truth as they saw it. It was also a source of anxiety because they tended to be very intellectually adventurous. That is how they had come to Catholicism in the first place, and they had remained intellectually adventurous when they got there.

There were several cases where converts got into trouble with the authorities because of their ideas. One was the evolutionary biologist called St. George Mivart; another was a theologian called George Tyrrell. Both of them continue to elaborate their ideas in a way which the Catholic authorities found very jarring. Each of them was ultimately ex-communicated. I would like to read you a little passage from Newman's book *The Apologia Pro Vita Sua*. In the '60s he was criticized by Charles Kingsley, the novelist, who was himself an Anglican clergyman. Kingsley couldn't believe that Newman, a clergyman, converted in good faith. Newman's *Apologia* is a spiritual autobiography in which he asserts that he is dead serious in his conversion and that it is based on a lifetime of religious study. It was quickly recognized as a masterpiece by Anglicans and Catholics alike, although you have to be very interested in these religious matters to read it attentively from end to end.

Here is a little glimpse of how Newman's life was spent. He is talking about his reading as a teenager.

> "Now I come to two words which produced a deep impression on me, each contrary to each and planting in me the seeds of an intellectual inconsistency which disabled me for a long course of years. I read Joseph Milner's Church History and was nothing short of enamoured of the long extracts of St. Augustine, St. Ambrose and the church fathers which I found there. I read them as being the religion of the primitive Christians. Simultaneously with Milner, I read Newton on the prophecies, and in consequence became most firmly convinced that the Pope was the antichrist predicted by Daniel, St. Paul, and St. John. My imagination was stained by the effects of his doctrine up to the year 1843. It had been obliterated from my reason and judgment at an early date, but the thought remained upon me as a sort of false conscience. Hence came a conflict of mind which so many have felt besides myself, leading some men to make a compromise between two ideas so inconsistent with each other, driving others to beat out one idea or other from their minds, and ending in my own case after many years of intellectual unrest at the gradual extinction and decay of one of them. I do not say it is a violent death, but why should I not have murdered it sooner if I murdered it at all?"

That is a typical passage, it is very involuted, and he is agonizing one by one over his history of the treatment of the doctrines. He was a great thinker about the process of thought. He wrote some interesting work on religious psychology later on. How is it that we come to an appreciation of faith itself? What is the connection between faith and reason?

In 1850, the Catholic Church decided that it was going to reinstitute a national hierarchy, its own system of bishops inside Britain. Ever since the Reformation, there hadn't been any legally recognized Catholic hierarchy in Britain. In doing so, it set off a great fury of anti-Catholicism. In several places, particularly in Liverpool, there were anti-Catholic riots in the streets. Lord John Russell himself, the Prime Minister, wrote a furious letter to the *Times* denouncing what he called the papal aggression. So, it was very widespread, at the highest levels of society. The Catholics are a terrible threat to the nation. Parliament passed legislation prohibiting the Catholics from duplicating any Anglican titles. Because the head of the Church of England was the Archbishop of Canterbury, the Catholics weren't allowed to have a bishop in Canterbury. Their head became the Archbishop of Westminster.

The second convert I mentioned earlier, Henry Manning, eventually became the Archbishop of Westminster. Fourteen or 15 years after converting, he became the head of the English Catholics and went on to become a luminous figure in English public life, widely loved, particularly in the Catholic working classes, for his sympathetic attention to the needs of the Irish working-class people in England. When he died in 1892, tens of thousands of Londoners—Catholic, Protestant, and sometimes alike—lined the streets. He managed to create once more for Catholicism the idea that it was a component of British life.

While all these things were going on, there were new intellectual trends disturbing the Christian sense of assurance. Darwin's publication of *The Origin of Species* in 1859 is the single most important one of these. Darwin's version of human origins was quite different from the one presented in the book of *Genesis*. It raised the possibility that *Genesis* wasn't reliable as history. Huxley was one of Darwin's most enthusiastic supporters. One of his nicknames was Darwin's Bulldog. He'd very often go and argue. Darwin himself was a shy and retiring man who suffered from bad health. Huxley was a great, healthy, enthusiastic controversialist, often out in public defending Darwin's ideas. He had a famous meeting in 1860 with the Bishop of Oxford, Samuel Wilberforce. They met in the new Oxford Museum of Science to debate the rights and wrongs of the theory.

Wilberforce said it was degrading to humanity to trace its descent to the apes, a point often made since by critics of evolution. Huxley answered him "If I had to choose, I would prefer to be a descendant of a humble monkey than of a man who employs his knowledge and eloquence in misrepresenting those who are wearing out their lives in the search for truth." In other words, let's face up to the shocking reality rather than act as though it wasn't true in the face of accumulating evidence.

Many Anglicans, rather than posing a stark opposition to evolutionary theory, found ways to adapt it to their faith, to say that Christianity is itself an evolving process and that the two are compatible. Here is an Anglican Darwinist called Stewart Headlam preaching in 1879, and he says, "Thank God that the scientific men have shattered the idol of an infallible book, broken the fetters of a supposed divine code of rules, so they help to reveal Jesus Christ in his majesty. He, we say, is the word of God. He is inspiring you, encouraging you, strengthening you in your scientific studies. He is the wisdom in Lyell or Darwin. In other words, he is abandoning biblical literalists and saying rather it is God's spirit which infuses the work of the modern scientists.

Another great furor developed in the Anglican Church in 1861 with the publication of a book called *Essays and Reviews*. It was a set of essays of critical study on the Bible, picking up techniques which were already becoming common in Germany, that is, particularly looking at biblical texts not with a lot of doctrinal preconceptions, but simply saying let's investigate these things in the way that we would investigate any other historical text. Let's be attentive to the fact that all the ancient religions of the Near East had a creation story; they all had a flood myth. Let's not assume that the story of Noah's flood is true and that all the others aren't. Let's just do a comparison of each of them in turn. The spirit of intellectual inquiry which governed this book, again set off a lot of controversy.

One contributor, C. W. Goodwin, a don at Cambridge said that the *Genesis* creation story shouldn't be regarded as history at all. It should be regarded as an old Hebrew myth. Several of the contributors, those who were clergymen, were put on trial in the church courts for heresy, that is, for writing in a way which violated the spirit and the traditions of the church. As one lay critic of these trials said in a letter to the *Times*:

> "What we all want is briefly not a condemnation but a refutation. The age when ecclesiastical censures were sufficient in such cases has passed away. A large portion of the laity now are unqualified for abstruse theological investigations or have competence to hear and decide theological arguments. These men will not be satisfied by an ex-cathedra shelving of the question nor terrified by a deduction of awful consequences. Philosophy and history have taught them to seek not what is safe but what is true."

This is the atmosphere in which Thomas Huxley gives the name to agnosticism. He and growing numbers of Victorians—another famous example would be the novelist George Eliot—had become doubtful about Christianity not only because of the new critical methods, and not only because of the Darwinian revolution, but also because of ethical objections. When they reread the Old Testament, they were horrified by God's brutality. Those of you who aren't familiar with it will realize that God often reacts with what seems like an extremely highhanded way. King Saul, for example, loses God's favor because he is not sufficiently ruthless in exterminating his prisoners. George Eliot and Huxley and others began to say "Do we really want to regard as absolutely reliable for our guidance a book which teaches us lessons of such a ruthless God as that?"

Huxley himself wasn't a defiant atheist. He admitted that all these were questions that were very much up in the air. He said, "We have no definite empirical evidence to support the idea of an afterlife or of a more powerful god, but we have no evidence against it either." He told one of his friends that the idea of eternal life "is not half so wonderful as the idea of the conservation of force or the indestructibility of matter. Whosoever appreciates all that is implied in the falling of a stone can have no difficulty about any doctrine simply on account of its marvelousness." So, there we are. Critical of theologians who are asserting the faith, but critical also of positives who are asserting the denial of God.

Another craze of the period which Queen Victoria herself became involved in was spiritualism, the holding of séances. She was a very enthusiastic party because she hoped to be able to communicate with Prince Albert after his death.

As the British Empire expanded around the world, it brought into its possession more and more people from different religions. It also was a motive for the development of comparative religion. I would like to end this lecture by giving you an example of a Victorian family which had representatives of several religions in it. This is an anecdote from Bertram Russell's autobiography. He is talking about his grandmother, Lady Stanley of Alderley.

> "Her eldest son was a Mohammedan, and almost stone deaf. Her second son Lyle was a free thinker and spends his time fighting the church on the London school board. Her third son, Algernon, was a Roman Catholic priest, a papal chamberlain. Lyle was a witty, encyclopedic, and caustic man. Algernon was witty, fat and greedy. Henry, the Mohammedan, was devoid of all the family merits and was, I think, the greatest bore I've ever known. At Sunday luncheons there would be vehement arguments. For among the daughters- and sons-in-law, there were also representatives of the Church of England, Unitarianism, and Positivism to be added to the religions represented by the sons. A favorite trick of my Uncle Lyle at these luncheons was to ask, "Who is there here who believes in the literal truth of the story of Adam and Eve?" His object in asking the question was to compel the Mohammedan and the Catholic priest to agree with each other, which they hated doing."

That is a little glimpse of the growing religious complexity of Britain as the 19th century progressed.

Lecture Ten
Work and Working-Class Life

Scope:

The Industrial Revolution accelerated through the Victorian period but not everywhere and not all at once. Big regional variations in the type of work done meant that many people continued with non-mechanized, non-factory work far into the 19th century. Pre-industrial work was irregular, contrasting intense work with periods of idleness. Gradually, capitalist ideas about value and pay replaced older ideas of the "just price" and "just wage." Industrial methods also forced working people to learn a new approach to work and to the organization of time. Every industrial occupation had its own characteristic hazards and illnesses, but the workers struggled, where possible, to retain a sense of dignified autonomy. Meanwhile, those who could afford it went into business for themselves or resorted to informal methods of raising their incomes. Alcohol, as much as unemployment, threatened working-class home life.

Outline

I. Pre-industrial working conditions in the trades were highly varied.

    A. Working hours were long but irregular.

    B. Pre-industrial workers had unofficial holidays, including, for example, patron saints' days and the monarch's birthday.

    C. Work in many jobs was irregular.

        1. Dockyard workers depended on the wind to bring in ships.

        2. Farm labor was highly seasonal and was paid by the day.

        3. Shipbuilders were often idle between contracts.

        4. Cornish lead miners had regular work but not regular pay.

    D. Payment was often not in money but in kind.

        1. Dorset quarrymen were paid in stone or bread.

        2. Fishermen often went shares in the fish from their voyages.

    E. Sharp status differences existed in most trades.

    F. Payment was often based on tradition and the notion of the "just price," rather than capitalist ideas of shifting value.

1. Pay scales often remained fixed for decades.
2. The notion of a wage rate commensurate with hours of labor developed gradually.

G. Each occupation had its own characteristic dress.
   1. Shepherds wore a distinctive smock.
   2. Fishermen wore hard-weather gear.
   3. Characteristically, working people wore the same clothes for days, and even nights, at a time.

II. Entry into mechanized factories and subdivision of labor made the old ways impossible.

   A. Workmen were unaccustomed to toiling the same number of hours every day; factory owners imposed heavy fines for lateness to try to create a new discipline suitable to the factory.

   B. Pay was low.
   1. Workers were generally paid piece rates (i.e., per completed piece or product).
   2. The rate of production was standardized by the workers: A low rate of production was common so that workers could leverage a higher rate per piece.

   C. Every occupation had its own characteristic illness.
   1. The phrase "mad as a hatter" came from the experience of hat workers poisoned by mercury.
   2. Miners suffered from silicosis and lung cancer.
   3. Sweeps' boys often failed to develop and had high cancer rates because they were subject to severe mistreatment. (Charles Kingsley's novel *The Water-Babies* was written in response to the particularly horrific working conditions of the sweeps' boys.)

   D. The working environment was polluted and dangerous.
   1. There were no safety regulations.
   2. There were no regulations against the use of child labor.
   3. Sickness and accidents were common.
   4. The consensus was that safety should not be the concern of government.

   E. Surveillance was tight.

III. Workers found ways to maintain some control over their working conditions even when they had no unions.

    A. Durham miners used a daily lottery to allocate work places.

    B. Skilled craftsmen in the factory system kept St. Monday where possible.

IV. Many working-class people struggled to move into "penny capitalism."

    A. Some became corner shopkeepers or street peddlers.

    B. Others ran cabs or bought shares in fishing boats.

V. Informal forms of economic activity were widespread.

    A. Thousands of people resorted at times to begging, poaching, shoplifting, pilfering from work, and prostitution.

    B. In coal-mining districts, "picking" was often the children's responsibility; in the countryside, children were sent out to steal fruit.

VI. Working-class neighborhoods were densely populated, smoky, neighborly, and gossipy.

    A. At times, they could be amicable and open.

    B. Husbands' drinking and economic stress were prime sources of social tension.

        1. Drink was closely connected to wife beating.

        2. Elite working men who joined the Methodists sometimes reformed their own trades.

Essential Reading:

John Benson, *The Working Class in Britain*.

John Rule, *The Labouring Classes in Early Industrial Britain*.

Supplementary Reading:

P. E. Razzell and R. W. Wainwright, eds., *The Victorian Working Class: Selections from Letters to the Morning Chronicle*.

Eric Hobsbawm, *Labouring Men: Studies in the History of Labour*.

Questions to Consider:

1. Why were pre-industrial work habits so irregular?
2. Did industrialization improve or worsen working people's lives?

Lecture Ten—Transcript
Work and Working-Class Life

The Industrial revolution continued to accelerate in the Victorian period, but not everywhere and not all at once. There were big regional variations of the type of work that people did, and there was a great deal of un-mechanized, non-factory work that people did far into the Victorian period, even after the factories became a more and more important component of the industrial landscape.

It's impossible to exaggerate the intense regionalism of British life. People living in different areas of the country rarely encountered one another. Their regional accents were very, very strong and distinct. Their mutual suspicions were strong and distinct as well. There was an intense localism about life. And even though the railways were beginning to break it down—still, to understand a subject like work, which is the issue in this lecture, you need to tour around Britain a good deal to sample work in different places.

Pre-industrial working conditions were also highly varied. Working hours, for example: if you didn't have a factory, you tended to have a variation in the number of hours that people would work and how they would use those hours over the course of the week. They were extremely irregular. Most trades, before they were subjected to factory discipline, tended to alternate between bouts of intensely pressurized work and long periods of idleness. From preference, people would work in that way. For example, among the cutlers— people who made knives and forks—coopers, barrel makers, and shipbuilders, there was a well-established tradition called Saint Monday. Monday wasn't really a saint, but the idea was that it was a saint's day, you take the day off. Saint Monday was a day that, routinely, people didn't come in to work. It was common, for example, in the shipbuilding yards for work to knock off on Saturday afternoon, for maybe the boss to bring in a barrel of beer and the men sit around drinking, for them to take the whole of Sunday off and sometimes the whole of Monday off as well, but then to work with accelerated determination and energy the rest of the week.

Joseph Matthew wrote a song called, "The Jovial Cutlers." This is about the men of Sheffield—a Yorkshire cutlery town—enjoying Saint Monday. "Brother workmen, cease your labor. Bring your files and hammers by. Listen while a brother neighbor sings a cutler's destiny, how upon a good Saint Monday, sitting by the smith fire, telling what's been done on Sunday, and in cheerful mirth, conspire."

It was very much like the way in which college students live today. Picture yourself as a college student. Only a very tiny minority work a systematic eight hours or ten hours every day. Most, for example, only do a writing project when they've absolutely got to. There are lots of last-minute deadlines (something I'm very familiar with.)

So, the rhythm of work was irregular. And as I mentioned in one of the earlier lectures, one of the stresses of switching over to a more mechanized system was having to learn a new kind of factory discipline of going at the same clock time every day, rather than according to the season and the day of the week. It was common for every trade to have its own traditions for days off—not only Saint Monday but also particular saints' days, especially if it was the patron saint of the trade in question. The shoemakers' patron was St. Crispin. The ironworkers' patron was St. Clement. Dockyard workers wouldn't go to work on the king's or queen's birthday. Coal miners had a tradition of Gaudy Day. When one of them heard a cuckoo for the first time in spring, he'd say, "It's Gaudy Day," and nobody would go to work, things like that. These were the kinds of customs that the first generation of factory owners were trying to break.

Access to work was also highly irregular in many trades. A good example here would be the dockyard workers. Before the invention of steamships, sailing ships were obviously at the mercy of the wind. That meant that, regularly, ships would be unable to get into harbor until they had favorable wind conditions. It was often a condition of feast or famine. There would be no ships coming in because of the wind and suddenly a whole lot would come in all at once and would need to be unloaded, re-laden, and so on. So, the workers would alternate between bouts of idleness and bouts of intense work.

Farm labor was highly seasonal. As the number of landless farm laborers increased, there would be times when there would be abundant work for everybody, particularly harvest time in the early autumn, and other times when there was very little farm work to be done—particularly in the winter.

Shipbuilders were very often idle between contracts. They had a contract to make a ship. When it was done, they then have to wait for another one. In 1849, one of the London newspapers, the *Morning Chronicle*, did a nationwide survey of the kinds of work that were being done all around the country. Its readership was middle class. The paper was telling its middle-class readership: "Here's what the working class is doing." It's a very valuable resource for historians as well, because we can still read these reports.

A boat builder told a journalist that was going around, "I'm not employed. Very few of us are three-quarters of the time. Taking the year as a whole, I don't earn more than a guinea a week [that's slightly more than one pound]. I may be hard at work this month, but I don't have anything to do for the next fortnight. I go from yard to yard only to be told that I'm not wanted"—so again, fluctuation between idleness and intense work.

In Cornwall—that's in the extreme southwest of England—the lead miners had regular work, but they didn't have regular pay. That was because they were actually paid only for the lead ore they brought up. All the time that they were digging tunnels and passages or the shafts to get to the lead ore, they had to do the work, but they weren't paid for it. So, it was very undependable when money was going to come in and when not. Once they encountered a good load, they might generate 100 pounds per month per man, but that might only happen for two or three weeks the entire year.

So, many occupations suffered from chronic underemployment and chronic uncertainty about when the money was going to be coming in. It was also common in many jobs for payment to be made not in money but in kind. It was becoming less common, but the tradition of payment in kind remained tenacious.

In the county of Dorsett, for example—the county that Thomas Hardy fictionalized as Wessex—the quarry men were actually paid in stone. They dug stone out of the ground; they were paid in stone. Sometimes if they were worn out, they would be paid in bread, but those were the two mediums of exchange—stone and bread.

Fishermen: the usual technique among the fishermen in all the coastal towns was to pay not money, even if you were an employee, but you were paid a share of the catch. In other words, you were actually physically given a lot of fish, which you could then use as currency in bartering in the local community for other things you needed.

There were great status differences within the working class. I mentioned this previously in talking about working-class women. It's certainly equally true of the men. In lots of trades, the aristocracy of labor—the men with the highest levels of skill—also had the steadiest work and were allowed to give themselves airs and graces. For example, carriage makers—the people who made horse-drawn carriages—there was a rigid hierarchy that the body makers—those who actually made the body of the carriage—were the most skilled. Below them were the trimmers. Below them were the smiths and the spring makers (blacksmiths.) Below them were the wheelwrights, then the painters, then the brace makers. The carriage makers at the top wouldn't dream of speaking to the brace makers unless they ordered them around within the works.

Payment itself is something we're familiar with now, but the idea of payment according to market value was itself only beginning to catch on. Rather, for most commodities, there was an idea that there was a just price. The payment for the creation of a commodity was sometimes fixed for decades and decades. Workmen would say, "That's the just price for this commodity." They didn't have any idea of market fluctuation, with which we're so familiar now. The notion of a wage rate which was commensurate with the number of hours of work done only developed gradually.

Each occupation had its own characteristic dress. If you were a shepherd, you had a very distinctive smock frock. There's a very interesting scene in Hardy's novel, *Far from the Madding Crowd*. Gabriel Oak, looking for work as a shepherd, buys a smock frock and then goes to stand in the market, and prospective employers are looking at him. "Oh, he's a shepherd." You can tell from the dress. And sure enough, he gets hired in that way.

One of the shocking aspects of this is that most working people had no change of clothes. They'd have the clothes they got, and that would be it. Here's the report again. The *Morning Chronicle* reports in 1849. It noted, "Farm laborers wear flannel whilst at work. But few ever change, even of that. The consequence is, they wear the same garment next to their skin day and night, although for many hours during the day it may have been soaked with perspiration."

They often sleep in their clothes as well. Do you remember in "My Fair Lady" Eliza Doolittle hates the idea of being undressed to be given a bath because she has no experience of it. As late as the 1930s, George Orwell commented that one of the reasons the English middle classes hated the working classes was because the working class smelled so bad. We have to take seriously that it was probably true.

The distinctive clothing of fishermen—hard-weather gear. Here's the *Morning Chronicle* again: "The fishermen wear enormous boots, form an expensive as well as prominent item in his attire. The poor fellows have generally their names marked upon the breast of their jersey jackets so that they may be recognized in cases of casualty." Because fishermen were often drowned, there was a way to tell instantly who it was.

All the irregular ways of work had to be abandoned once men began to go into the factories. As one by one industries switched over to factory work, they had to develop the new industrial discipline, which I've mentioned on several occasions. It was Adam Smith who realized, back in the 1770s, that the more you broke down the components of the job, the more efficiently it was going to be done, even though the price paid for that was an intensified boredom in the work itself.

A common metaphor used by working people themselves and writers watching work and the way it was becoming familiar was comparing people with machines, saying that the workers are being ground down until they're just like the machines. Here's an observer of a Manchester factory: "Whilst the engine runs, the people must work—men, women, and children are yoked together with iron and steam. The animal machine, breakable in the best case, subject to a thousand sources of suffering, is chained fast to the iron machine, which knows no suffering and no weariness," this idea that the machines are actually implacable and that the people being chained to them is a horrible destiny.

Inside the towns, particularly smoky places like Manchester, is the grinding sense of monotony and squalor. The one novel of Charles Dickens that is set in the north is *Hard Times*, where he takes up some of the issues of industrial work. The town is a fictional town called Coketown, but it's reminiscent of many of the northern manufacturing cities. Here is Dickens' description of it: "It had a black canal in it and a river that ran purple with ill-smelling dye and vast piles of buildings full of windows, where there was a rattling and a trembling all day long and where the pistons of the steam engine worked monotonously up and down, like the head of an elephant in a state of melancholy madness. It contained several large streets, all very like one another, and many small streets, still more like one another, inhabited by people equally like one another, who all went in and out at the same hours with the same sound upon the same pavement to do the same work. To home every day was the same as yesterday and tomorrow and every year, the counterpart of the last year and the next." A wonderful bravura of passages goes on about this awful feeling of blackness, monotony, repetition, and anonymity.

One of the ways that the factory owners tried to ensure discipline was by fining people very heavily for arriving late or stopping early. Sometimes you could lose half a day's pay for being a few minutes late at the factory. Of course, the pay was very low. In factories that paid according to piece rates, there was a constant squabble before—and some after—the creation of trade unions. What the boss wanted to do, obviously, was speed up the machinery as much as possible and make the piece rate low—in other words, make the workers make a lot of them to get paid for it, while the workers always tried to slow down the machinery and get a high piece rate, to claim, "We can't make very many, so you have to pay a good wage for each one that we make." This is the tension with the pacing of factories. We have lots of stories of workers intimidating one of their own brethren who was too enthusiastic. If a young man comes to a factory and says, "Oh, I can make a hundred of these in an hour," his older colleagues would say, "No, you can make 25, and we'll force you, if necessary."

I mentioned again, talking about the women, that each occupation had its characteristic illnesses. Coal mining was the single most dangerous job in Britain—and that remains true right up to the present. They suffered particularly from silicosis and lung cancer, if they even reached old age. If they weren't first killed in mines caving in or explosions or asphyxiation from methane gas or from fires, they were very likely to die prematurely from lung diseases, because the inhalation of coal dust was intense.

Another of the jobs that caused a great scandal in the mid-Victorian period was the work of the sweeps boys. You have to imagine this: every household in the country had a fireplace. They were used for heating and also for cooking. Because the coal that they were burning had a very high soot content, the soot would accumulate in the chimneys, and they would have to be cleaned very regularly, two or three times a year if the fire was constantly in use. Because very often there were labyrinth chimneys, it was difficult to clean them except by sending a small person up the chimney to clean out the soot. The sweeps' boys—there's a book about it by Charles Kingsley, *The Water Babies*—the sweeps boys were one of the most unfortunate groups of working people among English people. They had to start the job very young. Because they were the littlest ones, they could get into the tight corners in the chimneys. Repeatedly, Parliament passed laws to prevent the sweeps boys, but the fact that they kept having to pass such laws shows that they weren't being enforced. Obviously, you don't have to pass a law against an activity that isn't going on. The recurrence of the legislation shows us that it was going on, even when it was technically illegal. Regularly, the sweeps boys died. They'd get stuck in awkward parts of the chimneys and would be unable to get down. They'd become asphyxiated from smoke and fumes still in the chimneys. They'd have broken bones. Very often, what the master sweep would do would tie a rope around the boy's ankle so that he'd go up the chimney, and, if he got stuck, he'd pull on the rope to get him down again. There are stories of reluctant sweeps boys having a fire lit under them to force them to go up the chimney more quickly to get rid of the soot. These were horrible, horrible working conditions and an extremely high death rate.

Here's a master sweep giving evidence to a Parliamentary commission in 1863. He admitted that it was a horrible way of life, but he said, "I have lost a great amount of custom that I should otherwise have. I've been sent away, even from magistrates' houses, and even in some cases by ladies that profess to pity the boys, but refusing to use them. In other words, if you're a sweep and you said 'I'm not going to use the climbing boys; I'm going to use brushes with long attachments instead,' the prevailing wisdom from the customers was 'you're not going to do a very good job. You're only going to get a good job if you send the sweeps boys up there.'" So this master is claiming, "Well, I've got to do it because my customers are insisting upon it." This same man described the way in which he prepared the boys by rubbing brine—that's salt water—into the boys' joints to try to roughen the skin there and then holding them against the fire to make a thick and scabbed skin that's a bit more resistant to the abrasions of the work in the chimneys. It's very impossible to exaggerate the horrors of that way of life.

Nearly everybody doing industrial work was in a highly polluted environment, and a highly dangerous one, too, because of the size, scale, and power of the machinery with which they were working. There were virtually no health and safety regulations governing the way that work places should be run, because there's a tradition that that's not the role of the government. Although the government was gradually becoming involved in the regulation of some of these activities, the presumption was very strongly against it.

We have a wonderful book by a railway worker called Alfred Williams. He lived in Swindon, which is the place where the locomotives, the carriages, and the wagons were actually made to run on Isambard Brunel's Great Western Railway—Swindon. He wrote this book about his life as a workingman—very, very unusual, of course, to have a workingman's autobiography. Here's a little description of his working conditions: "Sickness and accidents are a frequent occurrence in the sheds. The first named can be attributed to the foul air prevailing, the dense smoke and fumes from the oil forges, and the thick, sharp dust and ashes from the coke fires. The tremendous noise of the hammers and machinery and the priming of the boilers have a most enduring effect upon the body as well as upon the nervous system. It's all intensely painful and wearisome to the workmen. As soon as you enter into the smoke and fumes, you are sure to begin sniffing and sneezing. The black dust and filth is being breathed into the chest and lungs at every moment. The percentage of sickness and accidents is higher at the stamping shed than in any other workshop in the factory. The accidents are of many kinds, though there are chiefly scalds and burns, broken and crushed limbs, and injuries to the eyes. When the workman is not feeling well, he's liable to meet with an accident at any moment. He does not have the keen sense of danger necessary under such conditions, or, if he has this, he has not the power in himself to guard against it. He has a vague idea that he's running risks, but he's too dazed or ill to fully realize it. He is, thus, often guilty of great self-neglect, amounting to madness, though he is ignorant of it at the time."

In other words, it impairs your mental capacity altogether when you're in this incredible smoky, rackety environment. And he says in another passage that, "So much oily smoke gets into your body that your skin is saturated by it." He says that however thoroughly he washes, whenever he wakes up there are black residues on the pillow, because it's under his eyelids, the back of his eyeballs, and so on. Only by stopping work altogether over the space of several weeks can you eventually work all this soot and smoke out of your bodily cavities.

The *Cornhill Magazine*—again, a magazine designed for middle-class readers—reported in 1862 on the life of coal miners in Tyneside. This is in the extreme northeast, near Castle-on-Tyne. "The real getters of coal are so-called hewers. In a small corner-like recess full of floating coal dust and noisome with bad air and miscellaneous refuse and garbage, glimmer three or four candles stuck in clay which adheres to the wall and roof. Close and deliberate scrutiny will discover one hewer—nearly naked—lying on his back, elevating his small, sharp pickaxe a little above his nose, and picking into the coal with might and main. If it is too hardly embedded, gunpowder is employed, and the mineral is blasted free, the dull, muffled, roof-shaking boom that follows each blast startling the air of the novice." He says, again, "After these explosions, an enormous cloud of acrid dust and smoke pours through the mineshafts, choking and making it utterly impossible, certainly for the observer who is not used to it, to breathe at all, always accompanied with the common threat that the explosions will bring down the roof altogether."

Another of the scandals over which there was a great deal of literary protest was coal mining, in particular, the use of women and children in coal mines. Here's Harriet Martin writing about it: "Women were employed as beasts of burden. Children were stunted and diseased, beaten, overworked, oppressed in every way. Women and children were made to crawl on all fours in low passages of the pits, dragging carts by a chain passing from the waist between the legs. All worked in an atmosphere of filth and profligacy, which would hardly leave a thought or a feeling untainted by vice." She describes also the work by one set of children—again, usually between the ages of five and nine—in the mines whose jobs were as trappers. The trapper was a child who sat by an underground door and opened it to let through the carts that were dragged by the older children and the women. The reason for these doors is to ensure that adequate air from the top could go through the ventilation system to the appropriate area of the mine, depending on which area was being used at the time. The trapper children would do 12-hour shifts. They were sitting in complete darkness. Candles were a luxury that they were entitled to bring in, but they didn't want to spend money on it. Candles themselves were quite expensive.

Workers struggled in the face of these kinds of hardships. always trying to keep some control over working conditions if they could. The Durham coal miners, for example, used a daily lottery to allocate work places. Some work places were more profitable than others. Some were more dangerous than others. Every day, they had an event they called caviling. One of the miners says this lottery gives everyone the chance for good and bad places and prevents union men and agitators from being victimized with bad and dangerous work places, and crawlers and gaffers men, that is, collaborators with the boss, from getting the good places as a reward for their collaboration.

Sometimes in the factory system—for example, in the Ireland steel system—skilled forge operators retained some autonomy over their work, even though they're now integrated into the factory. The boss said to them, "Here's what's got to get made. You can make it on your own schedule." They tried to keep up the tradition of Saint Monday, even though they're now working in the factory.

It was the dream of many working people to get out of the factories if they could and become entrepreneurs in their own right—penny capitalists. As I mentioned, [there were] women working as street peddlers or running cabs around city streets or buying shares in a fishing boat. This was a way of at least beginning to feel that they have some autonomy economically.

A historian called John Benson says that when we study people's work, we've got to take seriously the fact that people did things "like begging, in the countryside poaching and stealing fruit, scavenging, shoplifting, prostitution, and theft. These are all forms of work in the sense that they're activities to which people devoted lots of time and energy. We can't be solely content with looking at wage work." It's certainly true that, for example, shoplifting and petty theft were widespread. Here is an Edinburgh man talking to an interviewer just after the turn of the century and recalling his childhood in Victorian Edinburgh. "My mother used to send Jimmy or me for a couple of half loaves, a tin of milk, something like that, you know. Well, Jimmy and me would work out a plan of action and go into the shop to see if we could skim something off it. And my mother, she'd said, 'Get two apples.' I've seen me coming back with four. She said, 'Get a pound of taties'—potatoes. I'd see me coming back with a pack, seven pounds, things like that, see? We used to nab it, steal it in the shop." It's quite clear from the way he describes it that if you can get away with it, that's fine. There's no moral objection in his description of his shoplifting.

In coal mining districts, an activity called picking was the children's duty. That was to go to the slag heaps—the waste heaps of the mines—to look for little fragments of coal. In rural districts, children were required, if they could, to steal fruit from the orchards of the big farmers nearby, so scavenging, picking, and petty theft, really. There were severe laws to try to prevent poaching. It nevertheless went on all the time, particularly against game birds.

Working class neighborhoods were densely populated, smoky, neighborly, and gossipy. They weren't private at all. There were far too many people living in a concentrated place. Sometimes they could be amicable and quite open. Here's the *Morning Chronicle* again from 1849 talking about a Lancashire mill town in summer. "In most cases, the doors of the houses stand hospitably open, and young children cluster over the thresholds and swarm out upon the pavement. Every evening after the mill hours, these streets present a scene of considerable quiet enjoyment. The people appear to be on the best of terms with each other and laugh and gossip from window to window and door to door. The women, in particular, are fond of sitting in groups upon the thresholds, sewing and knitting. The children sprawl about beside them. There's an amount of sweethearting going forward, which is naturally to be looked for under such circumstances." So there we are: a glance of one of the few nice days in the summer that Lancashire is blessed with; things look quite good. But it's understood that behind the scenes there's an enormous amount of stress and tension, particularly when the men drank. Drink really was a great evil in Victorian Britain. Although temperance crusades had by now gotten a rickety look, it was easy to understand why temperance should generate so much enthusiasm at the time.

A woman from St. Helens in Lancashire recalled, "Men were tyrants. There was an awful lot of wife beating, and women were the underdogs. My mother slept in the outside lavatory at times to get away from him. The men who didn't drink and behaved like that were the worst of all. When it happened, women went to the neighbors' houses. Then the husband would come and kick the door down to get the wife out. It was just a way of life," so a very, very high degree of domestic violence.

But the amount of working-class drinking does seem to have been declining during the Victorian period. Among the shipbuilders, for example, an observer said, "Within these 20 years the shipbuilders generally were the hard drinkers, but now I'm assured that there are 50 steady men to one tippler." This is becoming rarer, or among the coopers—the barrel makers—they had a hard-drinking reputation in 1830 but decreasingly so as the century went on.

"There has been a great reformation in the drinking habits of the men. There are a few causes of this, in my opinion. One is the closing of the public houses at 12:00 on Saturday night and not allowing them to be opened until after church time on Sunday. The other is the cheapness of railway traveling so that the men are used to going a little way into the countryside on a Sunday instead of wasting their money and ruining their health in taverns." Among the Birmingham brass workers, here, from the evidence we got, it seems to be a generational shift. "The younger ones, who have grown up with the industrial system, aren't as hard drinkers as the older generation, who went through the switch from the old system to the new." The observer here says, "The habits here of temperance, carelessness, and irregularity, which is stated formerly to have prevailed among them, only linger among the older race of workmen and are fast disappearing among the younger men. The observance of Saint Monday and all such holidays is stated to be confined almost entirely to the older hands." "And it often frequently happens," said an intelligent journeyman, "that if one of the workmen absents himself for drunkenness, he returns to the manufacturer amidst the ridicule and hootings of his comrades, for the younger men have adapted themselves to the industrial work discipline; tend to be more sober and more regular in their habits than the older ones."

This is particularly true of those that had been impressed by the Evangelical revival, only a minority in the working class, but nonetheless an influential one.

We finish with a remark from a study of the Tyneside miners in 1862, which says that more and more of the men are becoming Methodists. "Men who might anyhow be buried alive in a dark pit, which will prove their tomb, may well think of that other world into which two of them went recently, without warning."

There we are. When you think about Victorian Britain, don't be distracted by visions of Masterpiece Theatre. Although what it depicts isn't wrong, the vast majority of Victorian people were people that had to work very hard for low pay in very bad conditions.

Lecture Eleven
Poverty and the "Hungry Forties"

Scope:

Poverty was common throughout British history and could be just as acute in the countryside as in towns. Urbanization and industrialization made poverty more visible and its effects more shocking. The new spirit of utilitarianism on one side, coupled with an evangelical reform impulse on the other, combined to make poverty seem more scandalous to the Victorians than it had to their predecessors. Underemployment and sickness often pushed working people into poverty; public health conditions were so bad that epidemics of cholera, typhus, and typhoid were common. Novelists, journalists, and radicals all studied and condemned poverty; the New Poor Law created the workhouse system in an attempt to alleviate the condition economically. The law's inadequacies, however, made philanthropy a necessary supplement.

Outline

I. Rural poverty was still common in Victorian England.

    A. The enclosure movement had created a class of landless laborers, many of whom were paid wages at or below starvation level.

    B. Benjamin Disraeli's novel *Sybil*, subtitled *The Two Nations* (1845), describes scenes of horrible rural poverty behind an apparently idyllic landscape.

II. Urban poverty was caused by numerous factors.

    A. Fluctuations in the business cycle and seasonal patterns of work led to periodic declines in the demand for labor.

        1. City dwellers were completely dependent on money for food but lacked money when out of work.

        2. There was no welfare state or unemployment benefit to compensate the unemployed.

        3. Mining needed more men in winter.

    B. Businessmen's belief in laissez faire policies was mixed with their belief that they could remain competitive only by paying the lowest possible wages.

C. Until the mid 19th century, the Combination Acts made the creation of trade unions illegal for fear that they would lead to revolutionary activity.

D. Sickness was often the push that sent a family over the edge from working poverty to starvation or crime. Unsanitary living conditions and overcrowding made epidemics common, and the cities were swept by periodic outbreaks of cholera, typhus, and typhoid.

E. The working poor found various ways to cope.

    1. If they were "known" they could get credit at local shops, buying "on tick."

    2. Pawnbrokers were universal in working-class districts, because families regularly had to raise a little money from their scanty possessions.

    3. The poorest people also moved often and were most likely to become criminals.

III. The persistence of poverty was studied and condemned by numerous groups.

A. Novelists used poverty as a backdrop for their stories; Mrs. Gaskell in *Mary Barton* (1848) described how members of the Davenport family were laid off, then became sick with typhoid fever.

B. Journalists, such as Henry Mayhew, were fascinated with the variety of ways poor Londoners found for making some sort of income and staying alive.

    1. Mayhew published *London Labor and the London Poor* in 1849.

    2. He was fascinated by the orphaned children of London, including the "mudlarks," who waded out into the river estuary at low tide to scavenge for anything of value that had dropped off boats into the muddy riverbed.

C. Radical observers, notably Friedrich Engels and later Karl Marx, described these conditions as part of their indictment of capitalism.

    1. Engels, a German, was sent by his father to manage his textile factories in Manchester and was appalled by urban slums there.

    2. His book *The Condition of the Working Class in England* (1845) became a classic indictment of early British capitalism.

IV. The political response to poverty was never adequate in the Victorian era.

  A. The New Poor Law, introduced in 1834, created workhouses.

    1. The aim was to be economical and to deter potential inmates.

    2. Dickens made them a byword for misery and privation.

    3. The sick, mentally ill, and the aged were often forced to go there.

    4. Historians have shown that some workhouses were well run and humane.

  B. The prevailing mood of laissez faire among the business classes discouraged state intervention, especially if financed through taxation.

  C. Civic reformers inside the British political system proposed public health and sanitation legislation.

    1. One of the most influential of these reformers was Edwin Chadwick, who belonged to the first generation of professional civil servants.

    2. He was a great collector of statistics and advocated the systematic application of efficient principles to the regulation of poverty.

    3. He encouraged cleanliness but was bitterly hated for it.

  D. A general rise in real wages after the 1850s made downright starvation less common, but aggravated poverty remained widespread.

V. Philanthropy sometimes alleviated the worst suffering but was often accompanied by preaching and moralizing that the poor resented.

  A. Middle-class Victorians widely believed that they were prosperous because they were more virtuous than the poor and that the poor were subject to that condition because they were less virtuous.

  B. In *Bleak House*, Dickens demonstrates his acute eye for charity recipients' resentment.

C. Seebohm Rowntree recognized poverty periods in the working-class life cycle.

   1. Poverty was likely during early childhood.

   2. It abated when a child could earn, increasing family funds.

   3. It recurred when a worker had to support his own children.

   4. It lessened when the worker's children joined the work force.

   5. It recurred again in old age when he was unable to work.

D. William Booth, founder of the Salvation Army, estimated in the 1880s that as many as three million people, "the submerged tenth," lived in permanent poverty. (See Booth's book on poverty, *In Darkest England* [1890].)

VI. As a percentage, the number of very poor was declining, but as a total it remained very high. In general, the standard of living, at least for people who could get regular work, did rise in the Victorian era.

Essential Reading:

W. D. Rubinstein, *Britain's Century: A Political and Social History, 1815–1905*.

J. H. Treble, *Urban Poverty in Britain: 1830–1914*.

Supplementary Reading:

Henry Mayhew, *London Poverty and the London Poor*.

Charles Dickens, *Oliver Twist*.

Questions to Consider:

1. What factors made the urban working class especially vulnerable to poverty?

2. How effective were Victorian efforts to remedy poverty?

Lecture Eleven—Transcript
Poverty and the "Hungry Forties"

Poverty has been a common condition throughout British history. Poverty could be just as acute in the countryside as it was in the new industrial towns. As we saw last time, the threat of falling into poverty was a constant possibility among a large part of the working class. Urbanization and industrialization brought a lot of people together in the cities and therefore tended to make poverty more visible than it had been previously and tended to make its effects more shocking. The new spirit of utilitarianism on one hand—that is, the philosophy that a society ought to be geared toward creating the maximum happiness for the greatest number of people—and the Evangelical reform impulse on the other side in the churches combined to make poverty seem more scandalous than it had done previously. As society is getting wealthier, the idea that a part of it is still so poor seems more objectionable than it had done previously.

The hard business conditions of the 1840s but also the amount of attention given to poverty by writers and politicians made it more visible and more controversial than ever before. Academic historians have a continuing debate about whether, with the Industrial Revolution, poverty was getting worse or whether overall economic conditions were being alleviated. Everybody agrees that in the long run, by the mid 20th century, poverty had been far less acute than it had been 100 years earlier. But did it get worse and then become better or were conditions becoming steadily better throughout the period? The evidence is very complicated and the nature of the debate is convoluted. Without trying to get too deep into the arcane aspects of that, let's just look at some of the evidence of poverty and its character and its consequences.

First of all, the rural poverty was still very common in the countryside. The enclosure movement had created a class of landless laborers, many of whom were paid just daily wages when work was available and were very, very close to starvation levels. Benjamin Disraeli, the man who eventually became the Conservative Prime Minister, in his early life was a successful novelist. Here's a quotation from one of his novels, called *Sybil*, published in 1845 in the middle of this decade remembered as the Hungry Forties. It's a description of a thatched cottage in the countryside which at first glance is picturesque, but in which, upon further inspections, conditions of poverty prevail:

> "With the water streaming down the walls, the light distinguished through the roof, with no hearth even in the winter, the virtuous mother in the sacred pangs of childbirth gives forth another victim to our thoughtless civilization. These swarming walls have neither windows nor doors sufficient to keep out the weather or admit the sun or supply the means of ventilation, the humid and putrid roof of thatch, exhaling malaria like all other decaying vegetable matter. Beside the door might be observed the dung heap on which every kind of filth was accumulated with the purpose of being disposed of for manure. So that, when the poor man opened his narrow habitation in the hopes of refreshing it with the breeze of summer, he was met with a mixture of gases from reeking dung hills."

That's an important insight for us. Today, if you go to England, especially if you go as a visitor, one of the attractions you might see is thatched cottages. Certainly, when the thatch is new, it looks very picturesque. But, of course, thatch wasn't used for picturesque reasons; it was used as an available material. As it decayed, it was not particularly weatherproof, and it was dangerous—certainly the home of vermin and fleas.

It was as bad in the city as well as the countryside. As I said last time, fluctuations in the business cycle and the irregularity of work, periodically large numbers of people were thrown out of work with no useful alternative source of income. They no longer had little vegetable plots of their own on which they could at least grow some vegetables. There was no adequate welfare system to compensate the unemployed. In trades like mining, there was a lot of seasonal variation, depending on what demand for the product was like.

In the factory system, the businessmen themselves believed very strongly in the philosophy of *laissez faire*, which really just means "leave us alone." The businessman's claim was that he was making an individual contractor of these workmen. They were free to accept or reject the contract depending on his judgment of its terms. Of course, it was a fiction, because workmen were in no position to bargain, especially against someone with the enormous economic power of the employer. Certainly, the belief was widespread that government ought not to be involved with matters of that kind. That's why, although legislation regulating things like hours and eventually wages did begin, it began haltingly and uncertainly.

Employers who were chastised for paying excessively low wages would say, "It's all very well to say that I should pay more wages. Sure, if it was just up to me, I'd be glad to do so. But, of course, if I pay bigger wages, I'd have to put up the price of the commodity I'm selling. If I did that, my competitors would all undersell me because they're still paying low wages, and therefore it wouldn't be long before I went out of business. If I'm making the same stuff and charging more for it, I'm lost." In other words, they could say that structural factors compelled them to pay very low wages.

Until the mid-19th century, the legal situation made it very difficult for working people to create trade unions. They were illegal altogether until 1824, because of the Combination Acts. Even after that, when those acts had been repealed, the legal obstacles against which a union worked were still very great.

So every family, or nearly every working family, was just a sickness away from absolute poverty. If the breadwinner was too sick to work, the family could rapidly fall into destitution. Because working conditions were so unsanitary, as we saw last time, because work was so undependable, and because public health conditions were so bad, typhoid and typhus and cholera swept continuously through the cities. People suffered chronically from dysentery and so on—you were always on the brink. Cholera first appeared in 1831, apparently coming from Asia. There were recurrent epidemics in 1849 and 1853 and 1864.

In those days, the theory was that cholera was caused by what was called a miasma—"bad air." Remember in that quotation from Disraeli he says "miasmatic fumes." The germ theory of disease didn't develop until the 1880s. It was true that the public health conditions, that disease was encouraged—contaminated places, standing cesspools, contaminated wells, and so on. One of the worst areas in the London area was a place just south of the Thames called Jacob's Island. An observer called Henry Mayhew called it "the Capital of Cholera." Here's his description of the area: "When I ventured to visit the last named district, would not have wondered about the pestilence in that malarious quarter, bound as it was on the north and east by filth and fever and on the south and west by want, squalor, rags, and pestilence. Spared by the Great Fire of London, the houses and comforts of the people in this loathsome place have scarcely known any improvement since that time." The Great Fire of London was way back in 1666.

"In the days of Henry II, the foul, stagnant ditch that to this day makes an island of this pestilential spot, was a running stream. But at this date, the running brook was changed to a tidal sewer." He says that, after the tide goes out, the sewage is carried away, and when the tide comes in, most of it comes back again.

Houses were built actually over the river on pilings, because building space was at such a premium. He says, "At some parts of the stream, whole rooms that have been built out over houses on opposite sides of the river nearly touch one another. There, with the very stench of death rising through the floorboards, human beings slept night after night until the last sleep of all came upon them years before its time."

He watches people emptying their toilet buckets into this river. At the same time, he sees a group of the local neighborhood boys swimming in the river not very far away. Then, to make matters even worse, he sees another kid lowering the drinking water bucket down into the river. He says, "And yet, as we stood gazing in horror at this fluvial sewer, we saw a child from one of the galleries opposite lower a tin can with a rope to fill a large bucket that stood beside her." He realizes that she's getting drinking water.

"In each of the rude and rotten balconies, indeed, hung over the stream, the self-same bucket was to be seen in which the inhabitants were wont to put their lucky liquid to stand so that they might, after it had been left to settle for a day or two, skim the fluid from the solid particles of filth and pollution which constituted the sediment." Well, isn't that gruesome? One of the reforms that was gradually brought about—I talk about this later on in the course when we deal with issues of public health—is the great problem of getting adequate drainage and adequate drinking water supplies. These are matters so basic we scarcely think about them. Of course, this society didn't have them.

The working poor—the people who were periodically on the brink of poverty—had various ways to cope. One of them was to get credit at the local shops. I mentioned previously, there's a lot of working people who, if they could, would become petty shopkeepers. To run a shop, you had to be willing to give credit, because you know that, periodically, people in your neighborhood would be out of work. From humane concern, you would have to give them credit. If you didn't, periodically, the shop would simply stop business altogether. If you were known in the neighborhood—often these neighborhoods were very gossipy and local; you'd be familiar with somebody— you'd be given "tick." Tick means being given credit.

Pawnbrokers were also very common. Every city was covered in pawn brokerages. Periodically, you'd have to take one of your few possessions to the pawnbroker and get a little bit of money for it. When you got some money, you'd pay a little bit more to get your property back again. A study made in 1870 showed that the average working-class family went to the pawnbrokers 30 times over a year. That's not far short of once a week. It was regular to be paid on Saturday, make it through part of the week, then eventually to run out of money, go to the pawnbrokers on Thursday. You know the song "Pop! Goes the Weasel." That's a song about going to the pawnbroker. "Popping," means pawning, and the "Weasel" is the iron. You can do without the iron for a day or two, so pop goes the weasel. Go to the pawnbrokers to give the iron and raise a bit of money.

The very poorest people of all were the ones that tended to move most often. They couldn't afford to pay the rent, so they were thrown out and moved to a new district. Because of that, they weren't known in the new district, so it was much harder for them to get credit at the local shop. Those are the poorest people, who are most likely to become criminals or prostitutes because it's becoming impossible for them to stay on the fair side of the law.

The persistence of poverty was widely studied at the time, and it was widely condemned as well by all sort of different groups. One group was the novelists. Mrs. Gaskell, who wrote *Mary Barton*—this is one of the great classic novels of industrial life, again published in the middle of the '40s, in 1848—she talks about how the Davenport family is laid off because of a drop in trade. Then Mr. Davenport is gotten sick with typhoid fever:

> "He lay on straw so damp and moldy no dog would have chosen it with preference for the flagstones. Over it was a

piece of sacking coming next to his worn skeleton of a body. Above him was every article of clothing that could be spared by mother or children in this bitter weather. In addition to his own, these may have given as much warmth as one blanket, could they have been kept on him, but as he restlessly tossed to and fro, they fell off and left him shivering in spite of the burning heat of his fevered skin. Every now and then, he started up in his naked madness, looking like a prophet of woe in a fearful plague picture, but soon fell again in exhaustion. Wilson appeared [this is one of his friends], carrying in both hands a jug of steaming tea intended for the poor wife, but when the delirious husband saw drink, he snatched at it with an animal instinct, with a selfishness he had never shown in health."

A journalist called Henry Mayhew was fascinated with the techniques poor people found for staying alive in the face of the most desperate circumstances. He wrote a classic book called *London Labor of the London Poor* in 1849. One of the groups of poverty-stricken individuals that particularly fascinated him were the orphan children of London. There were swarms of them—children that had been abandoned or whose parents had died in epidemics and now lived throughout the city. A lot of them appear in *Oliver Twist* as well. Henry Mayhew and Charles Dickens were friends, and they compared notes about their investigations of the life of the poor. One group who Henry Mayhew found were the "mudlarks." These were children whose way of life was to wait until the tide went out in the River Thames and then to wade out onto the muddy bed of the river to pick up anything of value that was in the river. Because it was a very busy shipping lane, a lot of stuff tended to get thrown off of the ships.

Now and again, they would find stuff of value—although not of very much value—little particles of coal, iron nails that had been used to hammer the copper cladding to the side of ships, bone that they could sell to a rag-and-bone man, and very often bits of glass. He said that they wade out barefoot, because then their feet will detect things. They're often knee or thigh deep in this mud, which itself is just sewage. It's just slimy sewage that's been tipped into the river. Sometimes they cut their feet on these pieces of glass and then they grovel down into the mud to pick them up and bring them to shore.

Then they can make a few pennies every day just to keep themselves alive.

Here is Mayhew's description of them: "I collected about a dozen of these unfortunate children. There was not one of them over 12 years of age, and many of them were but of six. It would be almost impossible to describe the wretched group, so motley was their appearance, so extraordinary their dress, and so stolid and inexpressive their countenances. Some carried baskets filled with the produce of their morning's work and some tin kettle with handles. Others, more needy still, had taken the caps from their own heads and had filled them with what they had happened to find. The muddy slush was dripping from their clothes and utensils and forming a puddle in which they stood." Here is Mayhew surrounded by this crowd of people who are literally just dripping with festering mud.

He wrote a chapter about another group, the London dustmen—people who, because they never washed, were always absolutely covered with dust and grime. One of the things Victorians loved was statistics, especially these researchers. He worked out that every year about 3,500,000 tons of coal that was brought into London, and that after it had been burned it left a residue of about 900,000 tons of ash. The dustmen were the people who dealt with the ash, taking it away from domestic and commercial properties and selling the particulate ash to the brick makers, who could actually recycle it. It was a very recycling-conscious society, incidentally, because nearly everything had some value. The stuff the mudlarks picked up—it's amazing that there was somebody there to buy it, but there was.

He found that entire communities of the dustmen actually lived in the ash pits, and they spent their time actually sifting through the ashes. Just as the mudlarks sifted the mud, so did the ash people sift through the ashes. He's a very good observer of the habits and the different appearances of the people. Here's his description of the dustmen: "The dustmen, in their appearance, very much resemble the wagoners of the coal merchants. They generally wear knee britches with ankle boots or gaiters, short, dirty smock frocks or coarse, gray jackets, and fantail hats. In one particular, however, they are at first sight distinguishable from the coal merchant's men, for the latter are invariably black from coal, while the dustmen, on the contrary, are gray with ashes." So you see these black people moving around—

they're the coal men— and the gray people moving around are the ash men.

Another group that Mayhew met were the sweepers. Again, it was very often orphan boys. In those days, only some of the city streets were paved. Some of them were still what we call dirt tracks. But all of them were covered in horse manure, because horses were the standard form of transportation. There were tens of thousands of tons of horse manure all over the city streets. So, every little street corner, every intersection, would have its crossing sweepers. These are boys who defended their own little patch of turf very tenaciously against others who tried to come in. They'd sweep the mess off the roads, and very often they'd run errands for the families that lived on that street, or, if one of the gentlemen came out of his townhouse, they'd hurry to open the carriage door in the hope of a little tip. Mayhew was still doing part of the research in the '50s, during the Crimean War. He said the sweeping boys would draw patriotic pictures in the dirt—the Union Jack or of one of the soldiers—in the hope of getting tips from passers-by.

Economical observers, people like Karl Marx and Friedrich Engels, who lived in England, described these conditions, these conditions of incredible poverty, as part of their indictment of capitalism. They believed that the inequities of capitalism were so great that the system couldn't possibly continue to exist and sooner or later the people would rise up to overthrow their oppressors, what they called the "bourgeoisie." Engels was a factory manager in Manchester, fascinated and appalled by what he found. His book, *The Condition of the Working Class in England*, also published in 1845, a decade that is very rich in these things, became one of the classic indictments of early British capitalism.

He talked about the very poor quality of the housing in which poor people had to live. Here's his description of a cluster of these houses on the banks of the River Irk. "The worst courts are those leading down to the River Irk, which contain unquestionably the most dreadful dwellings I have ever seen. In one of these courts, just at the entrance where the covered passage ends, there is a privy without a door. This privy is so dirty that the inhabitants of the court could only enter or leave it if they were prepared to wade through puddles of stale urine and excrement. It was the scene of a cholera outbreak in 1832. Nearby is the river. It is a narrow, cold, black, stinking river full of filth and rubbish which it deposits on the low-lying right bank. In dry weather, this bank presents the spectacle of a series of the most revolting blackish-green puddles of slime from the depths of which bubbles of miasmatic gases constantly rise and create a stench which is unbearable, even to those standing on the bridge 40 or 50 feet above the level of the water."

He says, "Everybody uses the river as a drain." Alongside the river are the tanneries—always very smelly places—the bone mills, and the gas works. Again, it's a great big reeking trench. We live in a world where pollution is an issue, but we've never had to deal with pollution on these kinds of levels. It's completely qualitatively a different thing.

The political response to poverty in the Victorian period was never adequate. The New Poor Law of 1834, passed just before Victoria became queen, created the workhouses. The idea of the workhouse was that it was meant to be an intimidating place. It was meant to be somewhere where you'd only go reluctantly when you're in the last extremity of poverty. In other words, what the government wanted was a poor relief scheme that would cost as little as possible to the taxpayers and which people would be deterred from entering unless conditions had reached the absolute breaking point.

If you went into the workhouse as a family, the family would be broken up, as men and women were placed in different areas. You had to put on a uniform, which is very much like a prisoner's uniform and was regarded as humiliating. The places were rife with rumors. One of them was if you died while you were there, your body would be cut up and served in pies that were served to the other inmates. There was a terrible scandal at Andover, a town just south of Oxford, when the inmates were given bones to grind, but they were so hungry they began chewing on the bones instead. They really were horrible places. Of course, it's in the workhouses that Oliver Twist is brought up and where he makes his famous request for more. Remember? The whole place just goes, "More?" It was Dickens that made the workhouse a byword for deprivation and misery.

If you were mentally ill—I suppose you didn't have relatives to look after you or you were chronically sick— you were very likely to end up in the workhouse. When I was a child in the town of Derby in the

English Midlands, I lived about three miles from a hospital called the Manor Hospital. I found out that it had been the workhouse. I was born in 1956, so people who were old in my childhood could remember the days when the workhouses had been in operation. The elderly people in my community dreaded that hospital. Even though it was no longer a workhouse, they wouldn't go there under any circumstances. That's the kind of terror and dread it had inspired in people. Regularly, the press in the Victorian period would report cases of people dying of want rather than go into the workhouse.

Ironically, more recently, some historians have said, "Actually, the workhouses weren't quite that bad." For example, in Liverpool and Manchester, two of the big northern cities, they were run by sensible committees and were quite effective. They had schools to give the children some elementary education and literacy, and they even had hospitals. Conditions varied depending on the humane attitudes of the local overseers of the poverty.

Sometimes—the central authority in London was always trying to enforce uniform regulations throughout the country, but they were never able to do so. Local custom proved too strong. For example, in some northern counties, particularly in Northumberland and parts of Yorkshire, the poor commissioners were supposed to require people to come into the workhouse, but didn't. Instead, they gave them what was called "outdoor relief." They paid them some money to tide them over hard times in the knowledge that it would be so humiliating and degrading if they did have to come into the workhouse and also for the pragmatic reason that it was usually a bit cheaper to pay outdoor relief rather than bring them into the workhouse.

Civic reformers became increasingly concerned with this range of poverty problems. One of the most influential was Edwin Chadwick. He'd been instrumental in the passage of the Poor Law legislation, and then later on he became very preoccupied with public health regulation. He was a great collector of statistics and a believer in the systematic application of efficient principles to the regulation of poverty. The historian G.M. Young, writing at just the end of the Victorian period, says this, a joking remark about him: "Born in 1800 in a Lancashire farmhouse where the children were washed all over every day, the mainspring of Chadwick's career seems to be the desire to wash the people of England all over every day by administrative order."

If you look at the history of the British death rate, you have to be struck by the fact that Chadwick is one of the great heroes. He clearly undertook the kinds of reforms that did diminish the death rate. Nevertheless, he was bitterly hated and resented. Working-class people didn't want to wash. They wanted not to because they were so unfamiliar with it. It may very well be that the legislation he helped to shepherd through Parliament was as contributory as anything else to gradual improvements in the life of working people.

Wages began to rise after 1850. That made downright death from starvation increasingly uncommon in Britain, but aggravated poverty remained widespread right up until the end of the Victorian period.

Another source of relief for poor people was philanthropy, that is, the generosity of the upper- and middle-class people. There was a great deal of Victorian philanthropy, but it was often accompanied by religious attitudes that the recipients found rather annoying or, even more, a moralizing attitude which they found particularly hard to deal with. It was widely believed among the Victorian middle classes that they were prosperous because they were more virtuous and the poor were poorer because they were less virtuous, an attitude that we still sometimes encounter today.

As usual, Charles Dickens has a wonderfully acute eye for this kind of thing. Here's a passage from *Bleak House* where the narrator goes to a poor brick worker's house, and he goes with Mrs. Pardiggle. Mrs. Pardiggle is a philanthropist. She's a terrible busybody, and she's visited this family before and given them some improving, Evangelical tracts. Anyway, when they go in, they find this disgustingly dirty house, and there's no furniture, and the man is lying on the floor, smoking. As soon as they come in, this is what the man says:

> "I wants an end of these liberties took with my place. I wants an end of being drawn like a badger. Now you're going to pull, pry, and question according to custom. I know what you're a-going to be up to. Well, you haven't got no occasion to be up to it. I will save you the trouble. Is my daughter a-washing? Yes, she's a-washing. Look at the water. Smell it. That's what we drinks. How do you like it?

And what do you think about gin, instead? Ain't my place dirty? Yes, it's dirty. It's naturally dirty, and it's naturally unwholesome. And we've got five dirty and unwholesome children as is all dead infants, and so much the better for them and for us besides. Had I read that little book what you left? No, I ain't read that book what you left. There ain't nobody here that knows how to read it. And if there was, it wouldn't be suitable to me. How have I been conducting myself? I've been drunk for three days. I would have been drunk for four if I'd had the money. And how did my wife get that black eye? Why, I give it to her, and she's a liar if she says I didn't."

Here's the recipient of the philanthropy hating and resenting the intrusion of the charity giver.

Another sophisticated investigator of poverty was a man called Seebohm Rowntree. He was a chocolate manufacturer from York and became very philanthropically inclined and statistically minded. He wanted to investigate what it was that caused poverty, not only from moment to moment but over the course of the life cycle. He was one of the first people to say we need to do longitudinal studies of poverty to find out the nature of how it occurs within families. He created a five-part picture of the life cycle. He said poverty is very likely during early childhood, because young children who can't work have parents that are overtaxed by the number of children they need to bring up. When a child is old enough to work, poverty tends to become a little bit less acute. When a young man is first married and hasn't got children, he's least likely to be sick and least likely to have too many mouths to feed. Then, as his family starts having children, the probability of poverty starts to increase again. It lessens when his children can help him. It increases again in old age, especially if he isn't well kept by members of his own family.

Rowntree concludes in this way: "The proportion of the community that in one period or other in their lives suffer from poverty to the point of physical privation is therefore much greater than it would appear from the consideration of the number that can be shown to be below the poverty line at any given moment." In other words, overall, it's worse as an affliction for working-class people than a look at any one moment might make you think.

Another investigator in the late Victorian period is William Booth, the founder of the Salvation Army. He found that about three million English people were living chronic lives of poverty. He called them the "submerged tenth." In those days, Africa was often referred to as "Darkest Africa"—this mysterious continent. He wrote a book called *Darkest England*, published in 1890, as a sort of expose of the continuation of extreme aggravated poverty.

We can conclude by saying that, although the percentage of the British people who were poor was declining slightly as the Victorian period persisted, the sheer number of poor people remained extremely high. The best avenues out of it—regular work and high wages—were still only accessible to a minority of people.

Lecture Twelve
Ireland, Famine, and Robert Peel

Scope:

Britain's oldest colony, Ireland, always resented English domination, and, by the 1840s, centuries-old resentments, political and religious, embittered relations between the two countries. A Protestant minority of landowners, the "ascendancy," enjoyed the profits of a system in which the Catholic peasant majority lived in severe and often degraded poverty. The peasants' dependence on potatoes (originally introduced from America) had led to steady population growth, but in 1846, a potato blight devastated the crop and threw millions into a condition of near or absolute starvation. The British government, hamstrung by its faith in laissez faire and its penny-pinching traditions where Ireland was concerned, took inadequate steps to alleviate the crisis. A large migration from Ireland to England, Canada, and the United States ensued, often aggravated by epidemics. At the same time, the Tory government of Prime Minister Robert Peel, already under pressure to dismantle protectionist trade policies, abolished the Corn Laws that had protected the interest of British landlords by keeping the price of imported food artificially high. This decision shattered the Tory Party, whose elements were unable to reunify for the next 25 years. Neither did it benefit the starving Irish, many of whom rarely or never ate bread.

Outline

I. British involvement in Ireland had always been a source of friction.

   A. The involvement began in the reign of Henry II in the 12th century.

   B. It intensified during the reign of Elizabeth I, when expeditions under Sir Walter Raleigh and others tried to bring more of the island under direct British control.

   1. Until then, the city of Dublin and the area immediately surrounding it was called "the Pale"—the area that England administered.

   2. Going "beyond the pale" originally meant going beyond the place where British rule in Ireland operated effectively.

C. Oliver Cromwell, leader of the parliamentary armies in the British Civil Wars of the 1640s, suppressed an Irish rebellion in 1649–1651.

    1. He massacred the inhabitants of Drogheda when they refused to surrender.

    2. He was unable to pay the members of his New Model Army in money but paid many of them in Irish lands instead.

D. Ireland had remained Catholic during the Reformation and supported the Catholic King James II in the Glorious Revolution of 1688–1689.

    1. Irish Protestants treasured the memory of James's defeat at the Battle of the Boyne (1690) by Protestant William III.

    2. The Ulster Protestant "Orange Parades" to this day commemorate that battle and continue to produce community friction.

E. In the early 19th century, the Catholic majority, mostly very poor, lived on lands owned by Protestants, many of whom were absentees.

    1. Local agents ran the estates and profited by multiple subdivision of plots.

    2. Owners often did not even know how many tenants lived and worked on their estates.

    3. Tenants were constantly liable to eviction without legal recourse and with no compensation for improvements.

    4. Secret societies, such as the White Boys and the Ribbon Men, avenged evicted tenants.

F. The Protestant Church of Ireland was a standing grievance to the Catholic people, who had to pay for its upkeep.

    1. The Catholic Association, founded by Daniel O'Connell in 1823, campaigned for Catholic emancipation.

    2. Catholic emancipation in 1829 gave Catholic property owners the right to vote and become Members of Parliament, ensuring that Irish Catholics would become an important (sometimes decisive) part of British political life for the rest of the century.

II. Population growth in Ireland was not matched by industrialization or agricultural diversification.

    A. By the early 1840s, the population was eight million.

    B. Most cotters lived on small rented plots, often housed with their farm animals in mud huts.

    C. Potatoes, introduced into Europe from America by Columbus, were the staple food of the rural poor; monocultures are unstable, because they offer the ideal conditions for the one crop's predators.

    D. Potato blight, beginning in late 1845, catastrophic in 1846, and again in 1848, denied millions their only supply of food.

III. Irish suffering in 1846–1849 intensified Anglo-Irish bitterness and has never been forgotten.

    A. Visitors were horrified by scenes of death by starvation and cholera, beginning in December 1846, that preyed on weakened survivors.

    B. Emigrant ships, often overcrowded and vulnerable to epidemics, sailed to America and England.

    C. A total of 1.5 million Irish went to America in 1845–1855, 300,000 to England, and another 300,000 to Canada.

    D. The British government, first under Tory Robert Peel, then under Whig John Russell, escalated public relief efforts.

        1. Unsympathetic bureaucrats in England, obedient to the prevailing market theory, prevented fast plentiful aid from being sent.

        2. Instead, they set up public works schemes that were not properly planned and that most Irish were too sick and weak to take advantage of.

        3. By early 1847, three million Irish people were on direct relief, being given food from local soup kitchens.

        4. The recurrence of crop failure in 1848 worsened an already desperate situation.

    E. Some Irish nationalists denounced the British response as callously indifferent.

    F. Historians debate the issue; some believe that the English did a great deal, considering that they had never encountered a similar situation before.

G. Irish-Americans continue to recall the famine in their indictment of Britain.

IV. The Irish famine coincided with a debate in Britain over free trade or protectionism.

    A. The Corn Laws protected British landowners against imports of cheap grain unless the domestic price was high. The policy favored landowners and support for it was central to Tory orthodoxy.

    B. Manufacturers, whose growing influence had been demonstrated in the Great Reform Act, favored low tariff barriers and a free-trade policy.

        1. They believed, correctly, that free trade would give them a competitive advantage in foreign markets.

        2. Working-class people would benefit from free trade by enjoying cheaper food and abundant work.

    C. Tory Prime Minister Robert Peel was the son of a Lancashire textile manufacturer and understood the appeal of the free traders' arguments.

        1. The Anti-Corn-Law League, led by Richard Cobden (1804–1865) and John Bright (1811–1889), pressured Peel's government in the early 1840s to repeal the laws.

        2. Bright believed that strong trade links (assisted by the absence of tariffs) would lessen the likelihood of wars between nations.

        3. The Irish crisis convinced Peel that the Corn Laws were indefensible.

    D. He finally achieved passage of the repeal, with the help of Whig and Radical votes.

        1. Within the Tory Party, Benjamin Disraeli led Peel's opponents, in speeches of venomous brilliance.

        2. The Lords also passed the repeal, led by the Duke of Wellington, but almost at once voted no confidence in Peel.

        3. The repeal of the Corn Laws represents one of the great turning points in mid 19th-century British politics. It shattered the Tory Party.

4. The Tory (Conservative) Party remained split for much of the next 20 years between a free-trade Peelite faction and a protectionist faction.

E. Ireland felt little immediate benefit from repeal because the Irish did not eat bread.

V. Throughout the 19th century, the British population rose rapidly, but that of Ireland never recovered from the famine. Eight million in 1841, it had fallen to six-and-a-half million by 1851 and continued to decline through successive censuses, because reduced fertility and high emigration forestalled population recovery.

Essential Reading:

R. F. Foster, *Modern Ireland: 1600–1972*.

Mary Daly, *Social and Economic History of Ireland Since 1800*.

Supplementary Reading:

C. Woodham-Smith, *The Great Hunger: Ireland, 1845–1849*.

Joel Mokyr, *Why Ireland Starved*.

Questions to Consider:

1. Who supported the Corn Laws, who opposed them, and why?

2. Why was the English response to the Irish famine so feeble?

Lecture Twelve—Transcript
Ireland, Famine, and Robert Peel

Britain had a large colonial empire in the 19th century and administered it better than most of their colonial rivals ran theirs. However, its closest and oldest colony, Ireland, was a standing challenge to the idea that Britain was a benign and enlightened master. Historian Paul Johnson, in a very memorable quote, says that Ireland was like Banquo's ghost at Macbeth's banquet, a standing refutation of the idea that Britain was good at governing other people.

It was a source of perpetual unrest. It had a very poor, resentful peasant population and had social antagonisms that were intensified by a sharp religious divide, because the majority of the Irish people were Roman Catholics.

In 1846, it suffered a catastrophic harvest failure in its one principle crop, potatoes. This threatened millions of people with starvation. British governmental aid to Ireland rose sharply in response to this crisis. However, it didn't rise sharply enough and couldn't prevent a very high death toll as well as a very high rate of emigration to Britain and America. Thus, the consequences of this catastrophe continue to be felt right up to the present.

It was one of things which contributed to the Tory Prime Minister Robert Peel deciding that it was necessary for him to repeal the government's protectionist policy as a way of encouraging importation of cheap food. However, in taking this decision, he split his own political party. Most of those members were desperately opposed to that kind of measure.

British involvement in Ireland had always been a source of friction. No matter how far back in history you go, you find recurrent and severe tensions. The earliest English intervention in Ireland begins back in the reign of Henry II, in the 12th century, and it intensified after the Reformation, particularly in the reign of Queen Elizabeth I, when a series of expeditions under Sir Walter Raleigh and others tried to bring more of the island of Ireland under the direct control of the British crown. Until then, the city of Dublin and the area immediately surrounding it was called the "Pale," the Palish Settlement, of which Britain was really in control. You probably know the saying "beyond the pale." That means going out beyond the place where the fact of British administration in Ireland ceased. It was one of his roles to try to extend that.

Probably one of the most dramatic Anglo-English confrontations came during the period of the British civil wars of the 1640s and 1650s. Oliver Cromwell, one of leaders of the Parliamentary armies in the British civil wars, suppressed an Irish rebellion between 1649 and 1651. He did it with terrifying thoroughness. Probably the most notorious episode of this war was his massacre of the inhabitants of Drogheda when they refused to surrender. Cromwell said to the people, "You can surrender now and I'll spare you, but if you continue to hold out I'll kill the lot of you." He claimed that this was in accordance with the rules of warfare at the time. It was simultaneous with the Thirty Years' War in Europe. The city refused to surrender, and, when it was captured, he massacred the inhabitants.

Now, one of Oliver Cromwell's great problems in the British civil wars was that the army he commanded, the new model army, probably one of the most effective fighting forces in Europe at the time, was that it was impossible to pay it. Although it had won, he couldn't persuade Parliament to raise sufficient money to pay off the army. Instead, Parliament paid them in Irish lands.

Earlier in the 17th century, in 1609, when King James I, the first of the Stuart kings, was on the throne, Protestant settlements in the Ulster counties of northeastern Ireland had created a local Protestant majority there. Protestant numbers were now increased in other parts of Ireland, which led to the foundations for the interreligious antagonisms; these are still not fully resolved there even today.

Ireland remained Catholic at the Reformation, and when, in the 1680s, King James II tried to bring the whole of Britain back into the Catholic fold, he failed catastrophically and was forced to abdicate. However, it was Catholic Ireland who was loyal to him, and, when King James II was replaced by King William III, William III had to fight a battle of the Boyne in Ireland against the Catholic army, which had French assistance. The fact that William III won made the Battle of the Boyne a symbolic moment of the triumph of Protestantism over Roman Catholicism. That, again, is an event, which is still commemorated in Ireland right up to the present. Every year, the Orange Parades, which take place among the Ulster

Protestants, in which they glory in the reminiscence of this battle, is a source of community friction.

In the early 19th century, the period we're concerned with here, the Catholic majority, most of them very poor, lived on lands most of which were owned by Protestant landlords. Many of them didn't live there; it was very common for the Protestant landlords to live in England, rather than Ireland, and simply to enjoy the rent which came to them from their estates. An example of this would be Lord Palmerston, who was one of the Whig prime ministers in the middle of the century.

Most of these landowners would have a local agent who ran the estates for them and collected the rent. They very often profited by subdividing the farmland without notifying the owner of what was going on. It was common for these absentee owners not even to know how many tenants they'd actually got living and working on land that they owned. One absentee went in 1846 to investigate his own estates, and he thought he'd got 60 tenants. When he got there, he found that he had something like 600, 10 times as many as his agents had let him know.

This was a situation in which national agricultural improvement, scientific farming, was very difficult to accomplish. The subdivisions of the lands made the plots too small. Besides, if you were a tenant farmer, you were constantly in danger of being evicted by the landlord. You could be evicted without getting any recourse and without being compensated for improvements you might have made. Thus, in that situation, you were unlikely to invest very heavily in improvements to the land, whose benefits you'd never enjoy.

Landlords who did attempt agricultural improvements were also vulnerable to attacks by secret societies. Throughout 19th-century Ireland, there were secret societies that sometimes would attack landlords who tried to evict their tenants, such as the "White Boys," or the "Ribbon Men." Therefore, most of these landlords didn't bother. They accepted the rents that the estates would generate and lived in England on the proceeds. Consequently, there was an enormous social, economic, and geographical distance between tenants and landlords.

The fact that the Church of Ireland, that is, the established church, was a Protestant church, which had to be paid for through taxation on all of the Catholic people, was a great grievance. If you were Catholic, you paid taxes to the state church, which you didn't belong to, as well as the Catholic church that you did belong to. It 1823, an association was founded called the "Catholic Association." It was led by a very charismatic lawyer, a very eloquent courtroom lawyer, called Daniel O'Connell. He led the campaign for Catholic emancipation, that is, the right for Roman Catholics to sit in Parliament. Some Catholics in Ireland already had limited voting rights, beginning in the 1790s. The Catholics were prevented by law from sitting in Parliament.

Members of the Catholic Association would pay a weekly penny for their membership. This was called "the Catholic rent." That meant that the Association was well funded, especially in view of the poverty of much of the country at the time. It campaigned very hard and very effectively for the abolition of all laws restricting Catholics from participation in political life.

O'Connell himself was not a revolutionary figure. He was a great admirer of the British constitution in many of its aspects. He certainly believed in due process, like all lawyers. He simply said, "At the moment, the walls of exclusion are keeping us out when we ought to be admitted." He put the political system to the test in 1828 by standing for a seat in Parliament. In America, you run for office, and in Britain you stand.

He stood for Parliament in County Clare. Thousands of people turned out and voted for him, with the result that he won the seat, even though he wasn't actually eligible to take it, because he was a Roman Catholic. In other words, he deliberately created a constitutional impasse.

Under these circumstances, the Parliament in London had to decide how to respond. The Prime Minister, the Duke of Wellington, although he wasn't any great enthusiast for Roman Catholics, realized that it was necessary to yield, because, if not, he was in danger of facing a Catholic rebellion in Ireland itself. Therefore, the Duke of Wellington guided through Parliament legislation to remove these disabilities on Roman Catholics.

One of the members of his own Tory Party, Lord Winchell's seat, was so enraged that the Duke of Wellington should be doing this that he charged him to a duel. This was just in the very last days of dueling in the British aristocracy. It was already illegal, but it was still practiced. Wellington accepted the challenge, and the two men met in a London field. We think that they both deliberately missed; they didn't make serious attempts to shoot one another, but honor could be satisfied in that way, and then he could go back to Parliament and resume his work.

Tory anger, concerted anger, came from the village that I mentioned earlier in one of lectures on religion. Catholicism was equivalent to treason, because the French and the Spanish, England's traditional Catholic enemies, had so often used the Irish Catholics against England. The Boyne, for example, was one of many cases. In addition, of course, the Tories recognized that if Catholics could sit in Parliament, it might mean that the Irish members of Parliament, who until then themselves had all been Protestants because of the law, the MPs might end up being Catholics instead. If that were true, the entire complexion of political life in Ireland would be changed. There was still no secret ballot at this point, but nevertheless the possibility of Catholic members now arose.

The legislation was passed—Catholic emancipation. This was one of the acts that also led to the protest of the Oxford movement in the Church of England against an idea that Catholics were now going to be participating, potentially, in the conduct of the Church of England. While only a minority of the more prosperous Catholics in Ireland had the right to vote even after this, nevertheless it was, symbolically, an important victory.

Historian Alvin Jackson writes this about it: "Emancipation was a Catholic victory, planned by Catholic leadership and won on the playing field of the Protestant constitution. The matter was passed not out of the magnanimity of the Wellington government but because that government feared, and was seen to fear, the consequences of resistance." In other words, if you were a Catholic Irishman, you could easily learn from that experience that concentrated political pressure was effective.

Ireland was very different from England, in this sense, but while the industrialization of the island of Great Britain was roaring along in the early 19th century, Ireland was not going through an industrial revolution. Instead, it remained overwhelmingly agricultural.

However, its population was rising. In fact, it was rising even faster than that of England. By the early 1840s, the population was over eight million, at a time when the population of the rest of Britain was about 15 million. Population pressure meant that emigration from Ireland was already quite common. A steady stream of Irish people had been going to America starting in the 1820s. Population pressure meant that people who stayed in Ireland tended to be very poor, living on these small plots, which I mentioned earlier, very often in houses which amounted to little more than mud huts and often with the farm animals living inside the house with the family.

Their chief source of food was potatoes. Before Christopher Columbus, there weren't any potatoes in Europe because the potato was a New World crop. It was discovered by Columbus's generation and brought to Europe. It was found to thrive in European conditions, particularly in a place like Ireland, which is never very hot and is very wet, a mild, damp, Atlantic climate. Thus, potatoes had become a staple crop of the majority of the Irish people. From a purely nutritional point of view, if your whole diet is going to be confined to one thing, potato is actually a very good thing for it to be confined to. It has a lot of nutritional value.

The great problem with growing just one crop, what's called a "monoculture," is that not only do you create ideal conditions for the crop to grow, you also create ideal conditions for predators on that crop. In other words, if a disease affecting the crop comes along, there isn't a diversity of crops to break spread of this disease. It was in 1843 that the potato blight was first discovered in America and spread very rapidly to Ireland, where it began to afflict the potato crop. It damaged the crop in 1845, damaged it much, much worse in 1846, and then again in 1848. This meant that suddenly millions of the Irish people were dramatically denied their one basic food staple. It's a fungus, and it's like other infestations. Because it had never been previously seen, it was unpredictable, unforeseeable, literally.

The Irish suffering that ensued from 1846 to 1850 was unprecedented. It greatly intensified Anglo-Irish bitterness. It's certainly something that has never been forgotten. Even people who had been hardened by scenes of English poverty, which I've described to you recently, were absolutely horrified by the scenes of death and starvation which they witnessed in many parts, particularly of Western Ireland, and then by the epidemic diseases which ravaged the weakened survivors. You're much more likely to die from cholera, dysentery, or typhoid if you've already been weakened by malnutrition.

This is a quote from a magistrate in the village of Skibbereen, in County Cork: "Being aware that I should have to witness scenes of frightful hunger, I provided myself with as much bread as five men could carry, and on reaching the spot I was surprised to find the wretched hamlet apparently deserted. I entered some of the homes to ascertain the cause, and the scenes which presented themselves were such as no tongue or pen can convey the slightest idea of.

In the first, six famished and ghastly skeletons, to all appearances dead, were huddled in the corner on some filthy straw, their wretched legs hanging about, naked above the knees. I approached with horror and found, by a low moaning, that they were alive. In a few moments, I was surrounded by at least 200 such phantoms, such frightful specters as no words can describe, either from famine or from fever. Their demonic yells are still ringing in my ears and their horrible images affixed upon my brain."

It was under these circumstances that anyone who could possibly afford to do so tried to emigrate. Huge numbers of people left Ireland altogether. About a million people, maybe even 1.5 million, went to the United States of America. At least 300,000 went to Canada, another 300,000 to England, and so on. There was a very, very rapid dispersal of refugees from the famine.

The British government itself, under the leadership of Robert Peel, the Tory Prime Minister, and then, after his fall in 1846, under Lord John Russell, quickly tried to escalate public relief efforts. However, this is only shortly after the passage of the legislation to create the workhouses. At first, the government said, "We've got a poverty relief scheme in place already, the workhouse scheme. It will have to take care of the problem." It wasn't long before the workhouses were completely swamped, and more drastic measures were necessary.

Even so, unsympathetic bureaucrats in England, unaware of the magnitude of the disaster and obedient to prevailing economic and political theories, resisted the idea that they should send massive quantities of food just to be distributed without reckoning to the suffering Irish people. They jockeyed about giving it away, and they didn't really think that famine relief was the government's job.

They'd never faced a crisis of such magnitude before, and they were fumbling for an appropriate response.

They set up public works schemes, with the idea that they'd pay a man about ten pence per day for his work. Of course, however, many of the weakest sufferers were simply incapable of working. They were literally on the brink of death from malnutrition and couldn't do vigorous manual labor of the kind that the government was offering. Thus, a lot of these schemes, which ran for a few months, had to be abandoned, because they couldn't find sufficient numbers of appropriate people to work in them. The Irish historian, Roy Foster, describes: "The celebrated piers, where no boats could land, were walls built around nothing, and the roads to nowhere." He says, "These are poignant reminders for policy that was neither consistent nor effective, which expressed economic beliefs held by the governing classes in both countries."

Gradually, the magnitude of the disaster started to be more fully appreciated. The case for direct aid became irresistible. In February of 1847, Parliament passed an act called the "Temporary Relief Act." It began shipping food directly to areas of Ireland where it could be distributed. In early 1847, three million Irish people—that's something close to half the population—were on direct relief, were being fed directly with food distributed at soup kitchens.

If you were a landowner on any scale, you weren't eligible for food handouts, and there were cases of people giving up their land, literally giving it away, so that they would become eligible for this food relief to be able to survive at all.

There's a very intense historians' controversy surrounding the British government's response to the famine. Some historians say that they were outrageously negligent. They could have done far more, more quickly and more effectively. Other historians say, "No, what's striking isn't how little they did but how much they did. They'd never encountered an event like this before. They'd never faced the potential starvation of millions. It's surprising that they did as much as they did. It was actually quite an administrative achievement."

I can't quite sort out the rights and wrongs about something that takes entire historians' careers and can still bring people to different answers. Certainly, from our point of view, what's so striking is how ghastly the whole situation was. The recurrence of the crop failure in 1848, the fact that the blight continued to afflict the crops, meant that there wasn't an opportunity for a rapid recovery.

Certainly, Irish nationalists themselves, people who wanted to get altogether out of the British Empire, reckoned that the British response was callously indifferent. The editor of a newspaper called the *United Irishman*, a man named John Mitchell, said, "The Almighty, indeed, sent the potato blight, but the English created the famine." Irish Americans, Irishmen who had already gone to America or who emigrated during the famine, continued to recall it as a central element in their indictment of Great Britain.

As recently as 1996, the New York State Board of Regents required schools in the state of New York to teach the episode of the Irish famine as an example of British genocide. Now, I think that's grotesquely unfair. Nothing on that scale had ever happened before. Nobody was ready for it, and certainly the intention of the British government was not to kill the Irish people. They'd merely been negligent in reacting to the suffering, but at least the intention was not one of mass extermination. Thus, "genocide" is the wrong word for it. Nevertheless, it's true that the officials didn't do as much as they might have done in view of an event of this scale. The death toll all together from famine and disease probably amounted to more than a million people, depending on how the figures accounted.

The Irish famine coincided with a debate in Britain over free trade, or protectionism. At that time, a set of laws was in place, the Corn Laws, which protected British landowners against the imports of cheap food from abroad. If you were a landowner in England, this was ideal. What it meant was that food you grew could be sold at a good high price. If the price became very high due to scarcity, those imports from abroad would come in. If you were a Tory landowner, you thought the Corn Laws were marvelous.

Conversely, manufacturers, whose growing influence was demonstrated by the passage of the Great Reform Act and other pieces of legislation, wanted low tariff barriers, or the elimination of tariffs altogether, to create a free trade policy. They could foresee that if Britain didn't have import and export duties—they could mass-produce goods, and sell them cheaply abroad, and they'd be paid for with the cheap imports of foods. That would mean that the price of food for their employees would go down, would take pressure off them to increase wages, and would generally increase the favorable conditions in which trade would operate. Thus, manufacturers had a free trade policy, by and large, and farmers had a protectionist policy.

The Tory Prime Minister, Robert Peel, was in a very awkward position. He was himself the son of a Lancaster textile manufacturer, and he understood the appeal of the manufacturers' arguments. In fact, probably privately, he had already been converted to the belief that they were right. However, he represented the Tory Party, was the leader of the party, most of whose members were protectionists, people who wanted to keep the import duties.

It was Peel, incidentally, who had antagonized Queen Victoria in the "Bedchamber Crisis." Do you remember this? It was when, a few years previously, he'd wanted to substitute his officials for hers, for Lord Melbourne's, when the government changed.

He was, in some ways, a rather stiff and diffident man. The Irish leader, O'Connell, himself, had a marvelous remark about him. He said, "Robert Peel's smile was like the silver plate on a coffin." He was not an instantly likable man.

He was feeling the pressure from an organization called the Anti-Corn Law League, which had been founded back in 1839 by Richard Cobden and John Bright, two of the most famous radical members of Parliament of the mid 19th century. They were both manufacturers, both interested in free trade, probably because they thought they would profit from it but partly because they felt that everybody else would profit from it as well. They were bitter opponents of what looked to them like a special and undeserved privilege for the landowners. Their rhetoric had a kind of evangelical intensity: "Why is it that the landowners, who often themselves don't do any work at all, should not only live off rent but should in addition be given these high prices for the food that their tenants are generating? Their wealth is being bought at the cost of everyone else's poverty."

The Anti-Corn Law League was an early pressure group, a lobby, and its meetings had a kind of evangelical intensity to them, particularly in the northern towns. John Bright himself was a Quaker, and he believed that free trade was not only good economic policy, it was also going to ensure the peace of the world. The more closely the different nations were entangled with one another, the stronger their motives would be in not fighting. Unfortunately, we now have the experience of two world wars to tell us that strong trade links are not enough to forestall international fighting.

Certainly, one of John Bright's hopes was that close trading relations, free trade, would make war that much less likely. He said, "As long as we've got tariffs, it's difficult for us and for our manufactures abroad to import food cheaply. That means that different countries are going to have to industrialize themselves, and, instead of becoming nations with which we can have mutually advantageous trade, they're going to become competitors. In the long run, we'll suffer from it." This proved to be prophetic.

In the end, the Irish crisis did convince Peel that the Corn Laws were indefensible. They had to be repealed. On one occasion, he was listening to a very powerful speech by Richard Cobden in the House of Commons, and getting ready to answer, but found that Cobden was actually expressing views in which he himself believed. He screwed up the notes he was holding for his speech and said to Sidney Herbert, one of his ministers, "You must answer this, for I cannot." In other words, he'd finally lost all faith in the policy position of his own party.

Finally, he achieved the repeal of the Corn Laws with the help of Whig and Radical votes. The Tory Party split over this issue. Benjamin Disraeli, the rising star of some of the conservatives, led Peel's opponents in speeches of venomous brilliance, and this is one of the moments when Disraeli's future was assured as a Tory leader. Disraeli accused him of betraying the interests of the men who had elected him.

Peel himself resorted to arguments about the primacy of a Member of Parliament's conscience. He said, "However strongly I may be indebted to my party, in the end I can't do violence to my own conscience. That must come first, even if it means I'm going to be ejected from office." He could foresee that that was going to happen. On two or three occasions, intensity of the vitriol poured upon him for his views made him absolutely stunned. On a couple of occasions, whenever others left the chamber, he was left with his head in his hands. He was one of the great turning points of mid 19th-century politics.

The House of Lords passed the repeal of the Corn Laws also, even though its membership was predominantly Tory. Once again, it was the Duke of Wellington, this very levelheaded man, who pointed out to the other members of the Lords that, although it seemed deplorable, the consequences of not doing it were probably going to be even worse. It was very shortly after that, however, that Peel endured a vote of "no confidence" and fell from office. He had foreseen it. He said, "When I fall, I shall have the satisfaction of reflecting that I do not fall because I've shown subservience to a party. I shall not fall because I prefer the interests of party to the general interests of the community."

It had a shattering effect on the Conservative Party, which for about the next 20 years remained factionalized and in disarray. The mid decades of the 19th century were a period of political realignment. Many people who had originally been Peelites, Tories, like Gladstone, ended up in the Liberal Party. It wasn't really until around the 1870s that an effective Tory government once again came into office, under the leadership of Disraeli, beginning in 1874. It pitched the Tories into the political wilderness, in effect.

Ironically, Ireland itself didn't derive much direct benefit from the repeal of the Corn Laws, partly because the Irish didn't eat wheat bread. It wasn't something they were familiar with, in any case.

Well, there we are. Throughout the 19th century, the British population as a whole rose rapidly. The population of Ireland, however, never recovered from the famine. It was about eight million in 1841. It had fallen to six million by 1851, and it continued to decline through the successive censuses until the end of the century. This was partly due to reduced fertility and partly because of high emigration, which had the combined effects of forestalling a population recovery. Even today, it's not as high as it was in the early 1840s.

Quotations from Queen Victoria

From Lecture Two

Journal comments after being notified of her accession:

"Since it has pleased providence to place me in this station, I shall do my utmost to fulfill my duty towards my country; I am very young and perhaps in many, though not in all things, inexperienced, but I am sure that very few have more real good will and more real desire to do what is right than I have."

Journal, 20 June 1837, cited in *Queen Victoria in Her Letters and Journals*, Christopher Hibbert, ed., (New York: Viking, 1985), p. 23.

Letter to her uncle, King Leopold of Belgium, regarding Lord Melbourne:

"Let me pause to tell you how fortunate I am to have at the head of the Government a man like Lord Melbourne. I have seen him now every day, with the exception of Friday, and the more I see him, the more confidence I have in him; he is not only a clever statesman and an honest man, but a good and kind hearted man, whose aim is to do his duty for his country and not for a party. He is of the greatest use to me both politically and privately …It is to me the greatest pleasure to do my duty for my country and my people, and no fatigue, however great, will be burdensome to me if it is for the welfare of the nation."

25 June 1837, ibid., p. 24.

Journal comments regarding her proposal of marriage to Prince Albert:

"I said to him …that it would make me too happy if he would consent to what I wished …we embraced each other over and over again, and he was so kind, so affectionate. Oh! To feel I was, and am, loved by such an Angel as Albert was too great delight to describe. He is perfection; perfection in every way, in beauty, in everything. …I felt it was the happiest moment in my life."

15 October 1839, ibid., p. 57.

Journal comments, a few days later:

"I signed some papers and warrants, etc. and he was so kind as to dry them with blotting paper for me. We talked a good deal together and he clasped me so tenderly in his arms and kissed me again and again."

27 October 1839, ibid., p. 58.

Comment on babies:

"An ugly baby is a very nasty object, and the prettiest is frightful when undressed, till about four months; in short, as long as they have their big body and little limbs and that terrible frog-like action."

From a letter to her daughter, Princess Frederick William of Prussia (i.e., Princess Victoria who had married the German Prince), 2 May 1859, ibid., p. 112.

Letter to her uncle King Leopold regarding the Great Exhibition of 1851:

"I wish you could have witnessed the 1st May 1851, the greatest day in our history, the most beautiful and imposing and touching spectacle ever seen, and the triumph of my beloved Albert. Truly it was astonishing, a fair scene. Many cried, and all felt touched and impressed with devotional feelings. It was the happiest, proudest day of my life and I can think of nothing else. Albert's dear name is immortalized with the great conception, his own, and my own dear country showed she was worthy of it."

c. May 1851, From J. B. Priestley, *Victoria's Heyday* (New York: Harper and Row, 1972), p. 78.

Journal comments on Albert's death:

"I took his dear left hand which was already cold …and knelt down by him …All, all was over …I stood up and kissed his dear heavenly forehead and called out in a bitter and agonizing cry 'Oh my dear darling' and then dropped on my knees in mute distracted despair, unable to utter a word or shed a tear …Then I laid down on the sofa in the red room and all the gentlemen came in and knelt down and kissed my hand, and I said a word to each."

Journal, 14 December 1861, *Letters and Journals*, p. 156.

From Lecture Three

Comments from Victoria's journal, when she was 13, on her travel through "the black country":

"We just passed through a town where all coal mines are and you see the fire glimmer at a distance in the engines in many places. The men, women, children, country and houses are all black. But I cannot by any description give an idea of its strange and extraordinary appearance. The country is very desolate everywhere; there are coals about, and the grass is quite blasted and black. I just now see an extraordinary building flaming with fire. The country continues black, engines flaming, coals, in abundance, everywhere, smoking and burning coal heaps, intermingled with wretched huts and carts and little ragged children."

Journal, 2 August 1833, ibid., p. 11.

From Lecture Six

Comments on the women's rights movement:

"The queen is anxious to enlist everyone who can speak or write to join in checking this mad, wicked folly of women's rights with all its attendant horrors, on which her poor feeble sex is bent, forgetting every sense of womanly feeling and propriety. Lady Amberley ought to get a good whipping."

Cited in Joan Perkin, *Victorian Women* (London: J. Murray, 1993), p. 213.

From Lecture Eight

Journal comments on evangelical Sundays:

"I am not at all an admirer or approver of our very dull Sundays for I think the absence of innocent amusements for the poor people a misfortune and an encouragement of vice."

Cited in Christopher Hibbert, *Queen Victoria: A Personal History* (New York: Basic Books, 2000), p. 295.

From Lecture Fourteen

Comments on the Great Exhibition:

"Some of the inventions were very ingenious, many of them quite Utopian. It has taught me so much I never knew before and has brought me in contact with so many clever people I should never have known otherwise, and with so many manufacturers whom I would scarcely have met unless I travelled all over the country and visited every individual manufactory, which I could never have done."

Cited in Asa Briggs, *Iron Bridge to Crystal Palace* (London: Thames and Hudson, 1979), p. 172.

From Lecture Sixteen

Journal comments on the death of Charles Dickens:

"He had a large, loving mind and the strongest sympathy with the poorer classes. He felt sure that a better feeling, and much greater union of classes, would take place in time. And I pray earnestly it may."

In Hibbert, *Queen Victoria*, p. 396.

From Lecture Seventeen

From a letter to Lord Canning, Governor-General of India, after the Indian Mutiny, in 1858:

"…[show] the greatest kindness [to the many] 'kind and friendly natives' who had helped restore order. They should know that there is no hatred to a brown-skin tone; but the greatest wish on the queen's part to see them happy, contented, and flourishing."

Ibid, p. 250.

From Lecture Eighteen

Letter to Mrs. Lincoln after the U.S. president's assassination:

"Though a stranger to you, I cannot remain silent when so terrible a calamity has fallen upon you and your country, and must express personally my deep and heartfelt sympathy with you under the shocking circumstances of your present dreadful misfortune. No one can better appreciate than I can, who am myself utterly broken-hearted by the loss of my own beloved husband, who was the light of my life, my stay, my all, what your sufferings must be; and I earnestly pray that you may be supported by Him to Whom alone the sorely stricken can look for comfort, in this hour of heavy affliction!"

29 April 1865, in *Letters and Journals*, p. 189.

From Lecture Thirty-One

Remark made after early defeats in the Boer War:

"We are not interested in the possibilities of defeat: they do not exist."

In Gwendolyn Cecil, *Life of the Marquis of Salisbury* (London: Hodder and Stoughton, 1922), vol. 3, p. 191.

From Lecture Thirty-Five

Letter to Prime Minister Lord Russell, explaining her reluctance to open Parliament in 1866:

"The queen must say that she does feel very bitterly the want of feeling of those who ask the queen to go to open parliament. …Why this wish should be of so unreasonable and unfeeling a nature, as to long to witness the spectacle of a poor, broken-hearted widow, nervous and shrinking, dragged in deep mourning, alone in State as a Show, where she used to go supported by her husband, is a thing she cannot understand. …she resents the unfeelingness of those who have clamoured for it."

22 January 1866, in *Letters and Journals*, p. 193.

Letter to Vicky after Albert's death:

"I feel so stunned and bewildered. He protected me so that I felt safe! And now all, all is gone in this world, and all seems unhinged again in thousands of ways…The shock, the blow, the blank, the constant missing at every turn of the one strong, powerful arm and head…This anguish that comes over me like a wave…is terrible. God's will be done, but I shall never be the same again."

Cited in Hibbert, *Queen Victoria*, p. 441.

Journal comments on her Diamond Jubilee of 1897:

"a never to be forgotten day. No one ever, I believe, has met with such an ovation as was given to me, passing through those six miles of streets…The crowds were indescribable…the cheering was quite deafening and every face seemed to be filled with real joy."

Telegraph message to British Empire after her Diamond Jubilee celebration:

"From my heart I thank my beloved people. May God bless them."

22 June 1897, *Letters and Journals*, p. 335.

Timeline

1819 .... Birth of Princess Victoria.

1829 .... Catholic Emancipation (permitting Catholics to vote and sit in Parliament).

1829 .... Opening of the Liverpool and Manchester Railway.

1831 .... Cholera epidemic.

1832 .... Great Reform Act.

1833 .... Abolition of slavery in the British Empire (Caribbean Islands).

1834 .... New Poor Law establishes the workhouse system.

1834 .... Fire destroys the old Houses of Parliament. Barry and Pugin win design competition for replacement (built 1837–1867).

1834 .... The Tolpuddle Martyrs, early trade unionists, convicted and transported for conspiracy.

1837 .... Death of King William IV; Victoria becomes queen.

1838 .... I. K. Brunel's steamship *Great Western* crosses the Atlantic.

1839 .... Parliament rejects the Chartists' first petition.

1839 .... British colonial army defeated in Afghanistan.

1839 .... Foundation of the Anti-Corn-Law League by Cobden and Bright.

1840 .... Queen Victoria marries Prince Albert of Saxe-Coburg-Gotha.

1840	Rowland Hill introduces the "penny post" cheap mail.
1842	The queen travels by train from Slough to London Paddington.
1844	Chancellor Gladstone specifies cheap "parliamentary trains" with fares pegged at one penny per mile.
1845	John Henry Newman scandalizes Oxford and the Church of England by converting to Roman Catholicism.
1846	Irish famine; abolition of the Corn Laws by Parliament.
1846	Publication of Friedrich Engels's *Condition of the Working Class in England*.
1848	A wave of revolutions in Europe—Marx and Engels write *Communist Manifesto*. Third great Chartist petition.
1850	Titus Salt founds model industrial community of Saltaire.
1850	An outburst of anti-Catholic prejudice when the Pope declares the re-creation of Catholic dioceses in Britain.
1851	The Great Exhibition in Joseph Paxton's Crystal Palace, Hyde Park.
1854–1856	Crimean War (France, Britain, and Turkey fighting against Russia).
1857	The Indian Mutiny.
1858	British government takes over direct rule of India from the Honorable East India Company.

1858 ....Publication of *Self-Help* by Samuel Smiles.

1859 ....Charles Darwin's *On the Origin of Species*.

1861 ....Death of Prince Albert.

1861–1865 ....American Civil War creates crisis in British cotton textile industry.

1863 ....Opening of the world's first underground railway (London).

1866 ....The "Sheffield Outrages," in which union cutlers intimidate non-union men.

1867 ....Disraeli as prime minister; the Second Reform Act extends franchise.

1868 ....Founding of the Trades Union Congress.

1869 ....Completion of the Suez Canal transforms strategic route to India.

1871 ....Parliament legislates for universal education of children.

1871 ....Abolition of the purchase of army commissions.

1872 ....The secret ballot.

1874 ....British victory in the Ashanti War.

1875 ....Disraeli buys a share in Suez Canal.

1876 ....Disraeli makes Victoria empress of India.

1879 ....The Zulu War; defeat at Isandhlwana, heroic British defense at Rorke's Drift, and victory at Ulundi.

1882 ....Legal reform permits women to maintain control of their own property after marriage.

1884 ....Third Reform Act further extends the franchise.

1884–1885 ....Expedition fails to rescue General Gordon in Khartoum.

1886 ....Liberal Party splits over Gladstone's proposal to grant Irish Home Rule.

1888 ....Jack the Ripper kills eight prostitutes in Whitchapel, London.

1888 ....Annie Besant leads the London match factory girls on strike.

1889 ....London dockyard workers' strike, arbitrated in the workers' favor by the popular Cardinal Henry Manning (another Catholic convert).

1892 ....Keir Hardie, first independent Labour Member of Parliament, takes his seat.

1896 ....Failure of the Jameson Raid provokes a crisis in South Africa.

1897 ....Queen Victoria's Golden Jubilee celebrations.

1899 ....Beginning of Boer War with humiliating British defeats.

1901 ....The Taff Vale Case stimulates TUC to create the Labour Party.

1901 ....Death of Queen Victoria.

Glossary

Anti-Corn-Law League: Richard Cobden and John Bright's pro-free trade, anti-protectionist lobby (founded 1839) whose objective was achieved in 1846 when Peel's Tory government defied much of its core constituency and repealed the laws.

Celtic fringe: An English politician's name for Scotland, Wales, Ireland, and (sometimes) the southwestern counties of England.

Chartism: The popular movement of the 1830s and 1840s, in the wake of the First Reform Act (1832), to achieve further reforms of Parliament, including universal manhood suffrage, secret ballot, equal electoral districts, payment of MPs, annual parliament, and abolition of property qualifications for MPs. Led by Fergus O'Connor, it presented petitions to Parliament in 1838, 1842, and 1848 but achieved no effective reforms.

Dissenter: A person who did not belong to the established Church of England. The word (and the word "nonconformist") was usually used of members of the Protestant sects, including Quakers, Presbyterians, Congregationalists, Seventh Day Adventists, and Baptists.

Establishment: The state-run Church of England was the established church. In the 19th century, however, "establishment" also came to mean the central elements of the government and the state and the institutions that supported them.

Evangelical: A member of the Church of England or one of the Protestant sects who had adopted the emotional idiom of a personal relationship with Christ and was involved in the attempt at national moral regeneration.

Evolution: The theory that human beings had developed from simpler organisms over an immense period of time. Charles Darwin's influential *On the Origin of Species by Natural Selection* (1859) codified evolutionary ideas and their compatibility with biological and geological evidence.

Free trade: Trade between nations unhampered by import and export duties. Britain, the world's first industrial nation, believed it would benefit from free trade and abolished most of its duties in the 1840s and 1850s, despite opposition from the landed gentry in the Tory Party.

Gothic: One of the architectural styles favored by many Victorians and exhibited in Parliament and many Victorian churches and civic buildings. It aimed at reviving the glories of medieval cathedral architecture.

Home Rule: The aim of the Irish Nationalist Party in the 1870s and 1880s was an Irish government but still inside the British Empire. Gladstone's decision to support it in 1886 broke the Liberal party into Home Rule and Unionist factions.

Imperialist: A supporter of an enlarged empire-building mission for Britain. Disraeli tried to make the Conservative Party self-consciously imperialist in the 1870s.

Industrialization: The process of concentrating and mechanizing manufacture on a large scale. In Britain, it was accompanied by the use of water and steam power and intense urbanization.

Mudlark: A London child who made a living by dredging metal, glass, and pottery scraps out of the Thames at low tide.

New Poor Law: The legislation of 1834 that created the workhouses. It was intended to be uniform throughout the country, to be economical for taxpayers, and to have a deterrent effect so that poor people would avoid appealing for help unless they were absolutely destitute. It was widely hated and feared by the English poor and satirized by Dickens and other writers.

Oxford movement: The attempt in the 1830s and 1840s by a group of Oxford dons to reinvigorate the Church of England, emphasizing its supernatural origins rather than its role as a department of state. Led by John Keble, Hurrell Froude, and John Newman, the movement scandalized "broad church" Anglicans when, in 1844, Newman (and others under his influence) became Roman Catholic.

Pre-Raphaelite: The artistic movement of the 1840s and 1850s that aimed to recapture the purity of early Renaissance art (i.e., before the era of Raphael). Artists in the movement included Millais, Rossetti, Holman Hunt, and Burne-Jones.

Radical: In the early Victorian era, supporters of free trade and political reform in a democratic direction. In the late Victorian era, the word began to carry connotations of socialism.

Rotten borough: A Parliamentary constituency with few or no electors and effectively in the hands of a landowning patron, who could appoint his client. The Reform Act of 1832 abolished more than 60 of them.

Sepoy: An Indian soldier in the service of the Honorable East India Company.

Thirty-Nine Articles: The list of doctrinal Christian principles drawn up under Queen Elizabeth I to which all clergy in the Church of England were required (by an act of Parliament, 1571) to subscribe. Designed to exclude Roman Catholics on the "right" and radical Protestants on the "left," the articles were intended to define a broad middle ground of Anglicanism and be as inclusive as possible.

Tory: A member of one of the two main political parties. Tories were mainly country gentlemen whose income came from rents and the sale of grain. They generally supported the Corn Laws and opposed Peel's repeal of them in 1846, which temporarily shattered the party. By the late 19th century, under Disraeli, the party had adopted the name "Conservative" instead, but Tory remained (and remains today) a widely used nickname.

Trade union: An organization of working people whose collective strength enables them to bargain effectively over wages, hours, and working conditions with their employers.

Uitlander: The Boer name for a non-Boer living and working in the Transvaal or the Orange Free State in the years before the Boer War. British dissatisfaction with the Boers' treatment of *Uitlanders* sparked the bloody Boer War (1899–1902).

Unionist: A supporter of the union between Britain and Ireland. In the late 19th and early 20th centuries, the Conservatives used "Unionist" as an alternative title. Unionism of this sort is unconnected with trade unionism.

Utilitarianism: The philosophical position associated with Jeremy Bentham and John Mill, which argues that a society should aim to achieve the greatest good for the greatest number of people. Highly influential among the early Victorians, it was criticized by evangelical Christians for its down-to-earth approach and by Mill's son John Stuart Mill for its neglect of minority rights.

Biographical Notes

Isambard K. Brunel (1806–1859). Premier Victorian engineer and railway and ship builder. Brunel, son of an emigre French inventor, grew up surrounded by engineering projects. His father, Marc, struggled to build the first tunnel beneath the River Thames, with his son as project manager. The young Brunel himself designed the Clifton Suspension Bridge, still standing across the Clifton gorge in Bristol, and in 1833, won the contract to design and build the 118-mile Great Western Railway from London to Bristol. Parliament passed the necessary legislation in 1835, and Brunel finished the project in another six years, building, among many other innovative structures, the longest tunnel in the country at Box, between Bath and Chippenham. This railway's seven-foot gauge deviated from the standard four feet, eight-and-a-half inches of other British railways, but its trains were more comfortable. Brunel was also an innovative shipbuilder and his paddle-wheeler *Great Western* (1838) was the first steamship to cross the Atlantic Ocean. Each of its two successors, the propellor-driven *Great Britain* (1845) and the *Great Eastern* (1858) marked a quantum leap in size and sophistication over all predecessors. The 700-foot-long *Great Eastern* could sail from Britain to Australia without refueling. Brunel, always a ruthless, tactless, work-obsessed overachiever, died just after its launch.

Edwin Chadwick (1800–1890). Civil servant, utilitarian, and poverty reformer who can be seen as a great benefactor of the poor but was hated by them in his own lifetime. Born and raised in the new industrial city of Manchester, Chadwick studied law in London and befriended the leading utilitarian philosophers Bentham and Mill. He became a member of a royal commission on poverty in 1832 and ultimately wrote a large part of its report, on which the New Poor Law was based. Working-class people loathed him for organizing the harsh workhouses on which the law depended and his fanatical and inflexible personality made him an easy target for satirists and critics. His next report (1842), written after he had discovered how high was the demand for workhouse places, showed that the nation's public health and wealth were menaced by poor sanitation. The Whig government of Lord John Russell responded to it with passage of a Public Health Act six years later and appointed Chadwick Commissioner of the Board of Health. He lost the job in

1854 when Home Secretary Lord Palmerston recognized that he was the focus of too much dislike to remain viable in office. Even in his retirement, Chadwick remained an immensely influential figure and advisor on projects of urban and civil service reform.

Richard Cobden (1804–1865). Reformer and free-trade advocate who led the Anti-Corn-Law League. Cobden, the son of a poor Sussex farmer, was raised by unkind Yorkshire relatives and went to work as a teenager in the textile business. His hard work and skill enabled him to start his own company at age 24, selling fabrics in London. Its rapid success made him wealthy. Cobden devoted his fortune to traveling throughout the world, then to campaigning successfully for a seat in Parliament, which he entered in 1841. An admirer of the United States, he believed Britain should become a democracy, too, and advocated the principle of universal manhood suffrage. He also believed that flourishing trade between nations helped to create wealth and prevent war.

The Corn Laws then in effect were designed to exclude foreign food from coming in to Britain, which gave a large economic advantage to British farmers. These laws, however, made it more difficult for British companies to export their manufactured wares, while forcing working-class people to pay more for their food than they would have had to under free-trade conditions. By 1845, the Anti-Corn-Law League, of which Cobden and his fellow orator John Bright were the leaders, was the most well organized lobby in Britain.

Parliament seemed unlikely to repeal the laws because most of its members represented landowners. However, the catastrophic Irish famine of 1846 forced Tory Prime Minister Robert Peel to recognize that Britain must have access to cheap and plentiful foreign food supplies at once. He defied many of his own party's members to repeal the Corn Laws, crowning Cobden's campaign with success. In later years, Cobden campaigned against British intervention in the Crimean War and continued to advocate free-trade policies.

Charles Darwin (1809–1882). Biologist and evolutionary theorist whose *On the Origin of Species* (1859) was one of the most important books of the 19th century. Born in Shropshire, Darwin was raised by a sister after his mother's death when he was eight. He would not devote himself to formal studies of medicine or theology but loved to collect plants and animals. His skills as a biologist led to his appointment on a navy expedition to South America on *HMS Beagle* from 1831–1836. There, he collected and studied exhaustively, notably on the Galapagos Islands, where he noticed small variations in species from one island to the next. His discoveries, when coupled with his reading of Lyell's geology and Malthus on population, helped him develop the theory of evolution by natural selection. Scattered theorists before Darwin had proposed the idea of evolution, but he was the first to find a viable mechanism that could explain the intricacy of the natural world. Knowing that a fellow biologist, Alfred Russell Wallace, was developing similar ideas, Darwin published his *Origin* in 1859, and it quickly became the center of an intense debate, both among biologists and among theologians, who recognized (and sometimes feared) its challenge to the creation story in Genesis. His later book, *The Descent of Man* (1871), specified what the first had left implicit: Mankind, too, was part of the evolutionary process. Darwin, despite suffering most of his life from Chagas's disease, first acquired in South America, wrote copiously on corals, orchids, insects, worms, plant breeding, and other biological issues.

Charles Dickens (1812–1870). Premier novelist of Victorian Britain. Born in Portsmouth and raised in London and Kent, Dickens's schooling was incomplete, because he was forced to go to work at a shoe-polish factory when his father was imprisoned for debt. Later, he became a court and parliamentary reporter and mastered high-speed shorthand. His first fiction, *Pickwick Papers*, serialized in 1836, was an instant success and made him famous throughout the English-speaking world. He went on to edit *Bentley's Miscellany* and, later, *Household Words*, monthly journals in which most of his subsequent 18 novels were serialized. Among his most famous books are the semi-autobiographical *David Copperfield* (1850); *Oliver Twist* (1839), with its attack on the New Poor Law and its picture of the London underworld; and the historical *Tale of Two Cities* (1859), set in the era of the French Revolution. Dickens toured the United States in 1842, speaking on behalf of an international copyright law and reading from his novels. His marriage to Catherine Hogarth produced ten children, but he abandoned her in 1858 in favor of Ellen Ternan, an actress from the traveling theater company he had founded 10 years before. His fiction is high-spirited, melodramatic, sentimental, and often highly satirical, providing a superb window onto many facets of Victorian life.

Benjamin Disraeli (1804–1881). Prime minister and founder of the modern Conservative Party. Disraeli, son of a Jewish convert to Anglicanism, was an unlikely man to succeed in British politics; it was even more surprising that he should rise to the leadership of the Conservatives, the party of the old landowning gentlemen. He did not go to one of the venerable public schools, nor to college. Instead, he traveled around Europe as a young dandy, ran up debts, enjoyed love affairs, and wrote a succession of novels that won him sympathetic notice among the upper classes. Entering Parliament as a Tory in 1837 after four unsuccessful attempts, Disraeli broke with his party leader, Sir Robert Peel, over the repeal of the Corn Laws in 1846. By the late 1840s, his organizational, oratorical, and parliamentary skills had pitched him into leadership of the protectionist Tory remnant in the House of Commons; he remained the leader of this minority throughout most of the 1850s and 1860s. Disraeli also made the most of brief intervals in office, as chancellor in 1852 and, finally, prime minister (briefly) in 1867, during which time he supervised the broadening of the electorate in the Second Reform Act. His victory in the 1874 election finally enabled him to dominate national affairs, which he did until 1880. His administration created a new mood of imperial pride, symbolized by his creation of Queen Victoria as empress of India, aggressive colonial expansion in Africa, and his purchase of a share in the Suez Canal.

William Gladstone (1809–1898). Liberal Party leader and four-time prime minister in the late Victorian era. Born to a wealthy Liverpool merchant, Gladstone was educated at Eton and Oxford and began his parliamentary career as an ardent Tory. He supported Peel on Corn-Law reform in 1846, an event that split the Tories, and in the late 1840s and 1850s, joined coalition governments under Whig leadership. Gladstone's skill as a parliamentary manager and orator led to his appointment as Whig (or Liberal) leader in the House of Commons in 1865, and by 1868, he was undisputed party leader, taking over the premiership when his party won that year's election. His administration introduced the secret ballot in 1871 and a national education act. Defeated by Disraeli's Conservatives in 1874, Gladstone spent his spare time writing books on religion and the classics and tried to "rescue" prostitutes from the London streets. He returned to national leadership in 1880, having demonstrated that he was skilled at appealing to the newly expanded electorate. His government extended votes to most working-class men by the Third Reform Act of 1884 and shocked conventional English opinion in 1886 by supporting the idea of Home Rule for Ireland. He lost an election fought largely over this issue but became prime minister yet again, at the age of 82, in 1892. His renewed attempt to introduce Irish Home Rule was defeated in the House of Lords, and he resigned in 1894.

Charles George Gordon (1833–1885). Soldier, imperial administrator, and evangelical Christian, who became the focus of world attention during the siege of Khartoum in 1885. While still a junior army officer in his early twenties, Gordon served with distinction in the Crimean War (where Britain's French allies awarded him the Legion of Honour). He moved to China and took command of the "Ever-Victorious Army" in the Taiping Rebellion and wars between 1860 and 1864. Fearless and always willing to lead his soldiers in person, Gordon became a respected commander of native troops in different parts of (and beyond) the British Empire. In 1873, seconded to the Khedive of Egypt, he worked as governor of the Sudan, where he struggled to impose elementary order and stamp out the Arab-African slave trade, policies that had largely succeeded by 1880.

At odds with the British government, which took direct control of Egypt in the early 1880s, Gordon resigned. However, the uprising of Mohamma Ahmed, a Dervish who was acclaimed in Sudan as a messiah, or "Mahdi," threatened Egypt's southern border. The failure of two Egyptian campaigns to suppress Ahmed led to Prime Minister Gladstone's decision to send Gordon, who knew the area better than any other Briton, to evacuate the Sudanese capital, Khartoum, in January 1884. On his arrival, however, Gordon fortified the city instead and tried to inspire its garrison to hold out against the Mahdi. Pressure of public opinion in Britain, which regarded Gordon as a Christian hero, forced the reluctant Gladstone to send a relief column under General Garnet Wolseley to his rescue. This slow-moving army arrived just too late to prevent the Mahdi's force from overrunning Khartoum. Gordon's death there, about which heroic legends soon grew up, made him a martyr to Christian imperial idealists.

James Keir Hardie (1856–1915). The first independent Labour Party MP. Born illegitimately in Scotland, Hardie grew up in desperate poverty and was forced to become a coal miner at the age of eleven. Self-educated as a teenager, he began organizing a trade union in his early twenties and led a strike in 1880. As ringleader, he was fired, but he became an organizer of the Ayrshire Miners' Union and, from there, rose rapidly to leadership of the Scottish Miners' Federation. Hardie's political beliefs were a mixture of socialism, pacifism, and Christianity; he became convinced that the ill-treated workingmen of Britain could not rely on Gladstone's Liberal Party but should form an independent political party of their own. Elected to Parliament in 1892, Hardie caused a sensation by arriving at Parliament in a tweed suit and cloth cap rather than the traditional morning dress. He formed the Independent Labour Party the next year and advocated a succession of controversial workers' issues in Parliament. Defeated in 1895, he remained a popular and charismatic speaker and played a key role in convening the Labour Representation Committee (1900), which developed into the modern Labour Party. He returned to Parliament that year as one of two MPs and witnessed the party's power jump to 29 seats, then 40, in the next two elections. He was not a particularly talented party manager, however, and many of his fellow MPs disagreed with his belief that women should be allowed to vote and that Britain ought not to take part in the First World War.

Charles Lyell (1797–1875). Leading Victorian geologist, whose work on the antiquity of the earth and the gradual nature of change over long periods of time was adopted by Darwin in his development of evolutionary theory. Lyell, the eldest of ten children born to an enthusiastic naturalist, was raised in comfortable circumstances, half in Scotland, half in England, and studied at Oxford to become a lawyer. His hobby, geology, became an obsession, however, and he devoted most of his adult life to geological fieldwork, coupled with extensive writings. The orthodox geological opinion in Lyell's youth was that the earth was a few thousand years old (as biblical chronologies suggested) and that its distinctive valleys, caves, cliffs, and mountains had been formed by catastrophic events, such as Noah's flood. Lyell theorized, to the contrary, that the same forces acting gradually in his own day, such as deposition and erosion, had always acted, transforming the world slowly and almost imperceptibly over tens of millions of years. His close study of exposed rock strata in cliffs, and the different fossils they contained, led Lyell to argue that extinction was a natural and continuing process. He traveled widely through Europe and North America, finally explaining his findings according to his new "uniformitarian" theory in *Principles of Geology* (1830–1833), part of which Darwin read en route to the Galapagos Islands. Widely admired in his own day, Lyell was knighted by Queen Victoria in 1848. Despite the importance of his work to Darwin, with whom he was on friendly terms, Lyell himself was distressed by the challenge that evolutionary theory presented to his Christian faith.

John Stuart Mill (1806–1873). Child prodigy, utilitarian philosopher, and advocate of women's rights. The son of a distinguished philosopher, Mill was educated by his father to an incredible standard at an early age, mastering Greek, Latin, and mathematics before the age of ten—an education brilliantly evoked in his autobiography. An influential journalist among the London radicals, Mill supported all the advanced causes of the early Victorian age: parliamentary reform, the abolition of slavery, women's rights, and justice for Irish farmers. However, he went through a crisis of confidence when he recognized that if all these hoped-for reforms were accomplished, he would not be made perfectly happy. He also worked for the East India Company, rising to the post of Chief Examiner, and later represented Westminster as a Member of Parliament. He conducted a long, intense, but possibly platonic love affair with his neighbor Harriet Taylor, whom he regarded as his intellectual superior, marrying her when her husband died in 1851. Among his most popular works, still widely read today, are *On Liberty*, *The Subjection of Women*, and *Principles of Political Economy*.

John Everett Millais (1829–1896). Pre-Raphaelite artist and portraitist. An artistic child prodigy, Millais entered London's Royal Academy school when only eleven. As a 17-year-old student, one of his paintings (based on an incident in Pizarro's conquest of Peru) was acclaimed at the Royal Academy exhibition. With two fellow students, Dante Gabriel Rossetti and William Holman Hunt, Millais created the Pre-Raphaelite Brotherhood, a club that declared its intention of recapturing the artistic purity of the early Renaissance, before Raphael. The brotherhood was supposed to be secret, but when news of its members' identity and pretensions leaked in 1850, a critical backlash made him the center of unfavorable publicity—Charles Dickens denounced his painting *Christ in the House of His Parents*. Millais reacted by asking John Ruskin, the era's most prominent critic, to support him, which Ruskin did in letters to the *London Times*. Later, however, he met and fell in love with Ruskin's wife, marrying her after she had won an annulment. Despite the claim of the Pre-Raphaelite Brotherhood to challenge accepted standards, the members soon proved amenable to assimilation, and Millais became an Academy member in 1853. He was one of the two or three leading portraitists in London during the 1860s and 1870s and grew rich from commissions. In later years, his style became sentimental, as can be seen from his painting *Bubbles*, which a soap-company adopted for its advertisements.

John Henry Newman (1801–1890). Anglican preacher who became a Catholic cardinal. As a young Oxford don in 1833, Newman joined Hurrell Froude and John Keble to create the Oxford movement, whose pamphlet series, "Tracts for the Times," argued the supernatural origins of the Church of England and tried to downplay its role as a branch of the state. By 1840, Newman had become convinced that Anglicanism was compatible in almost every way with Roman Catholicism, a view outlined in Tract 90, and he shocked many of his admirers by converting to Catholicism in 1845. He became an influential theologian and philosopher in the Catholic Church but often came into conflict with the Church hierarchy. His intellectual adventurousness clashed with the pope's and bishops' belief in the need to preserve and protect their faith from the powerful new intellectual currents of the 19th century. Newman lived in a community of Oratorian priests in Birmingham while his fellow convert, Henry Manning, went on to become the head of the Catholic Church in England. Newman's reputation as one of the greatest Victorian writers was assured by his *Apologia pro Vita Sua* (1864), a spiritual autobiography in which he denied Charles Kingsley's claim of religious insincerity and explained the tortuous mental path that had led to his conversion. In his old age, he was appointed cardinal by Pope Leo XIII and has remained one of the most influential English-language Catholic writers up to the present, inspiring generations of later converts.

Florence Nightingale (1890–1910). Pioneer nurse who made the job respectable for middle-class women and worked heroically for wounded British soldiers in the Crimean War. Born in Italy and named after a city her parents loved, Nightingale belonged to an upper-class family and was expected to cultivate the domestic, ladylike arts and find a suitable husband. She rebelled against this prospect and, despite parental opposition, visited Germany to study nursing. The outbreak of the Crimean War gave her a golden opportunity. By lobbying Sidney Herbert, a friend and government minister, she got permission to take 38 nurses to the temporary British military hospital at Scutari, Turkey. There, she discovered horrible conditions of neglect and set out to improve the food, laundry, and sanitation arrangements and to give proper care to the wounded. Nicknamed "Lady of the Lamp" by the grateful convalescent soldiers, whose death rate fell sharply under her supervision, Nightingale returned home a national hero, receiving a medal from Queen Victoria. She devoted the rest of her life to lobbying for improved hospitals, proper medical care for soldiers, and formal training for nurses. Her gender—and her later invalidism—prevented her from playing as active a role in politics as she would have liked, but her many loyal male supporters brought her ideas into public circulation throughout the later Victorian era.

Charles Stewart Parnell (1846–1891). Irish nationalist leader in the 1880s. A Protestant squire from County Wicklow who entered Parliament in 1875, Parnell was an unlikely candidate to lead the Irish Home Rule movement. However, his parliamentary and oratorical skill enabled him to displace the Nationalist Party's original leader, Isaac Butt. Under Parnell's guidance, Irish MPs filibustered endlessly in Parliament, trying to prevent any other business from moving forward; Parnell hoped that the English would grant Irish Home Rule as a way of ridding Westminster of their obstruction. He kept abreast of developments among Irishmen in America and in the Irish Land War of the early 1880s (he was president of the National Land League). He served a spell in prison in 1881 under a new Coercion Act but, by 1886, had convinced Prime Minister Gladstone that Irish Home Rule was necessary. Gladstone's Home Rule legislation failed to pass and split the Liberal Party. In 1887, parts of the British press insinuated that Parnell had been involved in the Phoenix Park murder of Lord Frederick Cavendish in 1881. He was exonerated in a sensational trial and resumed work for the Home Rule cause. His career in public life was ruined in 1889 when news spread that he had been having a long-running love affair with Katharine O'Shea and had fathered at least three children with her.

Robert Peel (1788–1850). Tory prime minister whose decision to repeal the Corn Laws in 1846 split and temporarily wrecked his party. The son of a wealthy cotton manufacturer in Lancashire, Peel was educated at Harrow and Oxford and entered Parliament in a "rotten borough" at the age of twenty-one. He was Home Secretary in the government of the Duke of Wellington and, in 1829, created the London police force, whose early nickname was the "Peelers." He also changed his mind that year over Catholic emancipation, introducing legislation for this reform that he had long opposed. Peel fought to prevent the Reform Act of 1832 on the grounds that the rotten boroughs enabled distinguished men to enter Parliament without having to fight wasteful election campaigns. After the act passed, he reconciled himself and his party to reform in the "Tamworth Manifesto" of 1834 (the year in which he first, briefly, became prime minister). Peel returned to power in 1841 and faced the great crisis of his life when the Irish potato blight caused widespread famine in 1846. Partly to alleviate the famine and partly in response to changing conditions of trade, Peel now promoted the repeal of the Corn Laws, enabling cheap food to flow into Britain from abroad and giving a corresponding boost to cheap British exports. Half his own party supported the repeal, but half, including Disraeli and many of the country gentlemen who had benefited from the law, opposed him fiercely, forcing his resignation. He remained influential among many Tories but died following a riding accident in 1850.

Cecil Rhodes (1853–1901). The leading figure in British South African expansion. Son of a Hertfordshire clergyman, Rhodes went to South Africa as a 17-year-old, planning to farm cotton with his brothers. Within a year, he had moved to the new diamond fields of Kimberley. He made an immense fortune there but spent parts of the 1870s back in Britain, at Oxford, where he finally finished his degree in 1881. Meanwhile, he created the DeBeers Consolidated Mining Company, which came to dominate the world's diamond trade, and invested in new gold discoveries around Johannesburg. An ardent supporter of expanding the British Empire during the "scramble for Africa" era, Rhodes dreamed of building a continuous British presence and a railway from "the Cape [of Good Hope] to Cairo."

His supporters fought off foreign and Boer rivals to develop the lands that were later named "Rhodesia" (now Zimbabwe) in his honor. He tried to force Britain to annex the Boer republic of the Transvaal in 1895 by launching the Jameson Raid. It failed in the short term and obliged him to resign as prime minister of the Cape Colony in 1896. The action prepared the way for the Boer War (1899–1902), however, which ended in a British takeover. Most of the six million pounds he left after his death from heart disease in 1901 was devoted to the Rhodes scholarships for study at Oxford. He imagined the holders as an idealistic society of Anglo-Saxon men who would build international links and rule the world according to benevolent imperial ideas.

Lord Shaftesbury (1801–1885). Pioneer of social reform and factory legislation. Anthony Ashley Cooper, who inherited the family title of Lord Shaftesbury in 1851 on the death of his father, was an earnest evangelical Christian and an opponent of child labor. Entering Parliament in 1826, he soon took over leadership of the movement to prevent children from being put to work in mines and factories. He supervised passage of legislation in 1833 and 1842 designed to exclude children from textile factories and coal mines. Because too few inspectors were appointed to make the laws effective, he continued in later years to campaign against the horrifying exploitation of child labor throughout the workforce. Shaftesbury also promoted "ragged schools" for children who would otherwise have received no education and was president of the Ragged Schools' Union for 40 years. Only in the last years of his life did universal primary education become compulsory.

Shaftesbury's political skills and aristocratic position entitled him to high government office. Although he was on good terms with most of the Victorian prime ministers (and was related to Palmerstone through his wife), he declined high office to dedicate his time to social and philanthropic reforms. Among his other achievements was legislation to improve the care of the mentally ill, many of whom he found to be cruelly neglected and abused; advocacy of Florence Nightingale's proposed army and nursing reforms in Parliament; and legislation to prevent the building of unsanitary and overcrowded lodging houses. For his own tenants in Wimborne St. Giles, Dorset, he built a model village and subsidized a large London housing estate, the Shaftesbury Park Estate, to demonstrate the viability of safe, decent working-class housing. In all these reform efforts, he was sustained by an intense evangelical piety.

George Stephenson (1781–1848). Pioneer of railway building and locomotive engineering. Stephenson was the son of a Northumberland mine engineer and, at the age of 21, became the engineman at Dewley Colliery (coal mine) near Newcastle-on-Tyne. Steam engines there, based on designs by Thomas Newcomen and James Watt, were large, aboveground devices used for pumping floodwater out of the mines. Stephenson overcame the technical obstacles to building a self-moving steam locomotive, which could pull wagons loaded with coal along a metal track. Primitive horse-drawn railways already existed in the area, but the steam locomotive represented a massive increase in power.

Stephenson was appointed chief engineer of the Stockton and Darlington Railway (1825), which is regarded by most historians as the world's first commercial steam railway. It prospered, taking advantage of Stephenson's many improvements in flat track-bed design, iron rail construction, and an improved engine, *Locomotion*. In 1829, now with the help of his equally gifted son Robert, Stephenson also designed and built the Liverpool and Manchester Railway, taking the line across the swampland of Chat Moss, a nine-arched viaduct, a two-mile-long cutting, and other obstacles. The father and son also built a locomotive, the *Rocket*, which won a competition for the fastest and most reliable source of steam power on the line (it traveled at the then-incredible speed of 36 miles per hour). In later life, Stephenson continued to prosper as a railway engineer but also worked to improve coal miners' safety and experimented in the cross-breeding of farm animals.

Queen Victoria (1819–1901). Queen of England for 64 years, between 1837 and 1901. Daughter of the Duke of Kent and a minor German princess, Victoria's gender and her place in the line of succession made her unlikely to succeed. But the death of the male children before her in line led to her accession on the death of William IV in 1837. Dependent at first on the advice and guidance of Prime Minister Lord Melbourne, Victoria later became a capable supervisor of her government and knew how to maximize her influence even though she, as monarch, no longer wielded actual political power. She married Prince Albert of Saxe-Coburg-Gotha in 1840, the man whom some of her relatives had groomed for exactly this role. Albert brought a Germanic seriousness and moral high-mindedness to court and soon won his wife's ardent affection and admiration. He was also able to impress senior figures in public life, overcoming their traditional xenophobia. His sudden death in 1861 plunged Victoria into a prolonged depression, and she wore black for the rest of her life. Among her later prime ministers, only Disraeli enjoyed her confidence and esteem—she disliked Gladstone. She also put great faith in a Scottish servant, John Brown, and later an Indian servant, "the Munshi." By the time of her death, her many children and grandchildren linked Britain to every royal family in Europe.

Arthur Wellesley, Duke of Wellington (1769–1852). Britain's premier hero of the Napoleonic Wars, prime minister, and grand old man of British politics in Victoria's early years. Wellesley, coming from an aristocratic family, mixed the advantages of rank with outstanding personal abilities as a soldier and statesman. After distinguished service in India in the 1790s, he returned to Britain, won a parliamentary seat, and accepted command of an expedition to Spain and Portugal against Napoleon. His victories in the Peninsula Campaign (1808–1812) made him a national hero, a position he consolidated by leading the victorious allied armies against Napoleon at Waterloo in 1815. He was granted a large Hampshire estate and the dukedom in 1814.

A strong conservative in politics, Wellington was also a political realist. He became Tory prime minister in 1828 and accepted the need for Catholic emancipation to forestall an Irish rebellion, even managing to persuade the king, George IV, of its necessity. He refused to lead the movement to reform Parliament (he considered the constitution virtually perfect as it was in 1830, his last year as prime minister) but acquiesced when Lord Grey's government carried out the Great Reform Act of 1832. Skeptical of railways at first, especially after being booed at the opening of the Liverpool and Manchester Railway, Wellington gradually realized their significance to the nation and made a good deal of money in successful railway speculation after his retirement from Parliament in 1846.

Bibliography

General Works

Asa Briggs, *The Age of Improvement, 1783–1867* (New York: Longman's Green, 1979). Briggs is a skillful writer and draws the reader into his own fascination with British history in this and many other books on Victoriana.

M. J. Daunton, *Progress and Poverty: An Economic and Social History of Britain: 1700–1850* (Oxford: Oxford University Press, 1995). Thorough exploration of the agricultural and industrial changes that culminated in Victorian Britain.

E. J. Evans, *Forging of the Modern State: Early Industrial England, 1783–1870* (New York: Longman, 1996). How the industrial revolution increased Britain's political power.

R. F. Foster, *Modern Ireland: 1600–1972* (New York: Penguin, 1989). A sympathetic account of the long anguish of modern Irish history.

Eric Hobsbawm, *Industry and Empire: An Economic History of Britain Since 1750* (London: Weidenfeld and Nicolson, 1968). Hard-headed analysis of nuts and bolts, trade, industry, and power, from a prominent Marxist historian.

K. Theodore Hoppen, *The Mid-Victorian Generation: 1846–1886* (Oxford: Oxford University Press, 1998). A huge survey of mid Victorian Britain—readable, too.

Philip Jenkins, *A History of Modern Wales* (London: Longman, 1992). An analysis of the smallest but linguistically most vigorous of Victoria's kingdoms, by a Welsh patriot.

Peter Laslett, *The World We Have Lost* (London: Methuen, 1965). A landmark work of social history and a lament for the passing of pre-industrial England.

James Morris, *Heaven's Command: An Imperial Progress* (New York: Harcourt, Brace, Jovanovich, 1973). The best history of the empire in Victoria's day, by an author (now Jan Morris) who is also famous for her sex change operation.

B. Porter, *Britannia's Burden: The Political Evolution of Modern Britain, 1851–1900* (New York: E. Arnold, 1994). The hesitant steps by which Britain became a recognizable democracy.

W. D. Rubinstein, *Britain's Century: A Political and Social History, 1815–1905* (London: Arnold, 1998). Start with this book for an overview of the whole subject.

Tom Steel, *Scotland's Story: A New Perspective* (London: Collins, 1984). A lively version of Scottish history with hundreds of illustrations.

Llewelyn Woodward, *The Age of Reform, 1815–1870* (Oxford: Clarendon Press, 1938). A superb example of the old-style institutional British history.

Specialized Works

Patrick Allitt, *Catholic Converts: British and American Intellectuals Turn to Rome* (Ithaca, NY: Cornell University Press, 1997). Why many members of three generations of British intellectuals followed John Newman's example and became Catholics.

P. Bailey, *Leisure and Class in Victorian England* (London: Routledge and Keegan Paul, 1978). The author shows vividly how each social class had its own way of spending its off-hours and how carefully defended its own leisure "turf."

David Bebbington, *Evangelicalism in Modern Britain: A History from the 1730s to the 1980s* (Boston: Unwin Hyman, 1989). How Wesley and his descendants transformed and "moralized" Britain.

Roger Beck, *The History of South Africa* (Westport, CT: Greenwood, 2000). A useful short introduction to the Boers, the Zulus and the English—Victorian-era rivals for South Africa's land and gold.

Kenneth Bendiner, *An Introduction to Victorian Painting* (New Haven, CT: Yale University Press, 1985). What the artists painted, who bought the pictures, how they were displayed and sold, and how the artists understood their world.

E. F. Benson, *As We Were: A Victorian Peepshow* (London: Longman's Green, 1931). A popular novelist's insightful memoir about his Victorian childhood. His father was Archbishop of Canterbury.

John Benson, *The Working Class in Britain, 1850–1939* (New York: Longman, 1989). A powerful reminder that the least articulate were the most numerous.

Christopher Brooks, *The Gothic Revival* (London: Phaidon, 1999). Why Victorian artists and architects venerated the works of the middle ages.

Raymond Lamont-Brown, *John Brown: Queen Victoria's Highland Servant* (Sutton: Phoenix Mill, 2000). Life story of the queen's favorite Scotsman.

Janet Browne, *Charles Darwin: A Biography* (New York: Knopf/Random House, 1995). Immensely informative account of the scientist's life and work.

W. L. Burn, *The Age of Equipoise: A Study of the Mid-Victorian Generation* (London: George Allen and Unwin, 1964). A classic; now slightly dated but still a pleasure to read.

David Cannadine, *The Decline and Fall of the British Aristocracy* (New Haven, CT: Yale University Press, 1990). One of the superstars of contemporary historical writing explains the aristocracy's long rearguard. All his other books are good, too.

Hugh Casson, *An Introduction to Victorian Architecture* (London: Art and Technics, 1948). Written at a time when Victorian architecture was totally out of fashion, it gives a hard look at what they built but ably explains the many styles, disputes, and debates.

Owen Chadwick, *The Victorian Church: 1829–1901* (2 volumes) (London: A. and C. Black, 1966 and 1970). A monument of erudition on every aspect of the Church of England and its rivals in Victoria's day.

John Chandos, *Boys Together: English Public Schools, 1800–1864* (London: Hutchinson, 1984). Flogging, sports, tyrannical teachers, and high-minded reformers all brightly explained.

Linda Colley, *Britons: Forging the Nation, 1707–1837* (New Haven, CT: Yale University Press, 1992). Excellent on social diversity within Britain just before Victoria's reign.

H. Cunningham, *Leisure in the Industrial Revolution* (New York: St. Martin's Press, 1980). How rural immigrants to cities brought their games, sports, and drinking habits with them, but found their culture changing in a changed world.

John Dawes, *Not in Front of the Servants: A True Portrait of Upstairs-Downstairs Life* (London: Hutchinson, 1973). Victorian and Edwardian servants' lives, based on interviews with elderly former servants with long memories.

Trevor Fisher, *Prostitution and the Victorians* (Stroud, UK: Sutton Publishing, 1997). He emphasizes the scale of prostitution, its variety, and the economic pressures that drew women into it.

Michael Freeman, *Railways and the Victorian Imagination* (New Haven, CT: Yale University Press, 1999). Beautifully illustrated account of how writers, artists, and architects responded to the new technology.

Norman Gash, *Politics in the Age of Peel* (New York: Longman's Green, 1953). Classic explanation of the mechanics of early Victorian parliamentary government.

Alan Haig, *The Victorian Clergy* (London: Croom, Helm, 1984). Who they were, why they became clergymen, what they did, and how they reacted to their age.

B. Harrison, *Drink and the Victorians: The Temperance Question* (Pittsburgh: University of Pittsburgh Press, 1971). Britain never had Prohibition, but its Victorian temperance movement was keen to try the experiment if possible.

Christopher Hibbert, *Queen Victoria, A Personal History* (New York: Basic, 2000). For "personal," read "gossipy."

Eric Hobsbawm and Terence Ranger, eds., *The Invention of Tradition* (Cambridge: Cambridge University Press, 1983). A lovely book, full of surprises, showing how many "ancient" traditions were really just Victorian inventions.

Richard Holt, *Sport and the British: A Modern History* (New York: Oxford University Press, 1989). How cricket, horseracing, soccer, and rugby changed to reflect changing social conditions.

Walter Houghton, *The Victorian Frame of Mind* (New Haven: Yale University Press, 1957). An intellectual history classic explaining how Victorians thought about literature and science.

Derek Hudson, *Arthur Munby: Man of Two Worlds* (London: J. Murray, 1972). Truth as strange as fiction; the man who married his servant but kept it secret all his life.

Lawrence James, *Raj: The Making and Unmaking of British India* (New York: St. Martin's Press, 1997). Superb one-volume history of the British Empire in India.

Richard Jay, *Joseph Chamberlain: A Political Study* (Oxford: Clarendon Press, 1981). The political life of a Birmingham industrialist and MP who split with Gladstone over Irish Home Rule and became a leading Tory imperialist .

T. A. Jenkins, *The Liberal Ascendancy, 1830–1864* (Basingstoke: Macmillan, 1994). Why Liberals dominated British politics between the First and Second Reform Acts.

Penny Kane, *Victorian Families in Fact and Fiction* (London: Macmillan, 1995). A clear-eyed sweeping away of the myths and an investigation of changing power relations inside Victorian families.

F. S. L. Lyons, *Ireland Since the Famine* (London: Fontana, 1985). Explains how Ireland prepared for Home Rule, revolution, and partition after the catastrophic 1840s.

Philip Mason, *The Men Who Ruled India* (London: Jonathan Cape, 1985). The airs and graces of men who were ordinary in Britain but magnificent in remote imperial India.

Henry Mayhew, *London Poverty and the London Poor* (orig. 1859, New York: Penguin, 1985). The classic story of a journalist's exploration of the working poor in London.

Donald Morris, *The Washing of the Spears: A History of the Rise of the Zulu Nation* (New York: Simon and Schuster, 1986). A classic (originally published in 1965) on the Anglo-Zulu wars of the 1870s.

A. E. Musson, *British Trade Unions, 1800–1875* (London: Macmillan, 1972). Just what you would expect from the title—a straightforward and reliable account of how trade unions developed.

Alan O'Day, *Parnell and the First Home Rule Episode, 1884–1887* (Dublin: Gill and Macmillan, 1986). Biography of the charismatic Irish leader—his spectacular rise and fall.

Henry Pelling, *Origins of the Labour Party* (Oxford: Oxford University Press, 1985). How the trade unions decided they must enter politics directly in the late Victorian era.

Harold Perkin, *The Age of the Railway* (Newton Abbot: David and Charles, 1971). How Victorian Britain was revolutionized by trains.

Joan Perkin, *Victorian Women* (London: John Murray, 1993). Feminist history writing at its best.

Kevin Phillips, *The Cousins' Wars: Religion, Politics, and the Triumph of Anglo-America* (New York: Basic, 1999). American pundit's view of the powerful Anglo-American special relationship, with an excellent Victorian section.

J. B. Priestley, *Victoria's Heyday* (New York: Harper and Row, 1972). Bright, pictorial, and anecdotal story of the 1850s from a north English radio celebrity.

Jane Purvis, *Hard Lessons: The Lives and Education of Working-class women in Nineteenth Century England* (Minneapolis: University of Minnesota Press, 1989). Unsentimental reality-check for anyone trying to romanticize the lives of poor people.

D. C. Richter, *Riotous Victorians* (Athens, OH: Ohio University Press, 1981). Men without votes often expressed themselves with outbreaks of direct action and demonstrations that could turn violent.

Mark Ridley, ed., *The Darwin Reader* (New York: Norton, 1996). Selections from the great scientist's works that give a sense of his life and literary idiom, as well as his ideas.

L. T. C. Rolt, *Victorian Engineering* (London: Allen Lane, 1970). Britain's premier engineering historian explains the era's innovative machines and the men who made them.

Phyllis Rose, *Parallel Lives: Five Victorian Marriages* (New York: Knopf, 1984). Gossipy, fascinating glimpse at the strange marriages of Dickens, Mill, Carlyle, Ruskin, and George Eliot.

Hugh Small, *Florence Nightingale: Avenging Angel* (London: Constable, 1999). As the subtitle suggests, the ultimate Victorian heroine had a tough and rather unlikable side!

Paul Smith, *Disraeli: A Brief Life* (Cambridge: Cambridge University Press/Canto, 1996). Excellent on Disraeli's use of his Jewish heritage as a speaker and writer and on his surprising leadership of the Tory Party.

Peter Stansky, *Gladstone: A Progress in Politics* (Boston: Little Brown, 1979). One of the good shorter biographies of the Liberal giant—there are hundreds of long biographies of Gladstone, too!

Lytton Strachey, *Eminent Victorians* (New York: Putnam, 1918). A famous book by a leading member of the Bloomsbury Group, deflating and making ruthless fun of four famous Victorians. Still wonderful despite its biases; Strachey wrote a good biography of Queen Victoria, too.

E. P. Thompson, *The Making of the English Working Class* (London: Gollancz, 1963). Half the professional historians in the world cite this as the most influential and inspirational book they ever read—vital for everyone really getting deeply into the subject.

Herbert Tucker, ed., *A Companion to Victorian Literature and Culture* (Malden, MA: Blackwell, 1999). An anthology of shrewd essays outlining the major themes, approaches, and topics of Victorian writers.

E. S. Turner, *What the Butler Saw: 250 Years of the Servant Problem* (London: Joseph, 1963). Humorous but insightful account of servants' lives intertwined with those of their employers.

Adrian Vaughan, *Isambard Brunel: Engineering Knight-Errant* (London: John Murray, 1991). Eccentric book by an admiring and talented amateur historian on the great engineer.

Stanley Weintraub, *Albert: Uncrowned King* (London: John Murray, 1997). Traces the immense influence of Victoria's husband and his role in creating "Victorianism."

Martin Wiener, *English Culture and the Decline of the Industrial Spirit: 1850–1980* (New York: Cambridge University Press, 1981). Brilliantly insightful study explaining why Britain lost its industrial lead as its elites pursued different goals.

Jeffrey Williamson, *Coping with City Growth During the British Industrial Revolution* (New York: Cambridge University Press, 1990).

Christopher Wood, *The Pre-Raphaelites* (New York: Viking, 1981). Sumptuously illustrated but also intelligently written account of the artistic and literary movement.

C. Woodham-Smith, *The Great Hunger: Ireland, 1845–1849* (London: Penguin, 1991). First-rate storyteller explores the human dimensions of the heartrending story.

———, *The Reason Why* (New York: McGraw Hill, 1953). Same author devotes the same skills to narrating the Crimean War and the Charge of the Light Brigade.

Philip Ziegler, *Melbourne: A Biography of William Lamb, 2nd Viscount Melbourne* (London: Collins, 1976).

Internet Resources

Victorian Art in Britain, http//www.victorianartinbritain.co.uk

Victorian Costume, http//www.victoriancostume.org.uk

The Victorian Web: Literature, History and Culture in the Age of Victoria, http//65.107.211.206